Individual Assessment

As Practiced in Industry and Consulting

Individual Assessment

As Practiced in Industry and Consulting

Erich P. Prien
Performance Management Press

Jeffery S. Schippmann
PepsiCo, Inc.

Kristin O. Prien
Christian Brothers University

2003

LAWRENCE ERLBAUM ASSOCIATES, PUBLISHERS

Mahwah, New Jersey   London

Lawrence Erlbaum Associates, Inc., Publishers
10 Industrial Avenue
Mahwah, NJ 07430

Cover design by Kathryn Houghtaling Lacey

Library of Congress Cataloging-in-Publication Data

Prien, Erich P., 1928-
Individual assessment : as practiced in industry and consulting / Erich P. Prien, Jeffery S. Schippmann, Kristin O. Prien.
    p. cm.
    Includes bibliographical references and index.
ISBN 0-8058-3975-5 (cloth : alk. paper)
ISBN 0-8058-3976-3 (pbk. : alk. paper)
1. Personnel management—Psychological aspects. 2. Psychology, Industrial. I. Schippmann, Jeffery S. II. Prien, Kristin O. III. Title.

HF5549 .P658 2003
158.7—dc21
                                    2002027860
                                          CIP

Books published by Lawrence Erlbaum Associates are printed on acid-free paper, and their bindings are chosen for strength and durability.

Printed in the United States of America
10 9 8 7 6 5 4 3 2 1

This book is dedicated to:

—Jay Otis, for his initiating contribution to the
practice of individual assessment
E. P. P.

—Deborah, for everything (12 & 24)
J. S. S.

—GLH & EPP, for introducing me to the practice
of individual assessment and teaching
me how to assess.
K. O. P.

Series in Applied Psychology

Edwin A. Fleishman, George Mason University
Jeanette N. Cleveland, Pennsylvania State University
Series Editors

Gregory Bedny and David Meister
The Russian Theory of Activity: Current Applications to Design and Learning

Michael T. Brannick, Eduardo Salas, and Carolyn Prince
Team Performance Assessment and Measurement: Theory, Research, and Applications

Jeanette N. Cleveland, Margaret Stockdale, and Kevin R. Murphy
Women and Men in Organizations: Sex and Gender Issues at Work

Aaron Cohen
Multiple Commitments in the Workplace: An Integrative Approach

Russell Cropanzano
Justice in the Workplace: Approaching Fairness in Human Resource Management, Volume 1

Russell Cropanzano
Justice in the Workplace: From Theory to Practice, Volume 2

James E. Driskell and Eduardo Salas
Stress and Human Performance

Sidney A. Fine and Steven F. Cronshaw
Functional Job Analysis: A Foundation for Human Resources Management

Sidney A. Fine and Maury Getkate
Benchmark Tasks for Job Analysis: A Guide for Functional Job Analysis (FJA) Scales

J. Kevin Ford, Steve W. J. Kozlowski, Kurt Kraiger, Eduardo Salas, and Mark S. Teachout
Improving Training Effectiveness in Work Organizations

Jerald Greenberg
Organizational Behavior: The State of the Science, Second Edition

Uwe E. Kleinbeck, Hans-Henning Quast, Henk Thierry, and Hartmut Häcker
Work Motivation

Martin I. Kurke and Ellen M. Scrivner
Police Psychology Into the 21st Century

Joel Lefkowitz
Ethics and Values in Industrial and Organizational Psychology

Manuel London
Job Feedback: Giving, Seeking, and Using Feedback for Performance Improvement, Second Edition

Manuel London
How People Evaluate Others in Organizations

Manuel London
Leadership Development: Paths to Self-Insight and Professional Growth

Robert F. Morrison and Jerome Adams
Contemporary Career Development Issues

Michael D. Mumford, Garnett Stokes, and William A. Owens
Patterns of Life History: The Ecology of Human Individuality

Kevin R. Murphy
Validity Generalization: A Critical Review

Kevin R. Murphy and Frank E. Saal
Psychology in Organizations: Integrating Science and Practice

Susan E. Murphy and Ronald E. Riggio
The Future of Leadership Development

Erich P. Prien, Jeffery S. Schippmann, and Kristin O. Prien
Individual Assessment: As Practiced in Industry and Consulting

Ned Rosen
Teamwork and the Bottom Line: Groups Make a Difference

Heinz Schuler, James L. Farr, and Mike Smith
Personnel Selection and Assessment: Individual and Organizational Perspectives

John W. Senders and Neville P. Moray
Human Error: Cause, Prediction, and Reduction

Frank J. Smith
Organizational Surveys: The Diagnosis and Betterment of Organizations Through Their Members

George C. Thornton III and Rose Mueller-Hanson
Developing Organizational Simulations: A Guide for Practitioners and Students

Yoav Vardi and Ely Weitz
Misbehavior in Organizations: Theory, Research, and Management

Contents

Series Foreword   xiii
Edwin A. Fleishman and Jeanette N. Cleveland

Preface   xv
      Overview and Contents   xvii
      Acknowledgments   xix
      References   xxi

PART I: THE PRACTICE OF INDIVIDUAL ASSESSMENT

Chapter 1   **Introduction to Individual Assessment**   3
      Historical Context   7
      Research Context   9
      The Individual Assessment Model   18
      References   23

Chapter 2   **Job Modeling**   27
      People Are Different   28
      Jobs Are Different   31
      Assessment Specifications   33
      Identifying Assessment Specifications   36
      Research Context   43
      Practice Examples   44
      References   50

Chapter 3   Establishing the Assessment Protocol   52
     Tests Are Different Too!   52
     Research Context   53
     Practice Examples   74
     References   89

Chapter 4   Conducting the Assessment   96
     Conducting the Interview   100
     Evaluating Interview Data   110
     Research Context   111
     Practice Examples   113
     References   120

Chapter 5   Integration and Interpretation   122
     Research Context   126
     Practice Examples   129
     References   139

Chapter 6   Feedback, Reporting, and Program Evaluation   141
     Assessee Background   147
     Foundations for Career Success   147
     Competency Evaluation   148
     Development Suggestions   150
     Research Context   152
     Practice Examples   154
     References   168

PART II: ADDITIONAL ISSUES AFFECTING PRACTICE

Chapter 7   Legal, Professional, and Ethical Issues   171
     Legal Issues   171
     Professional Issues   175
     Specific Ethical Issues   182
     References   185

Chapter 8   Final Thoughts and Prognostications   187
     References   199

Appendix A   Primer of Measurement Terms and Concepts   203
     Glossary of Terms   204
     Primer of Statistical Procedures and Definitions   215

Multitrait-Multimethod Approach   223
References   226

Appendix B   Management and Executive Model: 229
            Work Activities and Competencies
Work Activity Taxonomy   230
Competency Taxonomy   239

Appendix C   Supervisory Model: Work Activities   251
            and Competencies
Work Activity Taxonomy   252
Competency Taxonomy   258

Appendix D   Administrative Model: Work Activities   265
            and Competencies
Work Activity Taxonomy   266
Competency Taxonomy   274

Author Index   281

Subject Index   287

Series Foreword

Series Editors

Edwin A. Fleishman
George Mason University

Jeanette N. Cleveland
Pennsylvania State University

There is a compelling need for innovative approaches to the solution of many pressing problems involving human relationships in today's society. Such approaches are more likely to be successful when they are based on sound research and applications. This *Series in Applied Psychology* offers publications that emphasize state-of-the-art research and its application to important issues of human behavior in a variety of social settings. The objective is to bridge both academic and applied interests.

We are pleased to welcome the book by Prien, Schippmann, and Prien to the Series. Individual assessment is an active area of professional practice in today's business world. There is considerable variation on the methodologies and assessment procedures used by different professionals in this field, but the common objective is to make valid inferences about a person's fit for a job, usually a managerial job. These inferences are based on assessments and interpretations made, usually by a trained psychologist, employing and integrating combinations of interviews and psychological measures of abilities, personality, and background information.

Although there is widespread use of individual assessment, which represents a large segment of professional practice among industrial psychologists, this area has received relatively little attention in textbooks in industrial and organizational psychology and personnel management.

Individual assessment may be one of the least well-understood and re-ported-on areas in the entire field of industrial and organizational psychol-ogy. With thousands of practitioners, using many different methodologies and approaches, this has been an emerging business activity. There has been a need to organize this information and to emphasize the research un-derpinnings of the field.

Erich Prien, Jeffery Schippmann, and Kristin Prien have put together a re-markable book that draws on their rich and varied experiences over many years of management and executive assessment. Dr. Erich Prien was involved in the original Case Western Reserve research on individual assessment in the late 1950s. He has conducted several thousand assessments across a wide range of jobs over the past 40 years. For his work, he received the Distin-guished Professional Contributions Award from the Society of Industrial and Organizational Psychology. Dr. Jeffery Schippmann has made significant con-tributions to the research literature in the area of management and sales tal-ent, including work to identify the competency structure of management jobs as described in his recent book *Strategic Job Modeling: Working at the Core of In-tegrated Human Resources* (LEA, 1999). He has conducted hundreds of assess-ments for dozens of companies over the course of the past 15 years. Dr. Kristin Prien's expertise lies in all facets of job analysis related to managerial, profes-sional, and technical jobs. She has had significant involvement in an ongoing program of research on the components of the assessment process, and has been conducting assessments for the past 15 years.

In this book, these three authors present a clear, practical, research-based description of their approach to individual assessment. This is what the field has always lacked, a practical and methodologically sound model that can describe the diverse range of activities each step along the way and organize the diverse literatures that support and guide the assessment enterprise. Our expectation is that this book will take individual assessment to an en-tirely new level of understanding and practice, and into a new era of profes-sional research activity.

The book is appropriate for students in relevant fields of industrial and or-ganizational psychology and management, including classes dealing with psy-chological assessment, personnel selection and training, management development, and vocational counseling. Professionals engaged in individual assessment in the world of recruitment, selection, placement, and promotion of management personnel should find this book essential to their practice.

Preface

In the broadest sense, individual assessment refers to the process where an assessment practitioner measures or assesses the job-related characteristics of one job candidate (or job incumbent), one at a time or individually, for the purpose of making inferences about the individual's future job performance and organization-related behavior. Furthermore, there are two primary types of individual assessment: assessment for selection and assessment for development. In the former, the individual assessment practitioner's inferences concern whether to hire, promote, or outplace a particular candidate. In the latter, the practitioner's inferences focus on how, and how quickly, an individual may be developed (in their current job or for some future job) and how the individual might better utilize his or her talents. Of the two, individual assessment for selection is by far the more prevalent activity (Ryan & Sackett, 1987). For this reason, the prevailing focus of the book is on individual assessment for selection.

However, individual assessment for development is not ignored. Although the goals of selection and development-focused assessment are somewhat different, they are not mutually exclusive. For example, even when an assessment is conducted for selection purposes, there is typically some developmental feedback to the hiring manager for the successful candidate and, to a more limited extent, participating candidates in an effort to promote a positive reaction to the experience. A developmental assessment, conversely, may address the level and types of jobs that the candidate may aspire to. Furthermore, in both cases the assessment process itself is substantively the same. Thus, although we lead with a presentation of selection-based assessment throughout the book, in those places where there are meaningful differences, we note the difference and elaborate on the development aspects as necessary.

Why have we written a book on individual assessment? There are several reasons. First, from a very practical perspective, it is a business activity that can have a real and significant impact on individual and organizational performance. Second, at an intellectual level, it is a fascinating and complex realm of practice. A third reason is because of the intrigue—really. The practice of individual assessment is largely a cottage industry and has a very nearly invisible past and a ubiquitous, though covert, present, which is intriguing. In the 1950s and 1960s there was a small flurry of research and reporting that examined the practice, but, for the most part, it remained largely hidden from view, receiving scant recognition in the professional literature. Little has changed. There is still a high level of individual assessment effort and activity going on, but with little formal research attention or evaluation.

Moreover, there are no publicly available descriptions of how to conduct individual assessment work, other than through the limited distribution Society of Industrial and Organizational Psychology (SIOP) workshops (Jeanneret & Silzer, 1990; Prien, Miller, & Tamir, 1996; Prien, Schippmann, Hughes, & Sale, 1991; Silzer & Hollenbeck, 1992; Silzer & Jeanneret, 1987). Although there are other books available that discuss the practice of individual assessment in a general way (Hansen & Conrad, 1991; Jeanneret & Silzer, 1998), one could examine the descriptions provided therein and still not come away with an understanding of how to do it. In a nutshell, this is the overarching goal of the current book: to provide a structure and core set of principles for teaching others how to do it.

As such, this book was written with several potential audiences in mind. First, other practitioners, or would-be practitioners, in the field of individual assessment are targeted. These individuals may be in private practice, working as consultants in small boutique shops, or employed by one of the large assessment firms. Alternatively, they may be assessing individuals as part of their job responsibilities as an internal consultant within a private or public organization. Whatever the setting, it is a good bet that people from this group picking up the book are like their individual assessment brethren in several important ways: (a) They never had a graduate class dedicated to individual assessment, (b) they learned their craft at the shoulder of one or two mentors in a practice setting, and (c) since learning the craft they have had limited opportunity to compare notes with other professionals and further develop their competencies and techniques. These readers should gain additional understanding of the process and, hopefully, some ideas and concrete tools to incorporate into their practice. For aspiring service providers, this book will provide a structure for understanding the competencies that need to be developed in order to conduct individual assessment services in the context of consulting or business operations.

Second, the book should prove useful in teaching. Both students and scholars in graduate programs dealing with applied psychology, industrial relations, and human resource management should profit from the practice-oriented design of the book. Furthermore, although the practice orientation is a distinct characteristic of the book, there are important research literatures supporting various decision points in the individual assessment process: some better developed or more extensive than others. The research literature or context associated with these decision points are co-presented with the how-to-do-it descriptions in the book and gaps in the literature and opportunities for research are highlighted.

The third target audience is consumers of assessment services. With greater frequency, organizations are using external consultants to provide individual assessment services. Individuals who have been charged by their organizations with participating in the design of an assessment process, choosing a service provider, and managing an assessment program should expect to be better equipped to perform these activities after reading the book.

Clearly, this book has been written for a broad spectrum of potential readers, each with varying interests and backgrounds. What each target group shares is the desire to acquire, or extend, their knowledge and understanding of the individual assessment practice. In pulling together the diverse research literatures, and in presenting a very practice-oriented approach to the process, we hope we have satisfied the needs of these different groups. Ultimately, it is essential that the practice of individual assessment be practical, yet based on research, and conducted as a professional activity.

OVERVIEW AND CONTENTS

The book is divided into two sections. The focus of Part I, The Practice of Individual Assessment, is how to conduct this work in a practical, productive, and professional manner. Chapter 1, Introduction to Individual Assessment, provides some history for the practice, examines some of the research underpinnings, and defines some basic terms and concepts. In addition, this chapter presents a model or framework for thinking about individual assessment that summarizes important questions and decision points. Although the practice of assessment can be characterized as an open system, the practitioner should follow and adhere to certain standards when making decisions at each juncture in the process; these standards are based on research and years of best-practice learnings. The six-step model presented in this chapter reflects the flow of activities and decision points in individual assessment practice and serves as the organizing structure for the next five chapters (steps five and six are presented in combination in chap. 6).

Chapter 2, Job Modeling, begins where involvement of the individual assessment practitioner begins, with the effort to identify and define the important characteristics of the target job. The resulting definition and description essentially serve as a roadmap for each of the next steps of the individual assessment process. Although there is no single way to develop this mapping of requirements, there is, in a general sense, a right way to create this information foundation: in terms of both maximizing predictive power and ensuring adherence to professional guidelines.

Chapter 3, Establishing the Assessment Protocol, builds on, and logically follows, the content from previous chapters. With the mapping of the job requirements in place, the stage is set to begin the complex process of choosing the assessment tools that will be used to generate assessment information. This step is the figurative equivalent of building the lens to the eyeglass through which the assessment practitioner will be looking at the assessee. The material used to build the lens (i.e., the tests selected to create the assessment protocol) will govern and constrain the inferences that can be made about the assessee in subsequent steps of the process. Furthermore, a basic premise of assessment is that the measurement instruments must meet professional standards. Any test used in assessment must be supported by evidence of some form of validity, so that test scores represent meaningful information. Test scores cannot exist in a vacuum and the job modeling results, normative data, and validation data provide the essential framework to achieve understanding of the individual assessee.

Chapter 4, Conducting the Assessment, is concerned with just that: how to conduct the assessment and manage the assessment day. Suggestions about what and what not to include as prework, what to schedule when, how to conduct the assessment interview, tips for handling feedback to the assessee, and so forth, are covered in this chapter. There is more to managing the assessment day than just administering a lot of tests. These practical, operational issues are discussed at length in this chapter.

Chapter 5, Integration and Interpretation, addresses the complex series of decisions involved in integrating numerous pieces of information to arrive at some final judgments about expected outcomes. At this stage there are multiple streams of input information and, if one is not careful, it is possible to drown in the gushing, swollen river of data that is of one's own making. The key is to keep the assessment specifications (i.e., the product from chap. 2) always in sight and to work to reduce the massive amount of information into more discrete units. Thus, this step requires the co-consideration of information about jobs and people. This chapter also presents discussion on the clinical versus mechanical handling of assessment data. In the progression of the individual assessment process, there is a natural evolution from a descriptive, operational level to increasingly more complex and abstract levels of inference and decision making. In summary, this chapter presents all the steps in what is basically an intelligence-gathering operation that will ultimately lead to a characterization of the assessee with reference to some target job or jobs.

Chapter 6, Feedback, Reporting, and Program Evaluation, is concerned with the activities that follow the actual assessment. The product of the assessment process at this point is, first, an understanding of the assessee as a whole person and, second, an appreciation of the individual's strengths and weaknesses with reference to a target job. The challenge now is to provide verbal feedback and a written report to the client sponsor that are both comprehensive and precise. Numerous examples and tips for practice are built into the chapter. In addition, recommendations and guidance for managing assessment follow-up and program evaluation are covered.

Part II, Additional Issues Affecting Practice, examines a range of legal, ethical, service-provider training, and business management topics that influence the real-world conduct of individual assessment practice. For example, in chapter 7, we discuss in one place, and with greater depth, the relevant statutes and professional guidelines that apply to assessment and the nonconventional approach to supporting the practice. In addition, a review of applicable ethical issues and a model of assessor competencies are presented. The practice of individual assessment is defined in relation to the competencies required for different levels or standards of practice. In the final analysis, professional competence will determine the outcome.

Part II also includes capstone chapter 8. The individual assessment practitioner concept does not fit neatly into a mold or cubbyhole. It is a unique process that needs to be examined and understood if it is to thrive in the business marketplace. Furthermore, that marketplace is changing. How, and in what form, is the practice of individual assessment likely to survive? With this backdrop, we offer our thoughts for future research and our prognostications for the evolution of the practice.

Part II also includes four appendixes. Appendix A provides a primer of basic psychometric concepts such as reliability and validity. Although there is a clear practice emphasis in this book, a basic understanding of certain ideas related to testing and test theory are assumed. For individuals who need some brush-up or review in this area, Appendix A should fit the bill so the reader will not have to turn to a secondary resource.

Appendix B presents a comprehensive, research-based taxonomy of work activity and competency descriptors (factor, dimension, and item-level content) for management and executive jobs. These categories of work activity and competency content provide a structure for conducting individual assessments with this population. Similarly, Appendixes C and D represent variations on the basic theme and provide work activity and competency taxonomies for supervisory and administrative employee populations, respectively. Again, the reasons for including this content are to package a practical framework that may be used to improve the efficiency of the process when conducting assessments with these populations and, hopefully, to improve the quality and accuracy of the assessment outcome.

ACKNOWLEDGMENTS

Life is strange and unpredictable. When we started this project 10 years ago it was a team effort that included, as two of the authors, Fred Sale and

Garry Hughes. Then, as fate would have it, we lost Fred, in the prime of his career, in 1996. Then, 2 years ago, Garry passed away suddenly and we lost yet another colleague and friend. The final product in front of the reader now is the work of the final three-person team and is quite different from the early drafts of the text. However, the thinking and contributions of both Fred and Garry were important during the formative stages of the book and their fingerprints are evident in various places throughout the chapters. Both of these individuals were wonderful practitioners, strong researchers, and class-act people. Their professional and personal contributions are simply irreplaceable.

We also owe a special note of acknowledgment to Bill Macey for his support during the past two decades while we worked together on many of the foundation projects on which this practice is based. Bill provided the impetus, support, and encouragement for the various job analysis projects that are linked to the individual assessment framework presented in the book. Bill also took time from a very busy professional life to read and comment on early drafts of the manuscript.

In addition to Bill, Sally Hartmann, Ann Marie Ryan, and Nancy Tippins took the time to read and provide thoughtful comments on a prepublication draft of the book. The book is much improved because these individuals were willing to contribute some of their limited discretionary time to provide us with feedback. Of course, serving in a review capacity in no way suggests that they necessarily agree with all of the content of the book. Furthermore, any remaining faults in the book are entirely our own.

Next, we would like to express our appreciation to Kathy Thomas and Mrs. Donal Sutherland, who kept track of the various versions of this book, interpreted the hieroglyphic-like marginal comments and edits, and, finally, figured out where all of the inserts, references, and notes needed to go—no easy task these past several years.

Finally, developing this book has been as much a family effort as a professional one over the years, in which a number of people have participated directly and indirectly. Dolores Prien demonstrated untiring patience and support at many critical junctures during the past 10 years that we have at times agonized through the more than 25 manuscript drafts leading to this text. Deborah Schippmann carried a significant share of the load through all of these years, balancing the responsibilities for managing a home in addition to her active participation in reading manuscripts, critiquing content, and handling many of the administrative details that go along with a collaborative effort. Kristin Prien suffered through one after another versions of these manuscripts and had the good sense to maintain a comprehensive archive, not only of the various versions of the manuscript but also of the underlying statistics and analytical databases that constitute the underpinning of this technical work. Collectively, we acknowledge our appreciation for their assistance, which allowed us to work through all of the obstacles, conceptual shifts, and adaptations leading to this end. We hope that through this winding and sometimes laborious adventure, we have fulfilled some semblance of our dedication and sense of obligation to the field of industrial and organizational psychology.

—*Erich P. Prien*
—*Jeffery S. Schippmann*
—*Kristin O. Prien*

REFERENCES

Hansen, C. P., & Conrad, K. A. (1991). *A handbook of psychological assessment in business.* New York: Quorum Books.

Jeanneret, P. R., & Silzer, R. F. (1990, March). *Assessment of personality for selection and development.* Paper presented at the Society for Industrial and Organizational Psychology Workshop at the 38th convention of the American Psychological Association, Boston.

Jeanneret, R., & Silzer, R. (1998). *Individual psychological assessment.* San Francisco: Jossey-Bass.

Prien, E. P., Miller, L., & Tamir, L. (1996, April). *Individual assessment.* Paper presented at the Society for Industrial and Organizational Psychology Workshop, Nashville, TN.

Prien, E. P., Schippmann, J. S., Hughes, G. L., & Sale, F. (1991, June). *An introduction to psychological assessment.* Paper presented at the two-day workshop for the Society for Industrial and Organizational Psychology, Baltimore.

Ryan, A. M., & Sackett, P. R. (1987). A survey of individual assessment practices by I/O psychologists. *Personnel Psychology, 40,* 455–488.

Silzer, R. F., & Hollenbeck, G. P. (1992, April). *Executive assessment.* Workshop presented at the annual conference of the Society for Industrial and Organizational Psychology, Montreal.

Silzer, R. F., & Jeanneret, P. R. (1987, April). *Psychological assessment: Getting at job-related skills and abilities.* Paper presented at the Society for Industrial and Organizational Psychology Workshop at the 35th convention of the American Psychological Association, New York.

I

The Practice
of Individual Assessment

1

Introduction to Individual Assessment

Before jumping directly into a discussion of the practice of individual assessment for selection, it will be useful to provide some context by first discussing the broader practice of employment testing, given that testing is at the center of the assessment process. Few would disagree that selecting the right people to fill critical jobs in an organization is important to the long-term success of a business. The decisions made at the point of entry to an organization can have an effect that lasts for decades. Fortunately, a wide range of methods (e.g., paper-and-pencil tests, interview questions, performance simulations) are available to help improve the accuracy of selection decisions. In total, this range of methods refers to the realm of *employment testing*, which, when broadly interpreted, is probably as old as employment itself. Yet, employment testing as we know it today—objective, standardized, and validated procedures based on the results of some form of analysis of the target job's requirements—is a relatively recent development (i.e., in the past 85 years). Over the past 85 years, an extensive literature base has evolved, one that indicates that employment testing can be a reliable, valid, and fair method for choosing candidates who are likely to perform well on the job (Guion, 1991; Hunter & Hunter, 1984; Reilly & Chao, 1982; Schmitt, Gooding, Noe, & Kirsch, 1984; Schmidt & Hunter, 1998). This is important. Choosing the right candidate improves productivity.

In fact, a survey of research studies showed that using aptitude and ability tests increased productivity between 2.6% and 43.5%, with an average improvement of 10.4% (Kopelman, 1986). For many jobs, it is easy to see what a 10% improvement in performance per new hire would mean to the business' top line. For example, if selecting salespeople, after 10 hires, an organization would have the equivalent of an extra salesperson on the sales team with no additional headcount on the payroll. Other writers provide more detailed illustrations using actual dollar values (Boudreau, 1991; Schmidt, Hunter, McKenzie, & Muldrow, 1979). For example, Schmidt, Hunter, Outerbridge, and Trattner (1986) compared differences in performance of white-collar employees selected by employment tests with that of employees selected by other means. They found that test-selected entry-level white-collar employees outperformed the other employees by just under 10%, and this difference translated into annual productivity gains worth between $1,700 and $16,000 per person.

Of course, the economic benefits of employment testing are realized in less direct ways. For example, the primary reason for turnover in an organization is an individual's inability to perform adequately on the job and, although poor performance clearly has economic consequences, turnover itself is costly. At the very least, there are separation costs to contend with, including exit interviews, administrative functions related to termination, separation pay, and so forth. In addition, there are replacement costs for recruiting, head hunting, moving expenses, sign-on bonuses, costs associated with training the replacement, and so on. In total, replacement costs for mid-level executives are conservatively estimated to equal or exceed 1 year's salary in today's tight labor market.

It is precisely for the reasons just noted that employment testing is counted on more than ever to guide selection decisions in an increasingly competitive business environment. However, it is no simple task to develop a useful testing program that conforms to professional and legal guidelines. Building a conventional testing program requires an expert to conduct the sophisticated personnel research necessary to support the system. For example, in a criterion-related strategy, which is the most popular approach for establishing the reliability and validity of a testing program, this involves conducting the personnel research to show a systematic relationship between the test scores for a sample of employees in a given job and important measures of job performance from those employees. This research typically includes the eight steps listed in Fig. 1.1. The background work involved in developing a sound employment testing program is clearly not a simple exercise, but in situations where a large number of people are performing essentially the same work, it makes sense to invest the time and expense. (Those readers not familiar with these basic psychometric concepts should take a detour through Appendix A before tackling this chapter.)

Why all this discussion about employment testing? Well, the fact is that there are very few testing methods (again, broadly defined to include paper-and-pencil tests, interview questions, scored work history forms, performance in simulations, etc.) readily available for situations where few people are involved or where the issue of selecting replacement talent is not a recur-

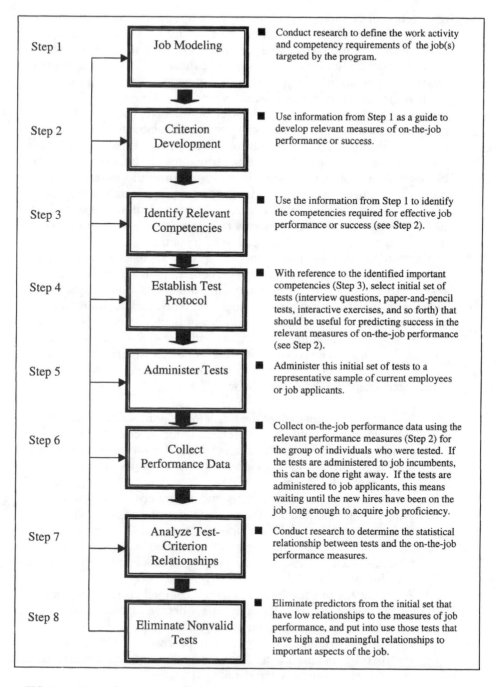

Step 1	**Job Modeling**	■ Conduct research to define the work activity and competency requirements of the job(s) targeted by the program.
Step 2	**Criterion Development**	■ Use information from Step 1 as a guide to develop relevant measures of on-the-job performance or success.
Step 3	**Identify Relevant Competencies**	■ Use the information from Step 1 to identify the competencies required for effective job performance or success (see Step 2).
Step 4	**Establish Test Protocol**	■ With reference to the identified important competencies (Step 3), select initial set of tests (interview questions, paper-and-pencil tests, interactive exercises, and so forth) that should be useful for predicting success in the relevant measures of on-the-job performance (see Step 2).
Step 5	**Administer Tests**	■ Administer this initial set of tests to a representative sample of current employees or job applicants.
Step 6	**Collect Performance Data**	■ Collect on-the-job performance data using the relevant performance measures (Step 2) for the group of individuals who were tested. If the tests are administered to job incumbents, this can be done right away. If the tests are administered to job applicants, this means waiting until the new hires have been on the job long enough to acquire job proficiency.
Step 7	**Analyze Test-Criterion Relationships**	■ Conduct research to determine the statistical relationship between tests and the on-the-job performance measures.
Step 8	**Eliminate Nonvalid Tests**	■ Eliminate predictors from the initial set that have low relationships to the measures of job performance, and put into use those tests that have high and meaningful relationships to important aspects of the job.

FIG. 1.1. Research steps required to support an employment testing program using a criterion-related strategy.

ring event. For example, it typically makes no sense to use conventional personnel research procedures such as those in Fig. 1.1 to develop a testing program for selecting a senior vice president (SVP) of marketing or a chief financial officer. For senior-level positions like these, even in the largest organizations, there are usually just a handful of people performing the work. Similarly, in smaller organizations, more junior-level positions like marketing or sales manager, accounting manager, or other entry-level staff and administrative positions may have relatively few incumbents. Consequently, the selection question is a relatively infrequent one. In these kinds of small sample and, in many cases, literally $n = 1$ situations, it is frequently not feasible to base selection or promotion decisions on conventional testing procedures: It is simply too difficult to generate the research sample sizes necessary to conduct criterion-related validation studies. It is into these niche employment testing situations that individual assessment practice has, over the years, quietly expanded to fill a void.

Unquestionably, there are a variety of specific approaches to individual assessment, some more directly tied to job content than others. The position taken in this book is that the most useful information is obtained when individual assessment is conducted as a logical extension of traditional validation research, as shown in Fig. 1.1. In other words, individual assessment is a process designed to measure a particular candidate's job-related competencies. Moreover, as in employment testing situations where there are large numbers of candidates, the proper job–person match resulting from an individual assessment can be best made by:

- Making a careful analysis of the target job requirements to identify the competencies most likely to be related to job success (as discussed in chap. 2, the definition of the target job may be a specific position or a broader job group, or even a job family like human resources (HR) or job category like Manager).
- Selecting a set of tests to reliably and accurately tap the job-related competencies identified in the previous step and administering them to the job candidate(s) (as discussed in chap. 3, the tests providing input information to the assessment process may be of the paper-and-pencil variety, or they may be in-basket tests, interactive exercises or simulations, and so forth).
- Analyzing the test results and making a comprehensive evaluation or assessment of a particular candidate's degree of possession of the job-related competencies identified previously (see chap. 5).
- Reporting the results of the assessment process to the client in such a way that the conclusions are clear, comprehensive, and unlikely to be misinterpreted (discussed in detail in chap. 6).

However, unlike a conventional validation study, the products of each of the first three steps just noted are, in part, derived by an assessment professional rather than empirically determined through personnel research. The final evaluation of a job candidate involves a subjective component on the assessment professional's part, rather than solely a reliance on the objective results of test scores. Together, these four bullet points define the process known as individual assessment and elaborate on the general definition provided in the preface. The characteristic that differentiates individual assessment from the traditional strategy of employment testing is the idiosyncratic procedure of conducting integrative and interpretive treatment of assessment data at the individual case level. However, it would be incorrect to interpret this as a license for the assessor to simply do what comes naturally. On the contrary, the practice of individual assessment must be consistent with sound measurement and decision-making methodology. Individual assessment is not an arbitrary and capricious activity. At this point, a brief sojourn to the historical and research roots of employment testing and assessment should help in our efforts to build a contextual platform for understanding current individual assessment practice.

HISTORICAL CONTEXT

The practice of assessment dates back at least 800 years. In 13th-century China, candidates for public official positions participated in an elaborate assessment process that yielded an evaluation of relevant knowledge, skills, and personal characteristics (i.e., competencies). This process has been written about in a number of places (DuBois, 1970) and appears to have been very sophisticated. In addition to employing the laudatory design feature of multiple measures to tap each of the job-related competencies, the process was quite protracted, lasting, from beginning to end, several years.

More recently, individual assessment practice was implemented and developed in the German military and in the British public service in the 1920s and 1930s (Ansbacher, 1941). Independently, the Office of Strategic Services (OSS) in the United States developed an extensive and intensive practice to select agents for assignments behind enemy lines (Murray, MacKinnon, Miller, Fiske, & Hanfmann, 1948). At the time, this measurement and prediction effort was unique in that the practice was developed and guided without the benefit of a definite target job. The assessment was conducted to select individuals who could operate, and survive, in an unstructured, unpredictable, and infinitely hostile environment, where failure had severe, if not fatal, consequences. In other words, a variant of assessment had evolved at this point, where the target job was not specified and the search for talent was more of an open-ended effort. A similar form of assessment then evolved in business and industry, where the target was broadly defined in terms of general fitness for employment, fit with a company or potential with reference to a broad job category (e.g., manager).

The practice of individual assessment in private industry was introduced in the United States, starting in the late 1930s and early 1940s. This initial work is most correctly described as clinical assessment. The practitioners were primarily psychologists and tended to be trained in clinical practice. Moreover, their approach to the assessment practice used primarily clinical tools and the process was geared toward accumulating information about individuals as individuals, with a very limited emphasis on the idea of job relatedness. Given this orientation, it is not surprising that the goal of assessment from this period centered primarily on helping executives fit into an organization and work effectively with their associates. A more structured, job-related approach, involving individuals trained as industrial psychologists, evolved in the 1940s and 1950s, when psychologists like Hemphill (1960), Rothe (1957), and Fleishman, Harris, and Burtt (1955) began to take into account job content, job requirements, and criteria of individual and group effectiveness—but we are getting ahead of ourselves.

The counterparts of the clinical psychologists, the industrial psychologists, initially had limited exposure to, and involvement with, individual assessment. Nevertheless, a few adventuresome individuals did practice in the early 1910s and 1920s, though their activity was not substantially integrated with the more clinically oriented practice. It is worth noting that the first assemblage of true industrial psychologists was represented by members of the Carnegie Tech group in 1912. Thus, in terms of generations, considering the 1910s through the 1920s as the first generation, the 1930s and 1940s as the second generation, and so on, it was not until the second generation that industrial psychology started to have an impact on individual assessment practice. Even then, the influence was typically one or two steps removed from any direct involvement in individual assessment activities. For example, although second-generation industrial psychologists like Burtt (1926), Munsterberg (1913), Ohmann (1961), Otis (1938), Stead and Shartle (1940), Strong (1934), Urbrock (1934), and Viteles (1932), and many others conducted work that is an essential part of the knowledge base that supports the practice of individual assessment, these individuals are seldom associated with the practice of individual assessment. The exceptions here are Oliver Ohmann and Jay L. Otis, who in the 1950s was president of Division 14 (Industrial and Organizational Psychology) and later of Division 13 (Consulting Psychology) of the American Psychological Association. Ohmann is particularly important because he was instrumental in initiating and supporting programs of research on executive assessment at the Standard Oil Company of Ohio.

This marks a transition point in our discussion of the history of individual assessment practice. Although there are few reported direct evaluations of the individual assessment process, and although much of the reported work is dated and has been conducted with reference to evaluative standards that prevailed at the time, there is a history here that is important to understand. The purpose of the next section is to briefly review those reported studies that directly address the question of whether an assessment practitioner, using the idiosyncratic procedures we have alluded to, can accurately forecast how an individual will perform in a future job.

RESEARCH CONTEXT

Ultimately, the critical component of the individual assessment process is the assessor's final prediction of performance for a candidate in specified activities or in terms of the whole job. This prediction of performance is what is observed by others and represents the end product of the process. As far as the customer or client is concerned, the accuracy of this prediction is all that counts. From this vantage point, it is conceivable to evaluate the process in terms of reliability and criterion-related validity. Unfortunately, although this is a very practical conclusion, it is deceptively attractive in that the answer does not necessarily lead to better understanding of the assessment process or to improved practice. Still, a brief examination of this research base will provide some context for ideas and discussion presented in later chapters.

As Table 1.1 indicates, the first reported evaluation of an individual assessment program was Vernon's (1950) study of the British Foreign Service and Civil Service selection program. This was an extensive project that involved various combinations of subject groups, assessors, predictors, and criteria. A representative subset of the results are reported in Table 1.1 for candidates for administrative jobs ($n = 147$), foreign service jobs ($n = 123$), and foreign service administrative officers ($n = 202$). Correlations between psychologists' overall evaluations and aggregated performance ratings for the three groups were .22, .21, and .14, respectively. These correlations are not particularly high, though it is very likely all the validity coefficients were lowered by severe attrition in the research samples as a result of the rejection of candidates. When corrected for restriction of range, the rs increase dramatically; specifically, the validity coefficients just noted jump to .49, .49, and .48. Other findings of interest were that most of the judgmental predictions were more effective than the purely mechanical predictions (i.e., strict actuarial interpretations; see chap. 3), and that psychologists' assessment ratings were less variable than assessments made by staff members.

The following year, Kelly and Fiske (1951) reported the second research study focusing on assessment, which included a validity coefficient of .37 between one psychologist's interpretation of credential and objective test data and ratings of job performance obtained 3 years later for 280 clinical psychology trainees. In spite of the fact that institutional variability interacted with job variability to confound the prediction problem, this study is unusual in that it involved an intimate familiarity with the criterion on the part of the assessor, a clinical psychologist.

Soon after, Holtzman and Sells (1954) reported a study that used 100 USAF aviation cadets as subjects, 50 of whom were judged by superiors as having successfully adjusted to the rigors of flight training and 50 who had failed to complete training due to a variety of psychological disturbances. Nineteen psychologists were split into five groups and each group was provided with the results of six group-administered projective tests and asked to identify the individuals that completed flight training. The number of cor-

TABLE 1.1
Individual Assessment Research

Reference	Sample	Criterion	Validities
Vernon (1950)	147 Civil Service candidates	Ratings by supervisors, 13 performance and personality dimensions, 1 aggregated grade	$r = .22$ for final grades
	123 Foreign Service candidates	Rating by Head of Foreign Office, based on reports by supervisors	$r = .21$ for final grade
	202 Civil Service officers	Ratings by supervisors, 10 performance and personality dimensions, 1 aggregated grade	$r = .14$ for final grade, 2 years after assessment
Kelly and Fiske (1951)	280 VA clinical psychologist trainees	Ratings by supervisors, 3 or 8 performance dimensions	$r = .37$ for overall performance rating
Holtzman and Sells (1954)	100 male USAF aviation cadets	Retention in flight training	Identification of successful graduates not significantly different from chance
Handyside and Duncan (1954)	44 male candidates for manufacturing supervisory positions	Ratings by supervisors, 1 overall	$r = .55$, 4.5 years later
Hilton, Bolin, Parker, Taylor, and Walker (1955)	100 males from PRI Personal Audit Program, representing 18 companies	Ratings by supervisors, 1 overall, 4 performance, and personality	rs from .21 to .38 (median = .28) across 5 dimensions
Stern, Stein, and Bloom (1956)	10 elementary school trainees	Rankings by supervisors, 1 overall	rho of .70
Meyer (1956)	190 supervisors from General Electric	Ratings by supervisors, 1 overall, 3 performance	rs from .11 to .38 (median = .77) across 4 dimensions
Holt (1958)	64 residents in training, Menninger School of Psychology	Ratings by supervisors and peers on 5 performance dimensions	rs from .13 to .58 for supervisors and from .15 to .55 for peers
Dunnette and Kirchner (1958)	26 male sales managers in 3M's production division	Rankings by supervisors, 1 overall	tetrachoric $r = .80$ for "high" and "low" potential classifications
	Two groups ($n = 29$ and $n = 16$) of 3M supervisors	Rankings by supervisors, 1 overall	rs of .52 and .62

Trankell (1959)	363 airline pilots with Scandinavian Airlines	Dismissal rate over 5-year period	Biserial rs from −.21 to .55 (median = .34) for 14 assessment dimensions
Campbell, Otis, Liske, and Prien (1962)	213 males performing manager, sales, and technical work for 37 companies	Ratings by supervisors, 1 overall, 7 performance and personality dimensions	rs ranged from −.05 to .50
Huse (1962)	107 males, partially overlapping with Campbell et al. (1962) sample	Ratings by supervisors, 1 overall, 7 performance and personality dimensions	rs from .13 to .44, (median = .28)
Phelan (1962)	94 males competing for supervisory positions with 18 different companies	Rankings by supervisors, 1 overall	median rho for all 18 populations was .70
Albrecht, Glaser, and Marks (1964)	31 district marketing managers assessed for promotion purposes	Rank composites for 1 overall and 3 performance dimensions	rs from .43 to .58
Flanagan and Krug (1964)	60 Lockheed engineers	Criterion group design	34 correct group assignments from 60 possible
Dicken and Black (1965)	31 first-line supervisors with manufacturing company and 26 managers and auditors with insurance company	Ratings by supervisors, 1 overall, 7 performances and personality dimensions	rs from .20 to .51 (median=.36) for manufacturing and .03 to .65 (median=.29) for insurance sample
Gordon (1967)	172 Peace Corps volunteers across 2 assessment sites, 103 males and 69 females	Placed overseas, includes dropouts and board deselections	rs .38 and .43 for two sites, rs of .46 for males, .28 for females
DeNelsky and McKee (1969)	32 government employees	Fitness reports revaluation. In terms of 25 performance and personality dimensions	r of .32 using composite index of effectiveness
Miner (1970)	Five groups of management and non-management business consultants; sample sizes range from 24 to 80	Tenure, mean increase in compensation, and 1 overall rating by supervisors	rs from −.05 to .18 for tenure, −.11 to .14 for compensation and −.14 to .05 for ratings
Silzer (1984)	1749 managers from many levels and organizations and 208 managers from two unidentified companies	Ratings on 7 trait dimensions by supervisors	rs from .10 to .28

11

rect classifications ranged from 4 to 14 with a median of 10.2, which is not significantly different from a 50:50 split (i.e., 10 of 20 classifications correct by chance alone). This study is often cited as a case against the use of clinical prediction. However, predictions can be no better than input data used as a basis for judgments, and the group-administered, projective personality tests used in this study (e.g., the Feeling and Doing test of psychosomatic symptoms and the group-administered version of the Draw-A-Person Test) have questionable psychometric quality. Furthermore, the 19 psychologists were one step removed from the actual test data and they had varying degrees of familiarity with the tests that were used.

The same year, in a study from the National Institute of Industrial Psychology in England, Handyside and Duncan (1954) reported an amazingly high validity of $r = .55$. In this case, the researchers were predicting overall ratings of performance by supervisors more than 4 years later for 44 candidates for supervisory positions. This level of validity is down from .68 as reported by Castle and Garforth (1951) using the same 44 candidates for supervisory positions in a large engineering works plant in an earlier 2-year follow-up.

The next year, Hilton, Bolin, Parker, Taylor, and Walker (1955) reported on the predictive validity of the Personal Audit Program at the Western Reserve University Personnel Research Institute. The study included 100 men, representing 18 companies, assessed in 1951 and 1952. Two psychologists reviewed test and interview data on file (which were generated previously by an unknown number of different psychologists) and rated assessees on five personality and performance dimensions. A variety of paper-and-pencil tests were used. Supervisor ratings of sociability, organization ability, drive, overall performance, and potential for advancement, obtained 2 to 3 years after the assessment, were used as criteria. Validities ranged from .21 to .38 (median $r = .28$) across the five dimensions. The median validity increased to .35 when corrected for criterion unreliability. Although these results, and those of Handyside and Duncan (1954), are encouraging, the predictive validities may be overestimates due to criterion contamination by raters through knowledge of previous assessment data. Furthermore, the correlations of a given predictor scale with other predictor and criterion scales were often significant, indicating halo effects and a lack of discriminant validity.

These same limitations also apply to the Stern, Stein, and Bloom (1956) study. A team of psychologists evaluated each of 10 elementary school teacher trainees with reference to a hypothetical model that included interpersonal relations, level of energy, and goal orientation. The rank-order correlation between overall rankings by the assessment team and faculty judgments was an exceptionally high .70 ($p < .05$).

The research reported by Meyer (1956) is atypical to the extent that it involved nonpsychologists making predictions. Actually, this study could be construed as a predecessor to the assessment center approach. One hundred ninety supervisors participated in the General Electric Supervisor Selection Program that involved appointing personnel specialists to help operating departments assess candidates for supervisory positions. Assessors made "recommend," "recommend with limitations," and "not recommend" judgments based on an interview and a wide range of general mental ability and specific aptitude tests. Predictive validities ranged from .11 to .38, depending on the criterion used, and five of seven validities were significant, although four of the correlations were below the predictive validity of the paper-and-pencil Wonderlic test alone (.27). Unfortunately, the criterion contamination problem reared its head here as well.

Holt (1958), using second- and third-year residents in training at the Menninger School of Psychiatry as subjects ($n = 64$), had two psychologists make predictive ratings in five performance dimensions (competence in psychotherapy, diagnosis, management, administration, and overall competence). Peer and supervisor ratings in the same performance dimensions were collected approximately 1 year after assessment. Across judges and dimensions, the validities ranged from .13 to .58 (median $r = .42$). However, one of the two assessors consistently outperformed the other across both groups and all performance dimensions. This finding, in conjunction with the wide variability in the accuracy of classifications reported by Holtzman and Sells (1954), underscores the likelihood that there are differences attributable to the assessor (e.g., training, experience, personal orientation, and insight) that affect the accuracy of different assessors' predictions.

The Dunnette and Kirchner (1958) study is interesting in that it used the clinical combination of personality and interest test scores in line with very specific hypotheses about what constitutes the requisite profile of effective management (e.g., broad interests, high intelligence, forceful personalities). Two psychologists used the results of an assessment test battery to classify 26 sales managers from 3M's Product Division into "favorable" or "unfavorable" profiles. The tetrachoric correlation between the classifications and paired-comparison rankings of effectiveness made by a divisional vice president was $r_t = .80$ ($p < .01$).

Trankell's (1959) work provides a look at an individual assessment procedure focusing on a quite different type of job, that of airline pilots. All airline pilots hired by Scandinavian Airlines System during the years 1951 to 1956 ($n = 363$) were assessed using various tests of intelligence, mechanical comprehension, social sensitivity, interests, and by autobiographical questions, an essay, and a scheduling-planning problem. The criterion was dismissal rate. By 1958 none of the 49 hires judged to be "particularly suitable" had been dismissed for unsuitable performance, whereas 8 of the 218 (3.7%) in the "suitable" category, 4 of 59 (6.8%) in the "doubtful" category, and 17 of 37 (45.9%) in the "unsuitable" category had been let go for unsatisfactory performance. Furthermore, biserial correlations between assessment ratings for 14 personality and performance dimensions and the remaining dismissed criterion ranged from −.21 to .55 (median $r_b = .34$). For the five specific assessment dimensions for which objective test data were collected, biserial correlations ranged from −.07 to .42 and, in all but one case, correlations for assessor ratings were higher than test-alone correlations.

A series of research efforts conducted at Case-Western Reserve presented evidence of the validity of the individual assessment process and of a number of specific components for assessees in sales and general management positions from 37 different companies (Campbell, 1962; Campbell, Otis, Liske, & Prien, 1962). Supervisor ratings on eight criterion dimensions were obtained for both a sales group and a general management group. Actually, two sets of supervisor ratings were obtained for both groups: First-level supervisors provided 44 sets of ratings and second-level supervisors provided 33 sets of ratings for the sales group, and first-level supervisors provided 73 sets of ratings and second-level supervisors provided 63 for the general management group. For the sales group, correlations between psychologists' ratings with first-level supervisors' ratings ($n = 44$) ranged from .08 to .39, whereas correlations between psychologists' ratings with second-level supervisors' ratings ($n = 33$) ranged from −.05 to .35. For the general management group, correlations between psychologists' ratings with first-level supervisors' ratings ($n = 73$) ranged from .04 to .41 and the psychologists' ratings with second-level supervisors' ratings ($n = 63$) ranged from .10 to .50. These results suggest that psychologists were able to make accurate predictions of successful job performance in spite of the fact that interinstitutional variability interacted with job heterogeneity to confound the prediction problem. On the downside, the fact that there were over four times as many inappropriate versus appropriate correlations suggests a lack of discriminant validity.

In related studies from the Case-Western Reserve assessment program, the interview showed slight but not strong validity (Prien, 1962) and the projective instruments showed questionable results (Hogue, Otis, & Prien, 1962). The work by Huse (1962), using a subsample of 107 subjects, found that ratings by the psychologists who conducted the assessments just described correlated from .13 to .44 (mean $r = .28$) with supervisor ratings on the same dimensions. Ratings by the author, based solely on a reading of the narrative assessment reports (i.e., no ratings or test data), ranged from .07 to .32 (mean $r = .21$) across the eight dimensions. Finally, the overall program evaluation provided conceptual support for the practice of individual assessment (Otis, Campbell, & Prien, 1962).

The same year, Phelan (1962) reported a follow-up on 94 men tested for first-line supervisory positions who were ranked by supervisors in terms of promotability after 18 to 36 months on the job. Upon completion of the testing, two personnel specialists read the reports produced by the psychologist assessors and then ranked the applicants in terms of promotability to management. Spearman-Brown rank correlations between specialist rankings and supervisor rankings were then computed for all 18 industrial populations. Of the 18 *rhos*, 8 were significant at the .05 level (median $r_s = .70$). There was a 66% agreement in the selection of those placed by top management and 83% of those judged second best were counted as correct choices.

The next contribution to the individual assessment research literature was from Albrecht, Glaser, and Marks (1964), who assessed 31 district marketing managers for promotion purposes. Three psychologists ranked the 31 subjects according to predicted job effectiveness on four job performance dimensions: forecasting and budgeting effectiveness, sales performance, interpersonal relationships, and overall performance. After 1 year on the job, each subject was ranked by two supervisors and by peers and the three sets of rankings were combined to form a composite index for each man on each dimension. Assessment predictions yielded correlations of .43, .46, and .58 across the three criterion groups and test score correlations ranged from −.07 to .41 (median $r = .20$). The finding that peer rankings were best predicted may be attributable to the fact that these rankings were based on the mean rankings of many judges rather than individual rankings. Furthermore, given the poor discriminant validity evidenced in previous studies, it is heartening that only 8% of the off-diagonal coefficients in heteromethod blocks exceeded the validity coefficients. Moreover, this study is particularly deserving of attention because the assessment data were not used in any way in the promotion process and no reports were given to company personnel. Thus, unlike other earlier studies, later judgments of effectiveness could not have been contaminated by prior assessment results.

Also in 1964, Flanagan and Krug (1964) reported a study involving 60 engineers with the Lockheed Aircraft Corporation, 30 of whom held management positions and 30 of whom were in primarily technical support positions. Fifteen subjects were selected to represent high promotion rate and low promotion rate groups for both the management and technical groups. Then 60 subjects completed the 12-hour SCOPES test battery, the results of which were evaluated by psychologists blind to the criterion group results. Based on this input data, the psychologists then assigned management and technical engineers to either high or low performing groups. By chance alone, 15 of the 60 classifications would be hits. However, psychologists assigned 34 individuals to the correct criterion group ($p < .05$).

The following year, Dicken and Black (1965) reported a study involving 31 first-line supervisors with a manufacturing company and 26 managers and auditors with an insurance company, who had been assessed at the Counseling Center at Stanford University. Each assessee was evaluated by a psychologist who produced a two-page report. These narrative reports were subsequently read by four psychologists who independently provided assessment ratings. Criterion ratings were obtained from supervisors 3½ years later for the manufacturing sample and 7 years later for the insurance sample. Validities ranged from .20 to .51 for the manufacturing sample (mean r =.36) and from .03 to .65 for the insurance sample (mean r =.29). When corrected for unreliability, the average validities rose to .43 and .33 for the manufacturing and insurance groups. The level of discriminant validity was also encouraging; correlations in relevant variables were, in all instances but one, a good deal higher than the average correlations with nonrelevant variables. In addition, it is likely that criterion contamination was minimal because, by the time the criterion data were collected, the assessment reports had not been looked at in years.

Two years later, Gordon (1967) reported a study with 172 Peace Corps volunteers who were assessed for 5 days for an overseas placement. The criterion was whether the volunteers were ever placed in an overseas assignment (25% of volunteers either quit or were terminated). Tetrachoraic validities for overall clinical assessment ratings for the two sites were .39 and .43 ($p < .05$). Up to this point, this is the only study that explicitly reports that women comprised part of the sample; there were 103 males and 69 females across the two sites. The validity for males was significant (.46, $p < .05$) and markedly higher than for females (.28, nonsignificant).

In the DeNelsky and McKee (1969) work, one of seven psychologists read assessment reports for 32 government employees who were assessed by one of eight psychologists 12 to 57 months earlier. The seven psychologists involved in the second step read two-page narrative reports generated by the first group of psychologists and, based on their reading of the reports, evaluated each subject in terms of up to 25 performance and personality dimensions. The fitness reports were then evaluated by the seven psychologists for each of the 32 subjects in terms of the same mix of performance and personality dimensions. The correlation between the overall predictions of effectiveness based on assessment reports and judged effectiveness as interpreted from the fitness reports was .32 ($p < .05$). In addition, 92 of 171 predictions of performance in specific personality and performance dimensions were judged to be hits ($p < .05$) relative to a 50:50 split. However, only three of seven judges were able to predict overall success with significant accuracy ($p < .05$). This highlights once again the variability in effectiveness of assessor performance. Moreover, this is another case where assessors were asked to formulate predictions on the basis of finished assessment reports. Thus, these assessors, similar to those in the Holtzman and Sells (1954), Hilton et al. (1955), Huse (1962), and Dicken and Black (1965) studies, were placed in a role similar to the typical consumer of assessment reports. In other words, they were asked to make predictions based on someone else's analysis and interpretation of first-hand data.

Then, to virtually close out an era, Miner (1970) described a series of five studies using management and nonmanagement industrial consultants from seven different firms. The sample sizes for each of the studies ranged from 24 to 80 and involved current and separated employees who had been assessed previously (1 month to 9 years) by one of approximately 10 different psychologists from one of seven different firms conducting assessments. The subsequent assessment reports were reviewed by Miner and evaluated using a 5-point scale ranging from 5 (*clearly outstanding*) to 1 (*definitely not recommended*). The criteria used in the five studies were tenure, mean increase in compensation, and a rating of overall performance that was completed by a supervisor. Correlations between Miner's ratings and those made by supervisors ranged from −.14 to .18 across the studies, none of which were significant. Although these results are discouraging, it should be noted that Miner's ratings were two interpretative steps removed from the original test data. Furthermore, variability in the tests, psychologists, and assessment firms used to generate the original reports seriously confounded the prediction problem. Miner himself raised additional issues that may explain the lack of validity in these studies. Together, these studies by Miner represent the end of a 20-year run of interest and research on individual assessment.

It was not until 16 years later that Silzer (1984) reported the results from two studies that constitute the last installment to the individual assessment research base. The first study involved 1,749 managers representing the full spectrum of management levels and functions. Using a mix of personality and cognitive ability tests as sources of input information, psychologists provided trait ratings of assessee motivation, problem solving, administrative ability, communication skills, interpersonal skills, leadership ability, and personal insight. The second study was a follow-up on 208 managers from two companies who went through an assessment process. Job performance ratings from each manager's supervisor were obtained 8 to 10 years after the assessment. In both cases, the level of reporting was fairly general, though it was clear that a large number of individual test scales and psychologists' ratings were correlated with ratings of success provided by supervisors, tenure, and salary increases over the years.

These 20 sets of studies constitute the sum total of the available research base directly evaluating the validity of individual assessment practice. Compared to the vast body of research in other areas of selection, such as paper-and-pencil testing or the interview, this, indeed, represents a puny amount of work. So, can an assessment practitioner accurately forecast how an individual will perform in a future job? As this research review illustrates, the studies that directly evaluate this question are dated and few. Furthermore, for the most part, the work that has been done represents casual, opportunistic, contaminated, psychometric evaluation. In spite of all of this, the results are still supportive of the process. Therefore, the answer would appear to be "yes."

However, the intriguing follow-up question is: "What would the results look like if we designed and carried out a sound, comprehensive evaluative study?" In other words, what if we used a job modeling effort to truly understand the nature of a target job's requirements? What if we then used the results of that job modeling effort not only to select a relevant set of predictor tests, but also to develop a meaningful and comprehensive set of performance criteria? What if we collected this criterion data over time in order to build adequate sample size? The kind of results we would get in this kind of (very basic) research context remains unknown.

Finally, as important as the tentative "yes" is with reference to the overall prediction question, it is a response to an overly simplistic question. "Can an assessment practitioner accurately forecast how an individual will perform in a future job?", a clearly practical question, is deceptively attractive because it leaves many important questions and lines of evidence unaddressed that would lead to improved practice. To achieve this higher order goal, what is required is a comprehensive and practical model to serve as the foundation for individual assessment practice.

THE INDIVIDUAL ASSESSMENT MODEL

The individual assessment process described in this book, and represented in Fig. 1.2, is not a theoretical model. Rather, it constitutes a description of the actual assessment process, step by step, as it actually exists. This same real world model is also a useful scheme for organizing the wide array of research that supports the different decision points in the process. The steps involved to ensure a comprehensive and rational basis for subjectively combining vast amounts of test data and personal information are complex and involve both breadth and depth in different content areas of knowledge. Furthermore, despite the range in practice, it is our view that there is a "best way" to conduct individual assessments. The steps involved in the process and the associated content areas of knowledge are described in the model for the individual assessment process below. This model also serves as the organizing structure for the next five chapters of the book.

Job Modeling

Before it is possible to predict who will succeed in a target role, it is necessary to know which work activities or behaviors are required in the job and which competencies are required to perform those work activities. Furthermore, not all jobs are alike, so the competency requirements will differ. The practice of individual assessment should include these two ideas to some extent. This does not mean it is necessary to conduct a large-scale analysis of the work requirements (i.e., Step 1 in Fig. 1.1). As chapter 2 covers in detail, there are efficient approaches for creating a job-related platform of information (e.g., an organization's business strategy, the work context, and the work activity and competency requirements of a particular job) to support an individual assessment program. However, the efficiency with which this information may be captured should not belie the critical nature of the content. This descriptive information is essential because it tailors the assessment protocol to the target job and establishes the rational relationship between the job and the assessment program.

It makes sense at this point to explain how we are using several terms. To begin with, there is the much maligned word *job*. It is vogue to speak as though the concept of a person holding a job in business and industry today is an outdated concept. Some professionals are going so far as to write about the end of the concept of a job in today's fast-paced, matrixed, restructured work environment (Aronowitz & DiFazio, 1994; Bridges, 1994; Rifkin, 1995). It is true that jobs, like everything else, are certainly changing, and

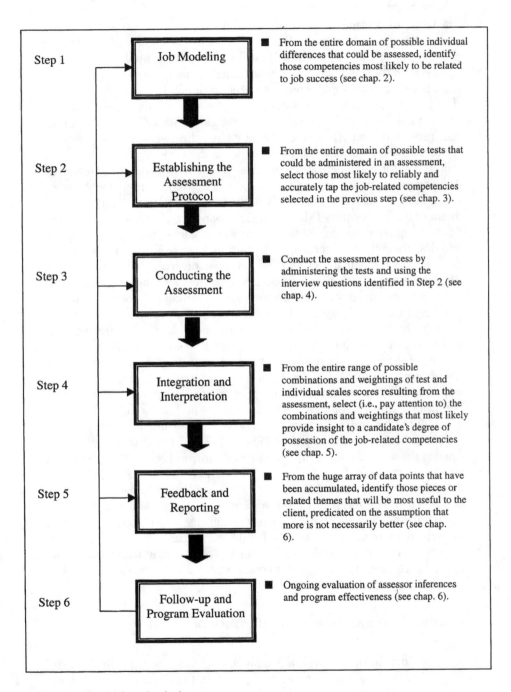

Fig. 1.2. Model for individual assessment practice.

the definition and measurement of the characteristics of jobs need to change as well (Peterson, Mumford, Borman, Jeanneret, & Fleishman, 1999), but the concept of a job, in our view, is still viable and essential.

However, there is a need for some updated thinking on the subject, which leads us to the next couple of terms we need to clarify: *job analysis* and *job modeling*. Job analysis refers to the systematic analysis procedures for describing job requirements that gained prominence in the early 1900s when their information-generating properties were recognized by industrial engineers, personnel specialists, and psychologists. Despite the prominence of job analysis as the foundation for many personnel practices (Prien & Ronan, 1971), including individual assessment, it is questionable whether conventional approaches are capable of delivering maximally useful information in the work environments of the 21st century (McLagan, 1990; Sanchez, 1994). Job modeling refers to an updated, more flexible, and forward-looking approach to identifying and describing the requirements of a position, job, job group, or job family as described by Schippmann (1999) and Schippmann et al. (2000), and it is this evolutionary approach that is integrated into the presentation of individual assessment in this book. Thus, any time we refer to conventional job analysis practices in the book, we use the phrase that was prevalent at the time: *job analysis*. On the other hand, when referring to the updated, OD-like approach to job analysis used in this book, the phrase *job modeling* is used.

One of the important products of the job modeling phase of the individual assessment process is a description of the *competencies* required to perform a job. When has a single term generated so much energy, angst, and confusion in the area of personnel management and research? As the reader is undoubtedly aware, competencies have been defined in various ways (Spencer, McClelland, & Spencer, 1994). However, in this text, they are defined as the measurable, occupationally relevant, and behaviorally based capabilities of people. In this respect, they can be thought of as behavioral descriptions of job-related knowledge, skills, and abilities (i.e., a more specific and behavioral version of the concept of *knowledge, skills, and abilities*, or *KSAs*). Competencies, then, serve as the job-related individual difference material to be measured or assessed and form the basis for establishing the assessment protocol. The detailed discussion on how to efficiently and comprehensively identify the important competencies associated with a particular job is presented in chapter 2.

Establishing the Assessment Protocol

An examination of the *Mental Measurements Yearbook* (Impara & Plake, 1998) reveals thousands of paper-and-pencil test options. Of course, when interpreting the word *test* more broadly to include work samples, interactive exercises, interview questions, and so forth, then the domain of potential measures becomes significantly larger. So, from the entire domain of possible tests that could be administered to a job candidate, how does the assessor select those most likely to be useful in an assessment?

In short, the requirements of the target job, which are operationally defined in terms of competencies, structure and drive the assessment protocol, in terms of the competencies and level of proficiency required. At this step in the model, the assessor is processing information about the requirements of the job and information about the reliability, validity, normative base, and so forth, of the tests at his or her disposal. It is this process of collecting, analyzing, and assimilating different types of information, at this step and elsewhere in the assessment process, that constitutes the uniqueness of the individual assessment practice.

For the sake of clarity, we need to further elaborate on how the word *job* is used in the discussion of the assessment protocol throughout the book. Unless otherwise stated, we use the word to refer to the target of the assessment in a general way. In fact, the target of the assessment process is often a specific *position* (i.e., a grouping of work activities performed by one person within a single organization, in one location, with one boss and one set of peers and direct reports). However, this is not always the case. In some assessment situations, the target job is broader and, in some instances, much broader. For example, the specifications for the assessment may be designed to tap the competency requirements for a job group (i.e., cluster of similar positions within one organization) like plant manager in a multiplant organization. Continuing up the broadness continuum, in still other situations the target job is even more general, where the competency requirements are determined based on those required for an entire job category or occupational class (e.g., managerial jobs, sales jobs, administrative jobs). This will be further addressed when we discuss the details of establishing the assessment protocol in chapter 3.

Conducting the Assessment

Typical assessments range from a half day to a full day, though some executive assessment programs last 2 days or more. Regardless of the duration, the assessment experience has some fairly standard stages, including: sending out and collecting prework, welcoming and orienting the assessee, explaining the process and administering consent forms, administering tests and inventories, conducting the assessment interview, and providing same-day feedback to the assessee. Suggestions and tips for managing the various stages of the assessment day are discussed in chapter 4.

Integration and Interpretation

The job-related competencies have been identified, the relevant tests have been selected and administered to the candidate, and now the assessor is awash in data. From the entire range of possible combinations of personal information and test scores resulting from the assessment, how should the assessor combine and weight the inputs so they provide the greatest insight into the candidate's degree of possession of specific competencies? Here, again, the assessor is required to collect, analyze, and assimilate different types of information, some clinical and some mechanical. Furthermore, the same set of assessment results may well be interpreted differently for two different candidates, with reference to similar jobs, in different areas of an organization or in different organizations.

In many respects, this step in the model is the heart of the individual assessment process. It is also at this juncture that the art of assessment becomes at least as important as the science. Nowhere is the complexity of the individual assessment process more evident than at this step. The idiosyncratic strategy representing the dynamic, integrative, and interpretive treatment of individual assessment is covered in chapter 5 and in its writing we have tried to stay true to one of Albert Einstein's familiar dictums: "Make everything as simple as possible, but not simpler." In the end, the assessor will address the all-important question: "What kind of person is this?"

Feedback and Reporting

This is where the rubber hits the road, the ball finally gets put into play, or any other metaphor indicating that the assessment results are about to be communicated and used. Depending on the level of complexity of the assessment, the assessor may have just spent several hours working with an assessee, may have accumulated hundreds of data points, and is now in a position to recognize all kinds of interesting trends and discrepancies in the information array. Furthermore, like most people, the assessor will be enamored with all the intricate richness and tempted to share all this terrific knowledge with the client sponsor. The challenge becomes how to organize and present the key themes so the critical messages get through, unclouded by wisps of tangential insights and nebulous possibilities. Although specific formats for feedback and reports vary, there are some basic rules of the road. These rules cluster around the need to keep one's bearings as one navigates through the vast expanse of data in the assessment landscape, with the roadmap of the job modeling results and the assessment specifications.

Program Evaluation

The measurement and tracking of individual assessment outcomes is a special case of the much broader challenge of change measurement reported elsewhere (Campbell & Stanley, 1963). Although it is deceptively attractive to slip into a dichotomous evaluation mode (i.e., the assessment intervention produces value or it does not), in practice, the geometry of evaluation does not run along such nice, straight lines. Consequently, it is necessary to measure the outcomes of individual assessment interventions in terms of degree and with reference to multiple definitions of success. Of course, the compounding difficulty is the slow rate at which individual-specific data points are accumulated over time. Nevertheless, a thorough, logical, and perhaps statistical analysis of the process and the outcomes is important to improve the functioning of the local assessment program. In addition, however, this evaluative information, when shared, will enrich the general body of information about assessment and propel the practice to the next level of sophistication as an organizational intervention.

REFERENCES

Albrecht, P. A., Glaser, E. D., & Marks, J. (1964). Validation of a multiple-assessment procedure for managerial personnel. *Journal of Applied Psychology, 48,* 351–360.

Ansbacher, H. L. (1941). German military psychology. *Psychological Bulletin, 38,* 370–379.

Aronowitz, S., & DiFazio, W. (1994). *The jobless future.* Minneapolis: University of Minnesota Press.

Boudreau, J. W. (1991). Utility analysis for decisions in human resource management. In M. D. Dunnette & L. M. Hough (Eds.), *Handbook of industrial and organizational psychology* (Vol. 2, pp. 621–745). Palo Alto, CA: Consulting Psychologists Press.

Bridges, W. (1994). *Jobshift.* Reading, MA: Addison-Wesley.

Burtt, H. E. (1926). *Principles of employment psychology.* New York: Harper Brothers.

Campbell, D. T., & Stanley, J. C. (1963). *Experimental and quasi-experimental designs for research.* Chicago: Rand McNally.

Campbell, J. T. (1962). Assessments of higher-level personnel: I. Background and scope of the research. *Personnel Psychology, 15,* 57–74.

Campbell, J. T., Otis, J. L., Liske, R. E., & Prien, E. P. (1962). Assessments of higher-level personnel: II. Validity of the over-all assessment process. *Personnel Psychology, 15,* 63–74.

Castle, P. F. C., & Garforth, F. I. de la P. (1951). Selection, training and status of supervisors: 1. Selection. *Occupational Psychology, 25,* 109–123.

DeNelsky, G. Y., & McKee, M. G. (1969). Prediction of job performance from assessment reports: Use of a modified Q-sort technique to expand predictor and criterion variance. *Journal of Applied Psychology, 53,* 439–445.

Dicken, C., & Black, J. (1965). Predictive validity of psychometric evaluation of supervisors. *Journal of Applied Psychology, 49,* 34–47.

DuBois, P. H. (1970). *A history of psychological testing.* Needham Heights, MA: Allyn & Bacon.

Dunnette, M. D., & Kirchner, W. K. (1958). Validation of psychological tests in industry. *Personnel Administration, 21,* 20–27.

Flanagan, J. C., & Krug, R. E. (1964). Testing in management selection: State of the art. *Personnel Administration, 27,* 3–5.

Fleishman, E. A., Harris, E. F., & Burtt, H. E. (1955). *Leadership and supervision in industry.* Columbus: Bureau of Educational Research, Ohio State University.

Gordon, L. V. (1967). Clinical, psychometric, and work-sample approaches in the prediction of success in peace corps training. *Journal of Applied Psychology, 51,* 111–119.

Guion, R. (1991). Personnel assessment, selection, and placement. In M. D. Dunnette & L. M. Hough (Eds.), *Handbook of industrial and organizational psychology* (2nd ed., Vol. 2, pp. 327–399). Palo Alto, CA: Consulting Psychologists Press.

Handyside, J., & Duncan, D. (1954). Four years later: A follow-up of an experiment in selection supervisors. *Occupational Psychology, 28,* 9–23.

Hemphill, J. K. (1960). *Dimensions of executive positions* (Research monograph No. 98). Columbus: The Ohio State University, Bureau of Business Research.

Hilton, A. C., Bolin, S. F., Parker, J. W., Taylor, E. K., & Walker, W. B. (1955). The validity of personnel assessments by professional psychologists. *Journal of Applied Psychology, 39,* 287–293.

Hogue, J. P., Otis, J. L., & Prien, E. P. (1962). Assessments of higher-level personnel: VI. Validity of predictions based on projective techniques. *Personnel Psychology, 15,* 335–344.

Holt, R. R. (1958). Clinical and statistical prediction: A reformulation and some new data. *Journal of Abnormal and Social Psychology, 56,* 1–12.

Holtzman, W. H., & Sells, S. B. (1954). Prediction of flying success by critical analysis of test protocols. *Journal of Abnormal and Social Psychology, 49,* 485–490.

Hunter, J. E., & Hunter, R. F. (1984). Validity and utility of alternative predictors of job performance. *Psychological Bulletin, 96,* 72–98.

Huse, E. F. (1962). Assessments of higher-level personnel: IV. The validity of assessment techniques based on systematically varied information. *Personnel Psychology, 15,* 195–205.

Impara, J. C., & Plake, B. S. (1998). *Mental measurement yearbook* (13th ed.). Lincoln, NE: The Buros Institute of Mental Measurement.

Kelly, E. L., & Fiske, D. W. (1951). *The prediction of performance in clinical psychology.* Ann Arbor: University of Michigan Press.

Kopelman, R. E. (1986). *Managing productivity in organizations.* New York: McGraw-Hill.

McLagan, P. A. (1990). Flexible job models: A productivity strategy for the Information Age. In J. P. Campbell & R. J. Campbell & Associates (Eds.), *Productivity in organizations* (pp. 369–387). San Francisco, CA: Jossey-Bass.

Meyer, H. H. (1956). An evaluation of a supervisory selection program. *Personnel Psychology, 9,* 499–513.

Miner, J. B. (1970). Psychological evaluations as predictors of consulting success. *Personnel Psychology, 23,* 393–405.

Munsterberg, H. (1913). *Psychology and industrial efficiency.* Boston: Haughton Mifflin.

Murray, H. A., MacKinnon, D. W., Miller, J. D., Fiske, D. W., & Hanfmann, E. (1948). *Assessment of men: Selection of personnel for the Office of Strategic Services.* Norfolk, VA: Rinehart & Co.

Ohmann, O. A. (1961). Some observations in executive selection research. In R. Tagiuri (Ed.), *Research needs in executive selection* (pp. 6–16). Boston: Harvard University Press.

Otis, J. L. (1938). The prediction of success in power machine operating. *Journal of Applied Psychology, 22,* 350–366.

Otis, J. L., Campbell, J. T., & Prien, E. P. (1962). Assessment of higher-level personnel: VII. The nature of assessments. *Personnel Psychology, 15,* 441–446.

Peterson, N. G., Mumford, M. D., Borman, W. C., Jeanneret, P. R., & Fleishman, E. A. (Eds.). (1999). *An occupational information system for the 21st century: The development of O*Net.* Washington, DC: American Psychological Association.

Phelan, J. G. (1962). Projective techniques in the selection of management personnel. *Journal of Projective Techniques, 26,* 102–104.

Prien, E. P. (1962). Assessments of higher-level personnel: V. An analysis of interviewers' predictions of job performance. *Personnel Psychology, 15,* 319–334.

Prien, E. P., & Ronan, W. W. (1971). Job analysis: A review of research findings. *Personnel Psychology, 24,* 371–396.

Reilly, R. R., & Chao, G. T. (1982). Validity and fairness of some alternative employee selection procedures. *Personnel Psychology, 35,* 1–62.

Rifkin, J. (1995). *The end of work: The decline of the global labor force and the dawn of the post-market era.* New York: Putnam.

Rothe, H. F. (1957). Matching men to job requirements. *Personnel Psychology, 4,* 291–301.

Sanchez, J. I. (1994). From documentation to innovation: Reshaping job analysis to meet emerging business needs. *Human Resource Management Review, 4*(1), 51–74.

Schippmann, J. S. (1999). *Strategic job modeling: Working at the core of integrated human resources.* Mahwah, NJ: Lawrence Erlbaum Associates.

Schippmann, J. S., Ash, R. A., Battista, M., Carr, L., Eyde, L. D., Hesketh, B., Kehoe, J., Pearlman, K., Prien, E. P., & Sanchez, J. I. (2000). The practice of competency modeling. *Personnel Psychology, 53,* 703–740.

Schmidt, F. L., & Hunter, J. E. (1998). The validity and utility of selection methods in personnel psychology: Practical and theoretical implications of 85 years of research finding. *Journal of Applied Psychology, 124,* 262–274.

Schmidt, F. L., Hunter, J. E., McKenzie, R., & Muldrow, T. (1979). The impact of valid selection procedures on workforce productivity. *Journal of Applied Psychology, 64,* 609–626.

Schmidt, F. L., Hunter, J. E., Outerbridge, A. N., & Trattner, M. H. (1986). The economic impact of job selection methods on size, productivity, and payroll costs of the federal workforce: An empirically-based demonstration. *Personnel Psychology, 39,* 1–29.

Schmitt, N., Gooding, R. Z., Noe, R. A., & Kirsch, M. (1984). Meta-analysis of validity studies published between 1964 and 1982 and the investigation of study characteristics. *Personnel Psychology, 37,* 407–422.

Silzer, R. F. (1984). *Clinical and statistical prediction in a management assessment center.* Unpublished doctoral dissertation, University of Minnesota, Minneapolis.

Spencer, L. M., McClelland, D. C., & Spencer, S. (1994). *Competency assessment methods: History and state of the art.* Boston: Hay McBer Research Press.

Stead, N. H., & Shartle, C. L. (1940). *Occupational counseling techniques.* New York: American Book.

Stern, G. G., Stein, M. I., & Bloom, B. S. (1956). *Methods in personality assessment.* Glencoe, IL: Free Press.

Strong, E. K. (1934). Classification of occupations by interests. *Personnel Journal, 12,* 307–313

Trankell, A. (1959). The psychologist as an instrument of prediction. *Journal of Applied Psychology, 43,* 170–175.

Urbrock, R. S. (1934). Attitudes of 4430 employees. *Journal of Social Psychology, 5,* 365–372.

Vernon, P. (1950). The validation of Civil Service Selection Board procedures. *Occupational Psychology, 24,* 75–95.

Viteles, M. S. (1932). *Industrial psychology.* New York: Norton.

2

Job Modeling

People are different. Many of the differences, such as height and weight, can be directly observed. Other individual differences such as intelligence, sociability, emotional stability, and job knowledge are less obvious, but can still be measured. In individual assessment the concern is with those differences in people that have consequences for job performance or are job related (Hellervik, Hicks, & Sommers, 1991; Schippmann & Vrazo, 1995).

Jobs are different. Sales jobs are different from accounting jobs, which are different from information technology jobs, and so on. Simply put, the measures of success, the work activities, and the individual competencies that line up behind each are different for different jobs. Furthermore, jobs are different across levels within the same general occupational class. For example, the array of activities and competencies required for an accounting clerk are different from, though similar to, those for a director of finance or for a chief financial officer. In fact, not only are there different types of competencies required across levels within a job group, but there are frequently level differences in the performance standards associated with the same competencies.

If the two working assumptions just noted—people are different and jobs are different—are combined, it logically follows that some people will perform certain jobs better than others. To a great extent, then, what explains different levels of job performance is the degree of possession of specific job-related competencies on the part of different individuals. Although this discussion may seem a bit abstract, the backdrop is important when one considers the fact that individual assessment is all about prediction. Specifically, it concerns using multiple sources of input information to predict who will succeed in the

27

whole job or perform best in certain facets of the job. Thus, ultimately, the individual assessment process must begin with a definition of what one means
by success or job performance. Stated differently, without a clear understanding of what the assessor is looking for, it is unlikely that it will be found.

The process of identifying and defining what is meant by success in a job,
and the competencies required for delivering that success, is job modeling.
At this point, it will be fruitful to present a brief discussion of the building
blocks that comprise the people component and the job component in the
individual assessment equation. These building blocks structure the input
information that serves as grist for the job modeling mill. Readers who would
like more detail on the subject are encouraged to review other sources
(Gael, 1988a; Schippmann, 1999; Schippman et al., 2000).

PEOPLE ARE DIFFERENT

The most important product of the job modeling step in the individual assessment process is the identification and description of the competencies required
to perform a job. It is this subset of job-related competencies that serves as the
specifications for the individual assessment to be performed and forms the basis
for establishing the assessment protocol. In this book, *competencies* are defined
as occupationally relevant capabilities or behaviorally defined individual difference capacities. In this respect, competencies can be thought of as reflecting
the evolution of knowledge, skills, and abilities (KSAs) to descriptors that, as
Barrett (1996) noted, have become more specific, behavioral, and ostensibly
linked to meaningful organizational outcomes. We have found it useful to classify competencies into two broad categories:

- *Can-do competencies:* Individual capabilities that tap into the basic
  ability to perform a work activity; can-do com-
  petencies include:
  - Skills: Individual capabilities that have been
    developed as a result of education, training,
    or experiences that underlie an individual's
    capacity to perform a work activity.
  - Knowledge: Individual understanding of
    ideas and concepts that have emerged as a
    result of education, training, or experience
    and that serve as a platform for performing a
    work activity.
- *Will-do competencies:* Personality and attitudinal characteristics that tap
  into an individual's willingness to perform a work
  activity; will-do competencies may be written as
  "willingness to," as in "willingness to persist in the
  face of obstacles or difficulties," for example.

As described elsewhere in more detail (Schippmann, 1999), competencies may be thought of as being comprised of three broad classes of individual difference characteristics: Abilities, traits, and interests/values/motivations. These three classes of characteristics constitute the deep structure, or foundation, on which education/training and experience opportunities are laid; these opportunities constitute the middle structure, or the bricks and mortar, that rest on the foundation. Competencies, then, constitute the occupationally relevant surface structure, which is the capstone to the People Pyramid. This model is illustrated in Fig. 2.1.

Starting at the top of the People Pyramid, competencies can be defined in varying degrees of specificity, and this variation impacts the extent to which they are generalizable across jobs and organizations. Three examples will illustrate the point:

- Example 1:   Thinking skills
  (Factor level,
  very general)

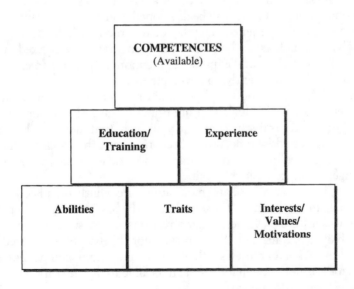

FIG. 2.1.   People pyramid. From J. S. Schippmann (1999), *Strategic Job Modeling: Working at the Core of Integrated Human Resources*, p. 22. Copyright © 1999 by Lawrence Erlbaum Associates. Reprinted with permission.

- Example 2:   Strategic thinking skills
  (Dimension level,
  somewhat general

- Example 3:   Skill in recognizing the broad or long-term im-
  (Item level,   plications of business decisions and plans
  fairly specific)

The formal educational or training opportunities represented in the pyra-mid can be either general or targeted. These opportunities are designed to build on basic abilities, interests, and so forth and enhance the acquisition of occupationally relevant knowledge or skills. A seminar titled *Strategic Deci-sions: Seminar for Analyzing the New World Competition* would be an example of a formal training opportunity.

On the other hand, experience is either informal exposure to the ideas and concepts or the opportunity to observe or practice the work activities related to a particular competency over time. *Serve on a task force designed to evaluate competitive technologies and identify opportunities for strategic alliances* is an example of a job-related experience.

At the base of the pyramid, abilities may be thought of as basic character-istics or aptitudes of individuals that constitute the present power of an indi-vidual to perform a fairly homogeneous set of related work activities. Abilities are similar to traits in that they are relatively stable over long peri-ods of time, though abilities can be developed over time as a result of educa-tion, training, or experience. The degree to which an individual possesses some abilities, such as mathematical reasoning, is relatively fixed, whereas other abilities, such as oral expression, are more responsive to exposure to situations and, subsequently, to development.

The next block in the People Pyramid refers to traits. Traits are basic characteristics of individuals that are primarily dispositional or "personal-ity-like" in nature. Traits are similar to abilities in that they are relatively sta-ble over long periods of time, probably even more so than abilities. Initative, defined as the willingness to self start and to take on responsibilities and challenges, is an example of a trait.

Finally, interests, values, and motivations are a fairly broad collection of individual difference characteristics that can be best understood as personal preferences. Interests, values, and motivations are less stable over time than either abilities or traits and, therefore, are more likely to be influenced by sit-uational events. Nevertheless, they are an important component in the model, for it is not enough for people to be able to do the work—they must also be willing to do the work.

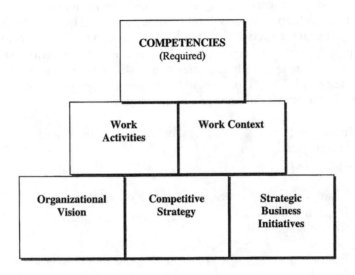

FIG. 2.2.   Job pyramid. From J. S. Schippmann (1999), *Strategic Job Modeling: Working at the Core of Integrated Human Resources*, p. 23. Copyright © 1999 by Lawrence Erlbaum Associates. Reprinted with permission.

JOBS ARE DIFFERENT

As in the people side of the assessment equation, the Job Pyramid in Fig. 2.2 is capped off with a competency building block. These competencies are the same as those defined previously as part of the People Pyramid. As such, they are occupationally relevant capabilities and knowledge that underlie an individual's capacity to perform a work activity or set of related work activities. However, there is one important difference. The difference is one of perspective: The competencies referred to here are those required by the job versus those possessed by, or available to, an individual.

Rather than reiterate the characteristics that comprise competencies, the focus here is to describe the underlying "drivers" that underscore certain competencies as being either more or less important in a given context. As Fig. 2.2 illustrates, work activities and work context determine competency requirements, and the organization's vision, strategic objectives, and initiatives form the basis for the work context and associated work activities.

After competencies, the next building block in the Job Pyramid involves work activities. A work activity is a set of tasks or behaviors that constitutes a job responsibility or discrete unit of work performed by an individual. The activity is goal oriented in that it is designed to lead to some outcome or the accomplishment of some objective (i.e., success or job performance). As with competencies, work activities can be defined in varying degrees of specificity. The level of specificity then makes them more or less generalizable across different jobs and organizations.

- Example 1:   General operations management
  (Factor level,
  very general)

- Example 2:   Supervise work operations
  (Dimension level,
  somewhat general)

- Example 3:   Coordinate work with other groups to ensure
  (Item level,   smooth progress and seamless integration of effort
  fairly specific)

The next building block involves work context variables. These are a broad mix of work role or job characteristics that help define the workplace. These characteristics can be broken down into four broad categories:

1. Work benefits of either an intrinsic or extrinsic nature (e.g., compensation, job security, job mobility, collegiality, recognition, development opportunities);
2. The work itself (which includes work variety, opportunities for creativity, coaching or mentoring possibilities, and tools and equipment used to complete work);
3. Work conditions (e.g., the work environment, travel requirements, time flexibility, autonomy, structure, level of work stress); and,
4. Organizational structure (e.g., organization size, hierarchy, degree of centralization, level of performance tracking).

These variables can be important for understanding the context in which work takes place. As such, these characteristics indirectly impact work activities performed and ultimately the competencies required in a particular role, job, or class of jobs in an organization. For example, collegiality is a job context variable and might be defined as the extent to which job incumbents interact with others and feel a part of a team.

The organization's vision includes two types of information: the organization's mission and the organization's core values or beliefs. Although vision and core values may be difficult to define and quantify, their role in influencing organization effectiveness and success is critical. Management can be more or less specific in articulating this information, although, once it is articulated, it can shed light on the fundamental ideas around which the business is built and guide the overall behavior of the firm, as well as the behavior of the people comprising the firm. This information leads naturally to questions about the organization's competitive strategy and strategic initiatives, which elaborate on, and provide an operational definition for, the language of the vision and values and beliefs statements.

ASSESSMENT SPECIFICATIONS

Up to this point, we have discussed the competencies available as part of an individual's portfolio of talents and the competencies required by the demands of a job as distinct components of the prediction equation. However, the all-important first decision point that the assessment practitioner has to make is this: From the entire domain of possible individual differences that could be assessed, which competencies are most likely to be predictive of success (i.e., in either the whole job or some important facets of the job)? This coconsideration of the competencies available and the competencies required is illustrated in Fig. 2.3, in which the models presented in Fig. 2.1 and Fig. 2.2 have been linked and are now building toward each other. Fig. 2.4 simply extends this illustration a little further by showing the overlap be-

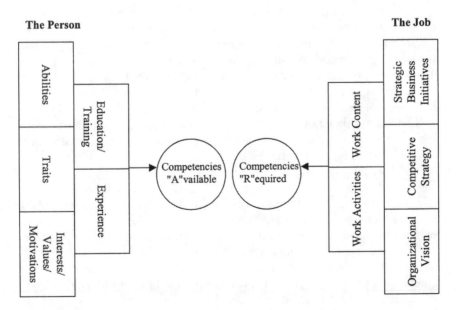

FIG. 2.3.   Interaction between the person and job domains. From J. S. Schippmann (1999), *Strategic Job Modeling: Working at the Core of Integrated Human Resources*, p. 25. Copyright © 1999 by Lawrence Erlbaum Associates. Reprinted with permission.

The Person   **The Job**

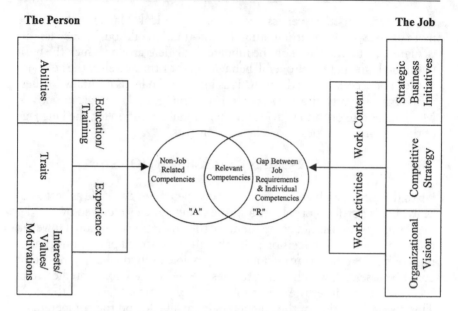

FIG. 2.4. Relevant competencies to target when building assessment specifications. From J. S. Schippmann (1999), *Strategic Job Modeling: Working at the Core of Integrated Human Resources*, p. 26. Copyright © 1999 by Lawrence Erlbaum Associates. Reprinted with permission.

tween competencies available ("A") and competencies required ("R"). The "R" domain identifies the competencies required by the job and represents the sweet spot for the assessment. This is where the predictive power of the assessment process is maximized. To the extent that the competencies available match the competencies required, the assessee will have a greater likelihood of performing successfully in the target job.

There is another, not unimportant reason for paying attention to the job modeling underpinnings of the individual assessment. The legal environment in which businesses operate has become a critical issue to be considered. A variety of laws passed in the last 35 years or so, including Title VII of the Civil Rights Act of 1964, The Equal Pay Act of 1963 (U.S. Department of Labor, 1971), and the Age Discrimination in Employment Act of 1967, have had the effect of increasing the importance of job analysis or job modeling as a vital part of establishing the job relatedness of various human resource practices.

Of course, the Civil Rights Act of 1991 and the Americans with Disability Act (ADA, 1990) created additional hurdles along what was already a challenging path. The ADA in particular has implications for the design of the assessment specifications. Specifically, ADA required that the employer identify the "essential functions" of jobs and make accommodations to workers with disabilities who can, with accommodation, perform the essential functions. For assessment, those implications include offering accommodation to assessees who request it, being able to adapt the assessment protocol to provide an accommodation if requested, and using assessment measures that are not proscribed under the ADA (e.g., interview questions or tests that could be construed to yield information that is medical in nature). This will be discussd further in chapter 3.

Although none of the statutes previously listed specifically legislates job analysis or job modeling, agency guidelines based upon some of these statutes do require a systematic analysis of jobs and work to establish the job relatedness of resulting procedures (Sparks, 1988). The most definitive statement of these guidelines is embodied in the *Uniform Guidelines on Employee Selection Procedures* (published jointly by the Equal Employment Opportunity Commission, Civil Service Commission, Department of Labor, and Department of Justice, 1978; hereafter referred to as the *Uniform Guidelines*). These administrative guidelines clearly establish job analysis as a prerequisite for demonstrating that an employment practice—including individual assessment—is job related. In part, these guidelines state:

> There should be a review of information to determine measures of work behavior(s) or performance that are relevant to the job or group of jobs in question. These measures or criteria are relevant to the extent that they represent critical or important job duties, work behaviors or work outcomes as developed from the review of job information. (p. 38300)

Further, the *Uniform Guidelines* state:

> There should be a job analysis that includes an analysis of the important work behavior(s) required for successful performance and their relative importance and, if the behavior results in work product(s), an analysis of the work product(s). Any job analysis should focus on the work behaviors and tasks associated with them. If work behavior(s) are not observable, the job analysis should identify and analyze those aspects of the behavior(s) that can be observed and the observed work product. The work behavior(s) selected for measurement should be critical work behavior and/or important behaviors constituting most of the job. (p. 38302)

The belief that accurately captured job information should precede most human resource management practice—again, including individual assessment—is also firmly expressed in the *Standards for Educational and Psychological Testing* (a document published by the American Educational Research Association, American Psychological Association, and National Council on Measurement in Education, 1999) and in the *Principles for the Validation and Use of Personnel Selection Procedures* (a practice guide published by the Society for Industrial and Organizational Psychology, 1987). Therefore, as various federal and professional guidelines indicate, the importance of job modeling information for supporting various human resource management and specific assessment practices is well established. In fact, in light of recent legislation, one could argue that quality job information appears to be gaining importance (Lozada-Larsen, 1992; Sanchez & Fraser, 1992).

Before moving on to the next section it should be noted that, in many cases, in individual assessment the target is a very specific job, that is, one position, in one organization, with one set of reporting relationships and individuals involved, and with one set of work activities to be performed and associated competency requirements (e.g., Division President, Natural Foods World Wide). Success in these cases means being an outstanding performer with reference to the important work activities of the position, which, in turn, is determined by the degree of possession of the associated competencies and their motivational components. When a position is the assessment target, the assessment protocol should include a detailed description of the competency requirements that roll up into the definition of job success. For example, the assessment results and reporting structure would be organized around the relevant subset of competency *dimensions* reported in Appendixes B, C, and D (for managerial, supervisory, and administrative jobs, respectively). At this level, the assessment specifications are likely to include some consideration of the specific functional competencies involved in the job.

In other cases of assessment, the target job is broader, perhaps a job group (i.e., a group of similar positions within one organization, such as supervisor) or even a job category (i.e., a grouping of jobs according to a broad occupational class, such as manager). As the assessment target becomes broader, the definition of success broadens as well. Therefore, in situations where a series of assessments are being conducted with reference to the generic job, a more general definition of the competency components involved in success will serve as the basis for establishing the assessment protocol. For example, the assessment results and reporting structure might be organized around the *factor* level components of the competency models presented in Appendixes B, C, and D (again, for managerial, supervisory, and administrative jobs).

We are returning to an important concept at this point. The selection of the assessment tools (i.e., establishing the assessment protocol) and the eventual organization and reporting of the assessment results all revolve around the assessment specifications, which may be thought of as the roadmap for the assessment. Unfortunately, conventional procedures for creating this roadmap (i.e., Step 1 in Fig. 1.1) are impractical in the individual assessment context. Fortunately, some practical, yet methodologically rigorous, procedures are available.

IDENTIFYING ASSESSMENT SPECIFICATIONS

Actually, the first set of questions to pose to a potential buyer of assessment services are premodeling questions, and they concern the purpose of the assessment. It is critical that the assessor have a clear view of the purpose of the assessment and a thorough understanding of how the assessment results will be used. These choices will have a controlling influence on how the assessment process is designed and carried out. In brief, there are two broad types of assessment: selection and development. Within the selection category, it is convenient to bucket the more specific options into the following three subcategories:

- **External selection:** The most typical assessment situations. In these cases the assessor's role is to evaluate candidates for an open position. More than likely, the developmental focus is minimal.

- **Internal selection:** Similar to external selection, though in these cases the assessor may be evaluating the top one or two internal candidates for a promotion or open position. Frequently there is a request for accompanying developmental feedback for these candidates.

- **Deselection:** A distinctively difficult and unsatisfying aspect of the selection assessment business where the assessor is evaluating individual or multiple current employees to identify keepers from a group of employees caught up in a reduction in force (RIF).

Then, of course, there are the developmental assessments. Here, too, there are several more discrete options:

- **Pure developmental:** In these cases the assessor is asked to evaluate and help prepare an individual for the next level. In many instances, they have a quick start intent to help the individual hit the ground running in the new role. As such, the assessor may be asked to help the individual prepare an action plan to address developmental opportunities likely to give the person the biggest and most immediate payoff.

- **Remedial developmental:** Here the person has been nominated for an assessment because they are currently, or are in danger of, failing. The assessment proposition also will include a heavy coaching component.

- **Talent searches:** In this assessment situation, employees who hold jobs that feed into key top-level positions are assessed to determine the organization's bench strength. The assessor will likely be asked

to help plan management's line of succession
with reference to the organization's projected
needs and requirements over the long term.

The selection and development options just described do not represent
an exhaustive list, but they do cover the predominant range of practice.
Again, when the call for an assessment comes in from a client (whether internal or external), it is essential to develop a clear understanding of the purpose of the assessment and of how the results will be used. The implications
of these options for design will become clear as this chapter continues.

Of course, when dealing with a new client, there are a number of questions that should be addressed that will allow the assessor to consult with the
customer and develop the most appropriate assessment intervention possible. Perhaps the first piece of information that should be determined is
whether the client and the organization have used individual assessment in
the past. If not, there needs to be an educational component up front to set
clear and realistic expectations. If there has been previous exposure to assessment practice, understanding what that experience was like, and
whether it was viewed favorably, can be helpful in maximizing the fit between expectations and deliverables.

After this, the assessor needs to know something about the organization
in which the job targeted by the assessment will operate. In short, jobs, job
requirements, and organizations do not exist independently. The organization environment has long been recognized as playing an important role in
the way coworkers treat one another, how they are supervised, how decisions get made, and so on (Boyatzis, 1982; Lawrence & Lorsch, 1986;
Mintzberg, 1979; Schneider, 1976). Although one could take the need to
know something about the organization context to extremes, the series of
questions presented in the Organization Modeling Worksheet in Fig. 2.5
should prove sufficient in most cases. This question set is brief enough that it
could be posed to the client as part of the get-to-know-you-a-little-better
conversation that occurs on a first time call.

In addition to learning something about the organization environment, it
is critical to get a clear picture of the requirements of the target job. Again,
the assessor should not go beyond the point of diminishing returns. However, if the picture of important work activities and competencies is vague, it
leaves the door open for misinterpretation about what is required to perform
successfully in a job. In the individual assessment context, one may proceed
along a couple of different paths to accomplishing this work and arrive at an
acceptable understanding.

At a minimum, we suggest that an assessor use some set of job modeling
questions, such as those posed in the Job Modeling Worksheet in Fig. 2.6, to
collect information from at least one person in the client organization who

Organization Modeling Worksheet

<u>Positioning</u>
<u>Statement</u>:   The purpose of my questions is to develop a better understanding of
the organization. Work roles, job requirements, and the
organizational context do not exist independently. To best tailor my
assessment service and produce information that will be most useful
to you, I need to know a little about the organization and work
environment.

<u>Background</u>
<u>Materials</u>:   If you have not done so already, ask for the following:

- Copy of the organization's annual report (it is crucial to know
  something about the client's business).

- Copy of the organization's mission statement or published
  values and principles (though only useful if they are operational
  and more than mere words on a page, they have the potential to
  shed light on the culture in which the target job exists).

<u>Organization</u>
<u>Assessment</u>
<u>Questions</u>:

- Briefly describe the *business and structure* of the
  organization.

- How does the target job contribute to, and fit in with,
  business *goals and plans*?

- Describe the work *culture* of the organization. What kinds of
  people stay with the company and advance? What kinds of
  people leave or are "managed out" of the organization? Why?

- Are there certain *values* that are widely held by the
  organization's founders or senior leadership team? What are
  they and how do they influence decision making?

- If you consider the current incumbents in the target job, and in
  the job one level up, as a human *talent portfolio*…what are the
  strengths of that portfolio? What are the weaknesses?

FIG. 2.5. Organization assessment worksheet.

Job Modeling Worksheet

Positioning Statement:

The purpose of my questions is to develop a better understanding of the work activities and individual competencies that contribute to success in the job. To best tailor my assessment service and produce information that will be most useful to you, I need to know what success "looks like" in this job, and what kinds of people have demonstrated the capacity to succeed in the past.

Background Materials:

If you have not done so already, ask for the following:

- Copy of organizational charts that start several layers above the target job and move a layer or two lower (this information will illustrate the span of control, reporting relationships, and career options for the target job, and may yield some insight into how decisions get made in the organization).

- Copy of existing job descriptions for the target job(s) (don't get your hopes up too high; often the information can be more misleading than helpful because it is outdated or poorly developed).

Job Assessment Questions:

- What are the four or five major duties or *work activities* performed in the target job(s)? Why are these activities important? In what way are they linked to business goals?

- What kinds of knowledge, skills, abilities, or personal characteristics (i.e., *competencies*) are required to perform the work activities we've just discussed? What competencies differentiate a top performer in this job from a marginal or poor performer?

- What are the recurring or inescapable *challenges* and difficulties associated with this job? Is there a lot of turnover or burnout in the target job? If so, why?

- What kinds of *people* skills are required? To what extent, and how, does someone in the target job get work done through others?

- What kind of *technical expertise* is required? Should the successful job candidate have a specialized degree?

FIG. 2.6. Job assessment worksheet.

has a deep understanding of the requirements of the target job. In most cases, this would be a direct boss or a person one level up from the target job. However, in some cases it might be a staffing director or a training manager (i.e., someone in a position to have seen a number of incumbents come and go in the target job). In still other instances, an experienced and high-performing job incumbent might be in the best position to have a clear view of the target job's demands, challenges, and competency requirements.

A 20- to 30-minute interview with a job expert, using the questions and follow-up probes in Fig. 2.6, will go a long way toward sharpening the resolution of the image the assessor is forming in his or her mind about the job's requirements. In our view, the minimal next step is for the assessor to complete some form of job modeling questionnaire to document and organize what has been learned. The best practice would be to have one or two job experts from the client organization also complete the same job modeling questionnaire. The second step here does two things. First, it provides a broader range of input into the definition of the job specifications. Second, the provision of a second and third perspective allows the assessor to test what has been learned via the job modeling interview by looking at the correlation between the two resulting modeling profiles.

The purpose for providing the management, supervisory, and administrative models in Appendixes B, C, and D is to facilitate the establishment of the assessment protocol, whether the target job is quite narrow and specific or more broad and general. In each case, part I of each appendix presents the associated model of work activities and part II presents the competency model. Furthermore, for each of the models presented, the taxonomic structure was based on research findings. For example, the management model is primarily the result of a research effort by Schippmann, Prien, and Hughes (1991), which included a systematic review of 35 years of research on the content of management work and used the results of 32 independent studies as input for analysis. Specifically, the taxonomic structures and descriptor statements in these two taxonomies were guided by the results of these 32 studies and involved an initial pool of 358 work dimensions, over 5,500 descriptor statements, and input and ratings from over 6,000 managers in a wide variety of different organizations. Enhancements to the original work activity and competency taxonomies have been made as a result of recent additions to the management literature, including Borman and Brush (1993), Spreitzer, McCall, and Mahoney (1997), and Tett, Gutterman, Bleir, and Murphy (2000). Similar research underpinnings support the models of work activities and competencies for supervisor and administrative jobs as presented in Appendixes C and D, respectively.

Descriptions of work content for additional occupational classes and job groups are available in other sources (Gael, 1988b). Furthermore, taxonomic solutions for the following two additional job groups are available from the first author:

- Sales and customer relations:

The sales and customer relations competency model differs somewhat from the supervisory competency model or the management competency model. To be sure, there is overlap of content, but the salient characteristics for the sales and customer relations job competency model include the following: The model incorporates a very broad range of job complexity in terms of the specifics, particularly with reference to the components of social and personal functioning, interpersonal relations, flexibility, innovativeness, and social and conceptual ingenuity. On the other hand, this model represents a relatively narrow range of technically oriented competencies in the general market. The exception is where positions are classified in terms of sales engineer with a substantially increased emphasis on technical and analytical facets of the model. There are, of course, hybrid target positions of all types, but with reference to the individual assessment paradigm, this model, in terms of work activities and the specific and detailed set of competencies, sets it apart with reference to the general scheme.

- Technical and analytical:

The technical and analytical competency model likewise shares some features with the general management model as well as with the sales and customer relations model. The technical and analytical model is again somewhat different in terms of components that are of a relatively higher level of complexity and involve general cognitive competencies as well as the similar features characterizing sales jobs in terms of innovativeness, ingenuity, flexibility, and ideational fluency. The technical and analytical jobs typically require a high level of abstract reasoning, quantitative analysis, and evaluation and competency in handling large and abstract databases. Although the competency model for the sales and customer relations and technical and analytical models may be very similar, the general education and experience and training will be quite different.

RESEARCH CONTEXT

Over 40 years ago, Hemphill (1960) pioneered the use of quantified job analysis results as the input data for developing an empirically based classification scheme for a particular occupational group: management jobs. Hemphill's questionnaire contained 575 work activity items that were factor analyzed to produce 10 separate dimensions of management work. Sixteen years later, Tornow and Pinto (1976) attempted to replicate Hemphill's findings while correcting some methodological limitations. The 10 factors from the Hemphill solution and the 13 factors from the Tornow and Pinto solution showed considerable overlap, although the factor labels were not identical. Nevertheless, the two studies demonstrated that human judgment (i.e., rating work activity descriptors on scales of "importance" or "time spent") can be reliably used as a basis for grouping similar activities. In addition, these studies demonstrated that managerial jobs do have common core dimensions. In the intervening years, numerous studies that are virtual line extensions of this original research have demonstrated the same results for other types of descriptor content (e.g., competencies) and for other classes of jobs (e.g., supervisory, clerical, trade, and craft).

The assumption underlying the research to identify common work dimensions is that such systems for classifying the "stuff" of work (e.g., work activities, competencies) would, in addition to providing a common vocabulary for talking about job requirements, provide a researcher or practitioner a basis for generalizing a set of results from one setting to another. This assumption has received a good deal of support from investigations on performance taxonomies in simple vigilance and visual monitoring tasks (Farina & Wheaton, 1973; Fleishman & Quaintance, 1984; Levine, Romashko, & Fleishman, 1973; Parasuraman, 1976; Theologus, Romashko, & Fleishman, 1973). Although there have been no direct tests of the usefulness of such classifications for improving the prediction of performance with more complex work activities and competencies, such as those comprising management jobs, the results from the studies on simple performance have been encouraging.

The implications are important and form one plank in the platform of research that supports the practice of individual assessment. As stated previously, the typical individual assessor rarely takes the time or uses the resources necessary to conduct a comprehensive job modeling study, in the conventional sense, to develop assessment specifications (Ryan & Sackett, 1987). In this regard, the taxonomies provided in Appendixes B through D provide detailed, comprehensive, and research-based structures for describing the dimensions of work, for three major job categories, which may be used to jump start the definition of a target job that falls into one of these broad job categories.

PRACTICE EXAMPLES

At this point we introduce "Practice Examples" as the capstone section of this, and the next four, chapters. To illustrate the concepts and tools discussed in chapters 2 though 6, we follow three case examples all the way through the assessment process. The first example involves Linda Jones, an external candidate for an entry-level sales associate position with Computer City. The second example involves the assessment of Peter Martin, an internal candidate for a department manager job with Barnes Stores. The third example involves Hector Dantos, an external candidate for a division president job with Natural Foods World Wide. In all three cases, the individuals and the organizations are fictitious, though they are based on a composite of issues from real candidates and actual clients.

Example 1: Sales Associate Assessment

The sales associate job for Computer City is an entry-level position with the company. There are several hundred sales associates across 20 store locations. Although it is somewhat unusual to employ individual assessment methodology with high head count (i.e., employee) jobs, it does happen. In this case, the senior leadership team of Computer City viewed the sales associate job as a key entry-level feeder job for other jobs throughout the company, and therefore worthy of this level of screening rigor. The organization assessment questions in Fig. 2.5 were posed to the company leadership team as a 2-hour focus group built in to a semiannual management off site. The job assessment questions from Fig. 2.6 were then posed to six store managers during individual 1-hour interviews. These same six store managers, plus eight others, then completed a job modeling questionnaire that used Appendix D (i.e., administrative model) work activities and competencies as starting point descriptors, which were then edited to reflect the input from the organization assessment focus group and the job assessment questions. The administrative model in Appendix D is a broadly applicable taxonomy, suitable as a starting point for a number of entry-level jobs. For educational purposes as part of this book, a written summary of the modeling results appears in Fig. 2.7. The actual trace-record documents that should be included in the assessment file are presented in chapter 3.

It should be noted that the extent of the modeling work described in this summary is unusual—unusually extensive, that is. In fact, because of the large number of incumbents, and the frequency of the selection screen assessments, the up-front modeling work approximates the level of review often seen in the development of more traditional, high-volume selection systems. Practice Example 3 is more indicative of traditional modeling in individual assessment work.

Modeling Results #1

Organization: Computer City
Target Job: Entry-Level Sales Associate
Date: September 7, 2000

**Organization
Assessment**:   Computer City operates 20 specialty retail outlets in a three state area. Each store employs approximately 30 full-time and part-time sales associates, as well as stock clerks and a small group of clerical workers. Each location is managed by a store director, who is assisted by three to four shift supervisors and five to six lead sales associates.

The company is in the business of selling computer hardware, software, and accessories. They also carry a line of consumer electronics and video tapes/DVDs. As a regional chain, Computer City is not in a position to compete directly on price with large national specialty retailers and general merchandisers, but instead emphasizes customer service and support. In fact, Computer City is well known for its knowledgeable and customer-oriented staff and, generally, once a customer makes an initial purchase at Computer City, they will return again and again.

**Job
Assessment**:   The majority of the sales associates are students and the majority are extremely knowledgeable about the products Computer City carries. A proportion of the sales associates leave Computer City within 2 to 3 years, normally to pursue a full-time career when their education is completed, but others stay with the organization and, as their education progresses or is completed, move into supervisory and managerial positions.

The primary responsibility of the sales associate is to provide customers with information, service, and support. Sales activities, such as actually closing a sale, are important, but less emphasized. Computer City management's goal is to provide a positive experience for each customer, even if that means that the customer is advised not to purchase an item, to purchase a less expensive item, or even to buy from a competitor.

FIG. 2.7. Modeling results #1, sales associate assessment (Example 1). *(continued on next page)*

Job
Assessment (cont'd):

> Strong interpersonal competencies are a must for sales associates. Technical knowledge is important, but more important is the ability to convey that knowledge to a technically naïve customer. The most successful sales associates are those who can adapt their communications and interpersonal style to a wide range of customers. Successful sales associates can debate the merits of rival video cards with sophisticated customers and can turn around and explain to an elderly lady how to read her grandchildren's e-mail without condescending or making the customer feel incompetent.

FIG. 2.7.   (continued)

Example 2: Department Manager Assessment

In this example, the department manager reports to the store director. The structure for the assessment was originally provided by the owner of the company, and supplemented over a 20-year period by discussions with all levels of management, as well as frequent visits to the various stores. Thus, this example illustrates assessment practice of an ongoing nature with a long-term client. Periodic updates to the original organization assessment and job assessment input were recorded as memos to the client file. In addition, the original job modeling questionnaire, which was a blend of the supervisory and the management models presented in the appendixes, was updated and readministered to a sample of managers and job incumbents every couple of years. In this way, the assessment target and the trace-record document were periodically refreshed. A written summary of the most recent modeling results appears in Fig. 2.8. The results from the most recent modeling questionnaire are presented and discussed in chapter 3.

Modeling Results #2

Organization:	Barnes Stores
Target Job:	Department Manager
Date:	September 24, 2000

**Organization
Assessment**:

Barnes Stores is a retail grocery chain, with 12 stores covering a major metropolitan area. Each store employs a management team of 8 to 10 employees, including the store manager, an assistant store manager, and department managers.

Barnes Stores is the up-scale grocery store in its market area; management places a high level of emphasis on customer service and each store has a florist, deli, bakery, and extensive produce, meat, and seafood selections. Video rental, pharmacy, and dry cleaning departments are rented out, although the store manager has some oversight.

The department managers are each in charge of an area of the store: Produce, Floral, Meat/Seafood, Grocery, Bakery, Deli, and Front End. In some stores, Produce and Floral are run as one department; several of the larger stores also have a department manager in charge of customer service.

The department managers have total responsibility for their areas, including selection and arrangement of products, staffing, and, to a certain extent, pricing, and their performance is normally assessed in terms of net profit and customer satisfaction (Barnes Stores conducts frequent and extensive customer satisfaction surveys).

The number of employees supervised varies in both number and level; for example, the Meat/Seafood manager supervises a relatively small number of employees, some of whom are highly skilled meat cutters. In contrast, the Front End manager supervises a large number of employees, predominantly young, part-time cashiers and baggers.

The department manager is viewed as the first full-time permanent management position. There are evening and weekend supervisors or leads in most departments, but these individuals have limited authority. The normal source for department managers is the evening and weekend supervisors and the department manager is viewed as the feeder job for both store manager and headquarters positions.

FIG. 2.8. Modeling results #2, department manager assessment (Example 2).

(*continued on next page*)

Job
Assessment: The skill set required for the department manager position is
extensive. The incumbents need a high degree of social judgment
and interpersonal expertise, both to deal with customers who
demand a high level of attention and service and to supervise a
predominantly young workforce with high turnover. In addition, the
department manager must have strong cognitive skills, including
quantitative problem solving, planning and organizing, and product
knowledge. A high degree of original thinking, flexibility, and
openness to experience is also necessary to ensure that Barnes
Stores can continually adapt and innovate to stay ahead of its
competitors.

FIG. 2.8.   (*continued*)

Example 3: Division President Assessment

The division president job reports directly to the CEO of Natural Foods World
Wide, a specialty food manufacturer and distributor. However, the CEO was
unavailable to provide modeling information to structure the assessment. Instead, the organization assessment questions in Fig. 2.5 were posed to the CFO
during a working lunch. In addition, the job assessment questions from Fig. 2.6
were directed to the senior vice president (SVP) of human resources (HR) and
the vice president (VP) of management development, during a 1-hour conference call. A summary of the modeling results appears in Fig. 2.9. After this telephone interview, the assessor, and the SVP of HR, independently completed
sections of a modeling questionnaire that included the items from the management model presented in Appendix B. The results from the modeling questionnaire are presented and discussed in chapter 3.

Modeling Results #3

<u>Organization</u>:   Natural Foods World Wide
<u>Target Job</u>:   Division President
<u>Date</u>:   September 28, 2001

<u>Organization</u>
<u>Assessment</u>:   Natural Foods World Wide is an international manufacturer and distributor of healthy snacks, portable meals, natural candies, and nutrient enhanced drinks, which also represent the company's four major operating divisions. They operate 40 plants and have 24,000 employees, marketing 35 brands in more than a dozen countries. Almost one quarter of their 1.4 billion in sales is from outside North America and their growth strategy is predicated on the premise that the world is ready for natural and nutrient enhanced foods.

The company prides itself on being flat (in terms of management layers), fast (in terms of moving from decisions to actions) and innovative. Because the management ranks are compressed, people have big jobs, and there are big expectations associated with them. Executives are expected to take calculated risks and to look for opportunities to "swing for the fences". An executive doesn't have to hit a home run every time, but the senior leadership team expects everyone to hit their share. As such, modest incremental gains in sales, volume, and profit in one's own area of responsibility won't cut it for long.

Across the divisions, the leadership teams are populated by people who are smart, creative, and ferocious about winning in their respective marketplace. The divisions themselves are pretty autonomous and getting things done across business boundaries is contingent upon who you know and what they think of you. In the world of body friendly products it is somehow incongruous that the internal joke is "If you are not a SCAD (Smart, Creative, Absolutely Driven) then you are just keeping a seat warm until somebody else moves into your office". As with most consumer goods companies that rely on marketing, personal presence and polish counts for a lot among the executive ranks.

<u>Job</u>
<u>Assessment</u>:   The open position being targeted by the assessment is Division President, Natural Candies. The job is open because the previous incumbent was managed out of the company after three consecutive years of subpar (though growing and profitable) division performance. As in the other divisions, the person in this job will

FIG. 2.9. Modeling results #3, division president assessment (Example 3).

(continued on next page)

<u>Job</u>
<u>Assessment cont'd</u>: have responsibility for mobilizing the 2,400 person organization to
achieve aggressive sales, volume, and profit objectives for both
domestic and international operations. It goes without saying that
mental horsepower, decisiveness, and creative ability are a must.
The ability to quickly build business relationships and influence a
group of smart, talented peers in a "run-and-gun" environment will
be critical. Responsibility for a broad, far flung part of the
organization will require both excellent planning and motivation
skills. It is worth noting that the previous job incumbent, though a
widely recognized functional expert (he was the former Chief
Financial Officer of the division), was ultimately judged to be too
narrow and unready to run a big business. Other internal candidates
are viewed as having similar shortcomings, which is why the search
has expanded to external candidates.

FIG. 2.9.   (*continued*)

REFERENCES

Age Discrimination in Employment Act of 1967, 29 U.S.C. § 621 *et seq.*
American Educational Research Association, American Psychological Association,
& National Council on Measurement in Education. (1999). *Standards for educational and psychological testing.* Washington, DC: American Educational Research
Association.
Americans with Disabilities Act of 1990, 42 U.S.C. § 12101 *et seq.*
Barrett, R. S. (1996). *Fair employment strategies in human resource management.*
Westport, CT: Quorum Books.
Borman, W. C., & Brush, D. H. (1993). More progress toward a taxonomy of managerial performance requirements. *Human Performance, 6,* 1–21.
Boyatzis, R. E. (1982). *The competent manager: A model for effective performance.*
New York: Wiley-Interscience.
Civil Rights Act of 1991, Pub. L. No. 102–166.
Farina, A. J., Jr., & Wheaton, G. R. (1973). Development of a taxonomy of human
performance: The task characteristics approach to performance prediction.
JSAS Catalog of Selected Documents in Psychology, 1973, 3(No. 323).
Fleishman, E. A., & Quaintance, M. K. (1984). *Taxonomies of human performance.*
Orlando, FL: Academic Press.
Gael, S. (1988a). *The job analysis handbook for business, industry, and government* (Vol.
2). New York: Wiley & Sons.
Gael, S. (1988b). Job Descriptions. In S. Gael (Ed.) *The job analysis handbook for
business, industry, and government* (Vol. 1). New York: Wiley & Sons.
Hellervik, L. W., Hicks, M. D., & Sommers, C. (1991). *The what and why of assessment.* Minneapolis, MN: Personnel Decisions.
Hemphill, J. K. (1960). *Dimensions of executive positions* (Research Monograph No.
98). Columbus: The Ohio State University, Bureau of Business Research.

Lawrence, P. R., & Lorsch, J. W. (1986). *Differentiation and integration in complex organizations.* Cambridge, MA: Harvard Graduate School of Business Administration.

Levine, J. M., Romashko, T., & Fleishman, E. A. (1973). Evaluation of an abilities classification system for integrating and generalizing findings about human performance: The vigilance area. *Journal of Applied Psychology, 58,* 147–149.

Lozada-Larsen, S. R. (1992). *The Americans With Disabilities Act: Using job analysis to meet new challenges.* Paper presented at the IPMA Assessment Council Conference, Baltimore, MD.

Mintzberg, H. (1979). *The structuring of organizations.* Englewood Cliffs, NJ: Prentice-Hall.

Parasuraman, R. (1976). Consistency of individual differences in human vigilance performance: An abilities classification analysis. *Journal of Applied Psychology, 61,* 486–492.

Ryan, A. M., & Sackett, P. R. (1987). A survey of individual assessment practices by I/O psychologists. *Personnel Psychology, 40,* 455–488.

Sanchez, J. I., & Fraser, S. L. (1992). On the choice of scales for task analysis. *Journal of Applied Psychology, 77,* 545–553.

Schippmann, J. S. (1999). *Strategic job modeling: Working at the core of integrated human resources.* Mahwah, NJ: Lawrence Erlbaum Associates.

Schippmann, J. S., Ash, R. A., Battista, M., Carr, L., Eyde, L. D., Hesketh, B., Kehoe, J., Pearlman, K., Prien, E. P., & Sanchez, J. I. (2000). The practice of competency modeling. *Personnel Psychology, 53,* 703–740.

Schippmann, J. S., Prien, E. P., & Hughes, G. L. (1991). The content of management work: Formation of task and job skill composite classifications. *Journal of Business and Psychology, 5,* 325–354.

Schippmann, J. S., & Vrazo, G. J. (1995). Individual assessment for key jobs. *Performance & Instruction, 35,* 10–15.

Schneider, B. (1976). *Staffing organizations.* Santa Monica, CA: Goodyear.

Society for Industrial and Organizational Psychology. (1987). *Principles for the validation and use of personnel selection procedures* (3rd ed.). College Park, MD: Author.

Sparks, C. P. (1988). Legal basis for job analysis. In S. Gael (Ed.), *The job analysis handbook for business, industry, and government* (Vol. 1, pp. 37–47). New York: Wiley & Sons.

Spreitzer, G. K., McCall, M. M., & Mahoney, J. D. (1997). Early identification of international executive potential. *Journal of Applied Psychology, 82,* 6–29.

Tett, R. P., Guterman, H. A., Bleir, A., & Murphy, P. J. (2000). Development and content validation of a hyperdimensional taxonomy of managerial competence. *Human Performance, 13,* 205–251.

Theologus, G. C., Romashko, T., & Fleishman, E. A. (1973). Development of a taxonomy of human performance: A feasibility study of ability dimensions for classifying human tasks. *JSAS Catalog of Selected Documents in Psychology,* 1973, 3(No. 323).

Title VII of the Civil Rights Act of 1964 (Pub. L. 880352), as amended, 42 U.S.C. 2000e *et seq.*

Tornow, W. W., & Pinto, P. R. (1976). The development of a managerial job taxonomy: A system for describing, classifying, and evaluating executive positions. *Journal of Applied Psychology, 61,* 410–418.

Uniform Guidelines on Employee Selection Procedures, 43 Fed. Reg. 38295-38309 (1978).

U.S. Department of Labor. (1971). *Equal pay for equal work under the Fair Labor Standards Act.* Washington, DC : Author.

3

Establishing
the Assessment Protocol

The previous chapter made the point that people are different and jobs are different. Well...

TESTS ARE DIFFERENT TOO!

Tests are different in terms of which competencies they purport to measure. They are different with respect to how they measure the competencies of interest (e.g., the administration of paper-and-pencil instruments, the observation of performance in work samples, the evaluation of verbal responses in an interview). The reliability and validity of the obtained information from ostensibly similar instruments can be quite different, more or less useful in certain contexts or with reference to certain populations than others (see Appendix A to brush up on psychometric terms and concepts), and so forth. Within this variegated test landscape it is incumbent on the assessor to pull together the mix of tests (again, using our broad definition of what constitutes a "test") that will prove most useful in a given assessment context (i.e., the assessment protocol).

The most useful assessment protocol will:

- Focus on more than a single competency (because even the simplest jobs require an individual to possess an interrelated mix of several competencies to perform at a successful level).

- Use multiple measurement instruments to assess an individual's degree of possession of each competency (because there should be measurement overlap in the protocol such that each competency will be measured at least twice, or from two different vantage points).
- Employ multiple types of measurement to provide assessees with different avenues for demonstrating their competencies (i.e., some mix of interview questions, work history information, speed tests, power tests, work samples, and interactive exercises will be used to provide assessment input).

As we discussed in chapter 2, the purpose of the job modeling step is to identify those competencies most directly related to eventual job performance. Therefore, related to the first bullet in the previous list, the effort to maximize the predictive power of the assessment is improved as a result of including the greatest number of the most important competencies in the assessment protocol. The balancing act occurs when one considers the second bullet: the need to have measurement overlap in the protocol. If the assessor creates an assessment protocol that doubles up on the measurement of every competency targeted by the assessment, and perhaps taps the most critical competencies using three or four measurement instruments, then the assessor is going to run out of time and assessee endurance fairly quickly. Thus, necessity dictates that the assessor focus on the critical competencies in the assessment process.

Together, the second and third bullets in the previous list refer to the domain of employment tests and, as noted in chapter 1, tests come in all shapes and sizes and include:

- Interviews
- Cognitive ability tests
- Personality tests and interest inventories
- Work samples
- Reference checks
- Biographical inventories
- 360° ratings

These categories will be used to organize our discussion of the base rate of validity of different methods in the Research Context section of the chapter.

RESEARCH CONTEXT

The research base underpinning this step of the individual assessment process is two pronged. The first aspect involves the base rate validity of the different methods that may be used to generate input data about individual differences. From a practical point of view, the most important outcome of the individual assessment process is the ability to predict future job performance in the whole job or the important decomposed facets of the job. The basis of these predictions will be assessee performance on some mix of tests. Thus, the specific instruments used to guide these predictions must be psychometrically sound.

The second line of support involves the ability of the assessor to estimate the validity of tests based on a description of the job's requirements. Making reference to Fig. 1.1, in a conventional prediction context, Steps 5 through 8 are used to empirically establish the usefulness of different tests. The individual assessment practitioner does not have this luxury, and consequently, must make some initial selection of tests judged to be useful for providing prediction information for a target job with a particular array of competency requirements, in the absence of an empirical research study to guide selections.

Base Rate Validity of Individual Difference Measures

Interviews. The interview is the most widely used component of individual assessment practice (Ryan & Sackett, 1987). Although there are a number of ways of organizing the different types of interview procedures, perhaps the most meaningful conceptualization is in terms of the amount of structure used to guide the process. In an unstructured interview, the assessor may have a general plan for conducting the interview, but for the most part follows his or her nose to track down information in response to the interviewee's responses. Similarly, the interviewee is given minimal guidance in terms of the direction of the conversation or how to frame his or her responses. On the other hand, in the structured interview, the assessor has a prepared set of questions and follow-up probes (Janz, 1982). These questions have been selected because they are likely to yield insights into competencies previously identified as important for a target job. Moreover, the interviewee is prompted as to how to provide responses that will be most useful (i.e., recent, behaviorally based activities that led to some job-related outcomes over which the individual had some direct control). Whereas early reviews of primarily unstructured interview procedures tended to provide minimal support for the validity of the procedure (Reilly & Chao, 1982; Schmitt, 1976; Ulrich & Trumbo, 1965; Wagner, 1949), the reviews of primarily structured procedures have been much more encouraging (Arvey & Campion, 1982; Harris, 1989; Judge, Higgins, & Cable, 2000). In fact, more recent meta-analytic reviews have supported the use of both unstructured and structured interviews, though they clearly establish the superiority of structured procedures (across studies, corrected validities for unstructured interviews ranged from .14 to .33 and from .35 to .62 for structured interviews; Huffcutt & Arthur, 1994; Hunter & Hunter, 1984; McDaniel, Whetzel, Schmidt, & Maurer, 1994; Schmidt & Hunter, 1998; Schmidt & Rader, 1999; Wiesner & Cronshaw, 1988; Wright, Lichtenfels, & Pursell, 1989).

Furthermore, the research strongly suggests using the results from a systematic review of job requirements (i.e., job analysis or job modeling) to

guide the selection and construction of the interview questions. Both narrative (Arvey & Campion, 1982; Campion, Palmer, & Campion, 1997; Harris,
1989; Schmitt, 1976) and meta-analytic reviews (Conway, Jako, & Goodman, 1995; McDaniel et al., 1994; Wiesner & Cronshaw, 1988) indicate improved reliability and validity when the interview content is linked to a
formal review of job requirements.

   Cognitive Ability Tests.   Standardized paper-and-pencil tests of
can-do competencies are widely used in the practice of individual assessment. These problem-solving tests provide the assessee with a series of written items designed to measure either a specific aspect of mental ability (e.g.,
vocabulary, reading comprehension, planning ability, mechanical reasoning, higher math or basic numerical proficiency) or more globally, mental
horsepower and the ability to learn. Of all the measures that could be included in the predictor mix comprising the assessment protocol, the research evidence for the validity of cognitive ability tests is the strongest. The
thousands of individual studies that have been conducted in the past 90
years and the dozens upon dozens of meta-analytic studies that have been
conducted in the past 20 years (e.g., Hunter, 1986; Hunter & Hunter, 1984;
Hunter & Schmidt, 1996; Ree & Earles, 1991; Schmidt, Gooding, Noe, &
Kirsch, 1984; Schmidt & Hunter, 1981, 1998) present incontrovertible evidence supporting the use of cognitive ability across situations and occupations with varying job requirements. For example, Schmidt and Hunter
(1998) reported a validity coefficient of .51 for a meta-analytic study that included 32,000 employees in 515 diverse jobs. In this study alone, the validity
of cognitive ability test measures for predicting job performance was reported to be .58 for managerial jobs, .56 for complex technical jobs, .40 for
semiskilled jobs, and .23 for unskilled jobs.

   In our view, the only question becomes: Which measures of cognitive ability
should be included in the assessment protocol? Just considering measures of
cognitive ability (i.e., discounting personality and interest measures for the moment), there are thousands of published tests to choose from. We offer some
suggestions in Table 3.1, but this is by no means a complete list of the potentially
useful instruments. The reader should review the critiques and published reliability and validity evidence in reference guides such as *The Mental Measurements Yearbook* (Impara & Plake, 1998) and *Tests in Print* (Murphy, Impara, &
Plake, 1999) to develop a more comprehensive list of potential measures, to be
narrowed down based on the results of the job modeling results.

   Before we leave this topic, we should note one of the very interesting
pieces of information concerning the base rate of correlation among tests
with similar and different dimensions and formats. Although it is true that
there are thousands of published tests that are available for the individual
assessment practitioner to draw on to develop a specific battery, the research
results in general indicate a very high degree of correlation between any one
of the General Aptitude Test Battery (GATB) tests and any one of the com-

TABLE 3.1
Available Tests

Test and Test Type	Description	Time	Target Population
COGNITIVE ABILITY			

General Mental Ability Measures

1. Adaptability Test (AT) • Reid London House (800-922-7343)	40 items designed to measure verbal, quantitative, and spatial abilities. Yields a single overall score.	15 minutes (timed)	• Supervisor • Operations • Administrative
2. Advanced Mental Ability Test (AMAT) • Performance Management Press (901-523-1265)	40 items designed to measure general information, vocabulary, logic, and basic arithmetic. Yields a single overall score.	25 minutes (untimed)	• Entry management • Supervisory • Administrative • Trade and craft
3. Thurstone Test of Mental Alertness (TMA) • Reid London House (800-221-8378)	Designed to measure the ability to learn new skills quickly and adjust to new situations. Yields scores of quantitative, linguistic, and general mental ability.	20 minutes	• Wide range of occupational groups
4. Wonderlic Personnel Test (WPT) • Wonderlic Personnel Test, Inc. (800-323-3742)	50 items designed to measure vocabulary, common sense reasoning, arithmetic reasoning and numerical facility. Yields general mental ability score.	12 minutes (timed)	• Wide range of occupational groups

Specific Ability Measures

5. Bennett Mechanical Comprehension Test (BMCT) • The Psychological Corporation (800-211-8378)	68 items designed to measure the ability to understand the relationship between physical forces and mechanical elements.	30 minutes (timed)	• Industrial employees • Various mechanical positions
6. Business Relations Skills Test (BRST) • Performance Managment Press (901-523-1265)	25 items designed to assess basic competency in dealing with other people in the work setting. The job competency areas or dimensions include customer relations skills, communication skills, employee relations, and human relations skills and knowledge of business conduct and propriety.	15 minutes (untimed)	• Manufacturing, clerical, entry-level supervisory

7.	Computer Programmer Aptitude Battery (CPAB) • Reid London House (800-922-7343)	Five subtests designed to measure verbal meaning, quantitative reasoning, abstract reasoning, number estimation, and diagramming.	75 minutes (timed)	• All levels of IT
8.	Critical Reasoning Test Battery (CRTB) • SHL (800-211-8378)	Three complementary subtests, 60-item subtest designed to measure verbal evaluation, 40-item subtest measuring data interpretation, and 40 items measuring diagrammatic reasoning.	Verbal: 20 minutes Data: 30 minutes Diagrammatic: 20 minutes	• Supervisor • Entry-level managers
9.	Critical Thinking Test (CTT) • SHL (800-899-7451)	Two complimentary subtests, one 52-item subtest designed to measure verbal reasoning and one 40-item subtest designed to measure numerical reasoning.	60 minutes (timed)	• Senior management • Middle management • Professional
10.	Differential Aptitude Test (DAT) • The Psychological Corporation (800-211-8378)	Suite of tests designed to measure ability to learn in nine specific areas (includes a total scholastic aptitude score): • Verbal reasoning • Numerical reasoning • Abstract reasoning • Perceptual speed/accuracy • Mechanical reasoning • Space relations • Spelling • Language usage	90 minutes (timed)	• Wide range of entry-level jobs
11.	Elements of Supervision (EOS) • Performance Management Press (901-523-1265)	70-item multiple choice measure of knowledge of generally accepted good supervisory practices. Yields a single overall score.	20 minutes (untimed)	• Supervisor • Higher level administrative
12.	Employee Aptitude Survey (EAS) • Psychological Services, Inc. (818-244-0033)	Suite of tests designed to measure specific components of mental ability, including: • Verbal comprehension • Numerical ability • Visual speed/accuracy • Space visualization • Numerical reasoning • Verbal reasoning • Word fluency • Manual speed/accuracy • Symbolic reasoning	5 minutes 10 minutes 5 minutes 5 minutes 5 minutes 5 minutes 5 minutes 5 minutes 5 minutes	• Technical • Production • Clerical • Some supervisory and professional

TABLE 3.1 (continued)

Test and Test Type	Description	Time	Target Population
COGNITIVE ABILITY			
13. Flanagan Industrial Test (FIT) • Reid London House (800-221-8378)	Suite of tests designed to measure specific components of mental ability, including: • Arithmetic • Assembly • Electronics • Expression • Ingenuity • Inspection • Judgment • Mathematics • Mechanics • Memory • Planning • Scales • Tables • Vocabulary	5 minutes 10 minutes 15 minutes 5 minutes 15 minutes 5 minutes 15 minutes 15 minutes 15 minutes 10 minutes 15 minutes 5 minutes 5 minutes 15 minutes	• Lower level jobs in industrial settings
14. Management and Organization Skills Test (MOST) • Performance Management Press (901-523-1265)	165 items designed to measure individuals' knowledge and understanding of the competencies and the requirements for management and supervisory positions. The test consists of a representative array of situation scenarios with an opportunity for a response or action, as well as a number of multiple-choice questions.	60 minutes (untimed)	• Entry- to mid-level management
15. Planning, Organizing, and Scheduling Test (POST) • Performance Management Press (901-523-1265)	40 items, based on situational scenarios from a variety of settings, designed to measure competency in planning, organizing, and scheduling activities.	20 minutes (timed)	• Industrial employees • Clerical and administrative • Technical and analytical • Supervisory and management
16. Raven Progressive Matrices (RPM) • The Psychological Corporation (800-211-8378)	60 items designed to provide nonverbal measure of thinking skills and trainability.	20 minutes (untimed)	• Wide range of norms available

17.	Sales Ability Test (SAT) • Performance Management Press (901-523-1265)	86 items built around 16 sales scenarios. Yields a single overall score.	30 minutes (untimed)	• Entry- to mid-level sales jobs
18.	Sales Professional Assessment Inventory (SPAI) • Reid London House (800-922-7343)	Designed to assess competencies and personal interests associated with sales success: work experience and training, sales interest, sales responsibility, sales orientation, energy level, self-development, sales skills, sales understanding, sales arithmetic, customer service, business ethics, job stability, and sales potential.	45 minutes (untimed)	• Sales, multiple levels
19.	Selling Skills Series (SSS) • SHL (800-899-7451)	71-item test designed to measure facility with written information and the ability to reason with data.	32 minutes	• Entry-level sales and retail • Call center staff
20.	Social and Business Judgment Skills (SBJS) • Performance Management Press (901-523-1265)	60 items designed to measure skills for dealing with people in both social and business settings. Yields both a social score and a factual or business score.	30 minutes (untimed)	• General population
21.	Supervisory Practices Inventory (SPI) • Western Psychological Services (800-648-8857)	20 situational items designed to assess knowledge of good supervisory practices, based on 10 management functions: setting objectives, planning, organizing, delegating, problem identification, decision making, subordinate development, performance evaluation, conflict resolution, and team building.	20–30 minutes (untimed)	• Entry-level supervisors
22.	Teamwork and Organizational Skills Test (TOST) • Performance Management Press (901-523-1265)	65 items designed to measure systems thinking and the ability to discern the requirements for individual behavior leading to work group effectiveness.	30 minutes (untimed)	• Entry management • Supervisory • Clerical
23.	Watson Glaser Critical Thinking Appraisal (WGCT) • The Psychological Corporation (800-211-8378)	80 items designed to measure ability to think and reason critically and logically. Yields single composite score based on following content areas: Inference, Assumption Recognition, Deduction, Interpretation, and Argument Evaluation.	40 minutes (untimed)	• Exempt and nonexempt populations

TABLE 3.1 (continued)

Test and Test Type	Description	Time	Target Population

COGNITIVE ABILITY

Basic Skill Measures

Test and Test Type	Description	Time	Target Population
24. Industrial Reading Test (IRT) • The Psychological Corporation (800-211-8378)	38 items designed to measure reading comprehension of written technical material.	40 minutes	• Entry-level employment
25. Mathematical Reasoning Test (MRT) • Performance Management Press (901-523-1265)	30-item, multiple-choice test, designed to assess mathematical competency up to the college graduate level. Test items include percentages, powers and roots, and algebraic problems.	30 minutes (timed)	• Middle management • Supervisory • Technical
26. Numerical Computation Test (NCT) • Performance Management Press (901-523-1265)	60 items designed to measure proficiency with addition, subtraction, multiplication, division, and the use of fractions and decimals.	15 minutes (timed)	• Supervisory • Wide range of entry-level office and retail jobs
27. Numerical Skills Profile (NSP) • Reid London House (800-221-7343)	25 items designed to measure basic business math skills.	15 minutes (untimed)	• Clerical • Entry level sales and retail
28. Wide Range Achievement Test (WRAT-3) • Wide Range Inc. (302-652-4990)	Designed to measure basic skills in reading, spelling, and arithmetic.	15–30 minutes	• Entry-level employment
29. Wonderlic Basic Skills Test (WBST) • Wonderlic Personnel Test, Inc. (800-323-3742)	Designed to measure work-related math and verbal skills taught in Grades 4 through 12. Yields scores of verbal and quantitative ability.	40 minutes	• Entry-level employment
30. Work Skills Series Production (WSSP) • SHL (800-899-7451)	Three subtests designed to measure numerical skills, visual checking, and the ability to understand instructions.	Numerical: 10 minutes Visual checking: 7 minutes Understand instructions: 12 minutes	• Entry-level employment in manufacturing and production environments

PERSONALITY, INTEREST, AND WORK STYLE

Personality

1.	California Psychological Inventory (CPI) • Consulting Psychologists Press, Inc. (800-624-1765)	434 item personality inventory based on the work of Harrison Gough. Designed to measure 3 structural scales, 20 folk scales, and 7 special purpose scales. The folk scales include dominance, capacity for status, sociability, social presence, self-acceptance, independence, empathy, responsibility, socialization, self-control, good impression, communality, well-being, tolerance, achievement via conformance, achievement via independence, intellectual efficiency, psychological mindedness, flexibility, and femininity/masculinity.	45 minutes (untimed)	• Wide range of norm groups
2.	Edwards Personal Preference Schedule (EPPS) • The Psychological Corporation (800-211-8378)	225 items designed to measure 15 dimensions: achievement, deference, order, exhibition, autonomy, affiliation, intraception, succorance, dominance, abasement, nurturance, change, endurance, heterosexuality, and aggression.	45 minutes (untimed)	• Wide range of norm groups
3.	Ghiselli Self Description Inventory (GSDI) • In the public domain and not carried by a publisher. (see Ghiselli, 1971)	64-item adjective checklist designed to measure 13 individual difference characteristics: supervisory ability, intelligence, initiative, self-assurance, decisiveness, maturity, masculinity–femininity, working class affinity, achievement motivation, need for self-actualization, need for power, need for high financial reward, and need for security.	10 minutes (untimed)	• Entry management • Supervisor • Administrative • Trade and craft
4.	Global Personality Inventory (GPI) • ePredix (800-447-2266)	300 items designed to measure 37 different dimensions of personality, including: adaptability, attention to detail, emotional control, energy level, optimism, risk taking, and work focus.	60 minutes (untimed)	• Norm base is being built, though instrument is somewhat unique in that it was designed to retain its psychometric properties across cultures.

TABLE 3.1 (*continued*)

Test and Test Type	Description	Time	Target Population
	PERSONALITY, INTEREST, AND WORK STYLE		

Personality

5. Gordon Personal Profile Inventory (GPPI) • The Psychological Corporation (800-211-8378)	38 items designed to measure nine dimensions: ascendancy, responsibility, emotional stability, sociability, self-esteem, cautiousness, original thinking, personal relations, and vigor.	25 minutes (untimed)	• Mid- and entry-level management • Supervisor • Higher level administrative
6. Guilford-Zimmerman Temperament Survey (GZTS) • Consulting Psychologists Press, Inc. (800-624-1765)	300 items designed to measure 10 dimensions of personality and temperament: general activity, restraint, ascendance, sociability, emotional stability, objectivity, friendliness, thoughtfulness, personal relations, and masculinity.	50 minutes (untimed)	• Management • Supervisor • Administrative
7. Hogan Personality Inventory (HPI) • Hogan Assessment Systems (800-756-0632)	206 true–false items designed to measure adjustment, ambition, sociability, likability, prudence, intellect, school success, service orientation, stress tolerance, reliability, clerical potential, and managerial potential.	20 minutes (untimed)	• Wide range of norm groups
8. Interpersonal Style Inventory (ISI) • Western Psychological Services (800-648-8857)	30 items designed to measure 15 dimensions of personality, grouped into five areas: interpersonal involvement (sociable, help-seeking, nurturant, sensitive); self-control (deliberate, orderly, persistent); stability (stable, approval seeking); socialization (conscientious, trusting, tolerant); and autonomy (directive, independent, rule free).	30 minutes (untimed)	• General population
9. Jackson Personality Test (JPS) • Sigma Assessment Systems, Inc. (800-265-1285)	300 true–false items designed to measure complexity, breadth of interest, innovation, tolerance, sociability, social confidence, energy level, empathy, anxiety, cooperativeness, social astuteness, risk taking, organization, traditional values, and responsibility.	45 minutes (untimed)	• Wide range of norm groups

10.	Manchester Personality Questionnaire (MPQ) • HRD Press (800-822-2801)	120 items designed to measure 14 dimensions (including Big 5): originality, openness to change, social confidence, communicativeness, rule consciousness, conscientiousness, decisiveness, rationality, assertiveness, empathy, independence, competitiveness, perfectionism, and apprehension. Short form (MPQ-5) measures Big 5 only.	20 minutes (untimed)	• General population
11.	16PF • Institute for Personality and Ability Testing (IPAT) (217-352-9674)	185 items designed to measure 16 personality dimensions: warmth, reasoning, emotional stability, dominance, liveliness, rule consciousness, social boldness, sensitivity, vigilance, abstractedness, privateness, apprehension, openness to change, self-reliance, perfectionism, and tension.	45 minutes (untimed)	• Wide range of norm groups
12.	Thurstone Temperament Schedule (TTS) • Reid London House (800-922-7343)	Designed to measure six individual difference characteristics: activity, impulsiveness, dominance, stability, sociability, and reflectiveness.	20 minutes (untimed)	• Wide range of occupational groups

Interest

13.	Campbell Interest and Skill Survey (CISS) • Reid London House (800-221-8378)	377 items designed to measure career interests based on the Holland typology: realistic, investigative, artistic, social, enterprising, and conventional; under each dimension, scores indicating congruence of interests are provided for a variety of potential occupations. In addition, four personal style scales (work style, learning environment, leadership style, and risk taking/adventure) are scored.	45 minutes (untimed)	• Wide range of occupational groups
14.	Kuder General Interest Survey (KGIS) • National Career Assessment Services (800-314-8972)	Designed to measure 11 broad interest areas; outdoor, mechanical, computational, scientific, persuasive, artistic, literary, musical, social, service, clerical, and verification.	60 minutes (untimed)	• Wide range of occupational groups

TABLE 3.1 (continued)

Test and Test Type	Description	Time	Target Population
PERSONALITY, INTEREST, AND WORK STYLE			
Work Style			
15. Customer Relations Skills Test (CRS) • Performance Management Press (901-523-1265)	45 situational questions designed to measure a range of competencies related to customer service jobs.	30 minutes (untimed)	• Entry-level sales and customer service
16. Customer Service Inventory (CSI) • ePredix (800-447-2266)	64 items designed to measure customer service orientation.	20 minutes (untimed)	• Entry level service and front-line sales
17. Leadership Opinion Questionnaire (LOQ) • Reid London House (800-221-8378)	40 items designed to measure two facets of supervisory leadership. Yields scores of consideration and structure.	10 minutes (untimed)	• Entry management • Supervisor • Higher level administrative
18. Work Styles Questionnaire (WSQ) • SHL (800-899-7451)	162 items designed to measure relationships with people, thinking style, emotions, and energies.	30 minutes (untimed)	• Administrative • Retail • Operations/manufacturing

parison tests in the marketplace (U.S. Department of Labor, 1970). Although the GATB tests are linked to several hundred commercial tests, there is a degree of specificity (from general to very specific dimensions) that differentiates among those test measures. Examining only tests of dimensions comparable to one or another of the GATB measures and linking those tests to specific commercial tests, the average correlation is on the order of .65. When the comparison tests from the commercial measures are of different dimensions, then the average correlation drops to .37. The third and most critical comparison is where GATB tests are linked to commercial measures of a different format (written tests vs. physical manipulation tests); in these cases the average correlation drops to .05. The obvious conclusion to be drawn from this work is that the GATB is a cognitive ability measure developed to measure a spectrum of cognitive competencies. For the hundreds and hundreds of tests with the same format and the same or different dimensions, it is not difficult to imagine and to conclude that there is very significant redundancy in the commercial test inventory. The final and obviously important conclusion is that, when measures are made of different dimensions (in comparison to the GATB) and of different formats (written paper-and-pencil and the physical manipulation tests), the measurement properties and results of these measures can be very different.

A useful resource providing guidance on various test options for assessing cognitive and other abilities is the *Handbook of Human Abilities: Definitions, Measurements, and Job Task Requirements* (Fleishman & Reilly, 1992b). This volume brings together comprehensive definitions of 21 cognitive abilities identified in previous research. For each ability, information is provided about the specific kinds of tasks and jobs that require each ability, as well as descriptions of the tests that can used to measure each ability. In many respects, this book is more of a comprehensive extension of Table 3.1. It identifies appropriate commercially available assessment instruments to measure the specific abilities required for successful performance on particular jobs, and it provides test publisher information and an index of tasks and jobs classified according to ability requirements. In addition to the coverage of the full range of cognitive abilities (e.g., written and oral comprehension, deductive reasoning, spatial orientation, visualization, time sharing, etc.), the book provides similar information for abilities, tests, and job tasks in the physical, psychomotor, and sensory-perceptual domains of human performance.

A nice feature of the Fleishman and Reilly (1992b) taxonomy is that a job analysis system was developed for describing any job in terms of these same ability requirements. The instrument developed for this, the *Fleishman Job Analyses Survey (F-JAS)* (Fleishman, 1992), provides behaviorally anchored rating scales for all the abilities in the taxonomy. These scales have been widely used for developing profiles of ability requirements which have been shown to yield valid tests for use in personnel selection (for a review see, e.g., Fleishman & Mumford, 1991). Extensive research summarizing the reliability and validity of this instrument may be found in Fleishman and Mumford (1991) and Fleishman and Reilly (1992a). The most comprehensive review of research leading to these developments is described in Fleishman (1975, 1982) and in the book *Taxonomies of Human Performance: The Description of Human Tasks* by Fleishman and Quaintance (1984).

Another feature of the F-JAS system is the linkage to O*NET, an occupational information system developed for the U.S. Department of Labor to replace the Dictionary of Occupational Titles (DOT). The O*NET system includes a database of job requirements of thousands of jobs in the U.S. economy. The ensuing research involved in the initial development of O*NET is described in Peterson, Mumford, Borman, Jeanneret, and Fleishman (1999). In analyzing the ability requirements of new jobs using the F-JAS, it is possible to access Internet sites to compare the profiles of ability requirements obtained with jobs in this O*NET database.

Personality Tests and Interest Inventories.   In chapter 2 we made the distinction between can-do and will-do competencies. Whereas cognitive ability measures are designed to tap into the can-do competency domain, personality predictors yield information related to the will-do aspects of job performance. Personality tests can be divided into two categories: projective and objective. Projective measures present assessees with ambiguous stimuli, such as ink blots, photographs, or incomplete sentences. Assessees are then asked to describe what they see, tell a story, finish the sentence, or otherwise compose a response. Some examples of projective tests are the Rorschach Ink Blot Test and the Thematic Apperception Test. However, in our view, the resulting scores and interpretations from these measures are more unreliable than their objective counterparts, not to mention that they have typically been designed and normed with reference to a clinical rather than a business population. Furthermore, the rather amorphous projective-type tests are considerably more likely to arouse suspicion, skepticism, and resistance among assessees, as well as among consumers of assessment practitioner services. Although there are undoubtedly practitioners who are enamored with particular projective techniques, both the research evidence and the history of legal challenges mitigate against using such instruments.

On the other hand, a number of objective, psychometrically sound measures of personality are available that have appropriate content for use in business settings and are accompanied by relevant norms. For the most part, these instruments are self-report questionnaires that require "true" or "false" responses to descriptive statements such as: *You find it easy to approach and speak to strangers.* In other cases, these measures require the test taker to select a descriptive statement from a pair or group of statements that best describes them. In this way, these objective measures are thought to get at individual difference constructs that are related to "typical behavior" (Cronbach, 1990) or behavioral dispositions.

The research evidence supporting the usefulness of objective measures of personality has taken an interesting turn in the past 15 years. The tone of early reviews of the research literature was skeptical if not outright critical (Ghiselli, 1966; Guion & Gottier, 1965; Reilly & Chao, 1982; Schmidt, Gooding, Noe, & Kirsch, 1984). However, in recent years there has been a surge of research that supports a link between objective personality measures and job performance (Christiansen, Goffin, Johnston, & Rothstein, 1994; Gellatly, Paunonen, Meyer, Jackson & Goffin, 1991; Hough, Eaton, Dunnette, Kamp, & McCloy, 1990; House, Shane, & Herold, 1996; Mount & Barrick, 1995; Tett, Jackson, & Rothstein, 1991; Vinchur, Schippmann, Switzer, & Roth, 1998). For example, meta-analytic reviews have reported validities of .31 for personality scales that measure various aspects of conscientiousness (Mount & Barrick, 1995; Schmidt & Hunter, 1998). In fact, although the evidence is not uniform (Sackett, Gruys, & Ellingson, 1998), there are data to suggest that personality instruments not only are good predictors in their own right, but also provide incremental validity over cognitive ability predictors (Day & Silverman, 1989; Goffin, Rothstein, & Johnston, 1996; McHenry, Hough, Toquam, Hanson, & Ashworth, 1990; McManus & Kelly, 1999; Schippmann & Prien, 1989).

Similar to objective personality tests, interest inventories provide the assessee with true–false or forced-choice response options that compare the test taker's interests to the interests of individuals engaged in different occupations. There is a fairly large base of research indicating that these tests are useful for predicting occupational choice and occupational satisfaction. As such, these tools are frequently used to help individuals make career choice or career change decisions. However, there is evidence that these predictors may also prove useful for selection purposes (e.g., Vinchur et al., 1998).

Work Samples.   Work sample tests directly measure an assessee's performance in doing an important part of the target job. For example, asking a candidate for an administrative assistant position to complete a typing test is essentially asking the individual to perform one aspect of the job as part of the pre-employment evaluation. Other fairly concrete examples include asking a mechanic to rebuild part of a motor or an architect to read a blueprint. For higher level positions, it makes sense to divide work sample tests into two categories: interactive (i.e., simulations requiring the assessee to interact with other people) and noninteractive.

By far, the most prevalent noninteractive work sample approach for higher level jobs is the in-basket test, a method that is the product of over six decades of research and application (Schippmann, Prien, & Katz, 1990). As the name implies, this test asks the assessee to arrange, evaluate, and respond to materials (e.g., memos, brief reports, summaries of business data) of varying importance and urgency that might appear in a manager's in-basket. In most cases the assessee assumes a hypothetical position in a new management role, where there has been an accumulation of in-basket material requiring a response (e.g., from 30 to 60 memos, brief reports, and so forth). The assessee has between 60 and 90 minutes to work through these items and jot down notes, list action items, and prepare to-do lists, all of which is turned in to the assessor at the end of the time period for scoring. Commercially available in-baskets are available; however, most assessment practitioners develop their own instruments that may be used again and again for fairly broad occupational groups or within a particular organization. A variety of discussions of in-basket development and design exist in the literature and will not be duplicated here (Crooks, 1971; Crooks & Mahoney, 1971; Lopez, 1966; Ward, 1959). Furthermore, although the reported evidence supporting the usefulness of the in-basket as a measurement tool is modest and mixed (Schippmann et al., 1990), there is some unpublished work that provides more impressive predictive validities within an individual assessment context (Schippmann, 1995).

One of the categories of noninteractive individual difference measurement that is somewhat nonconventional is small job sample testing, which is a spin-off of the in-basket procedure. Work sample tests are exactly what the name implies and the hallmark of this approach is represented in the four-volume manual entitled *Principles of Work Sample Testing* by Robert Guion (1979). In brief, work sample testing follows very conventional test construction and development practices based on a thorough and comprehensive modeling of the content universe for a defined job or family of jobs. However, the strategy and tactics are somewhat different in that the focus of a small job sample is intended to achieve absolute fidelity of the test content domain with reference to the job itself. Thus, work sample tests are designed to measure the individual's actual competence, not an abstract or hypothetical assessment of competence. An alternative conceptualization is that a work sample test represents a highly standardized version of performance appraisal that is concrete and absolute, rather than representative of a judgmental evaluation of the performance capability. Work sample testing certainly has advocates, but the approach has very high requirement hurdles for fidelity and for comprehensiveness of measurement. As a result, work sample tests are considerably more expensive to develop but, in many cases, they can be a valuable adjunct to more efficient means of deriving information about individual difference characteristics.

It should be noted, however, that there is some evidence that a combination of paper-and-pencil tests measuring the different abilities required for a particular job can predict performance as well as a complex work sample test (Fleishman, 1988; Fleishman & Mumford, 1991; Hogan, Ogden, & Fleishman, 1991). Also, high correlations have been obtained between combinations of tests of general abilities and work sample tests designed for the same job (Fleishman, 1988; Fleishman & Mumford, 1991; Gebhardt & Schemmer, 1985; Hogan et al., 1979; Myers, Gebhardt, Price, & Fleishman, 1981).

Interactive work samples include a wide array of simulations like one-on-one role plays, leaderless group discussions, and mock presentations. For example, in a role play, the assessee might be asked to play the role of a new bank manager who must coach a bank teller on how to improve performance (this role is played by the assessor or other assessment associate). Alternatively, the candidate may be asked to prepare a presentation to be delivered at a fictitious senior management meeting describing a sales initiative. In this case, the candidate is provided with an overhead projector, blank transparencies, and flip charts, and he or she must prepare and deliver a presentation to the assessor in a meeting room. These kinds of simulations have been a staple of assessment center methodology for years (Bray & Grant, 1966; Thornton & Byham, 1982). Their use in the practice of individual assessment has been more limited due to designing and delivering challenges in $n = 1$ settings. However, meta-analytic research indicates that these kinds of interactive work samples add significant predictive value in the assessment center context (Gaugler, Rosenthal, Thornton, & Benson, 1987). Specifically, meta-analytic coefficients of $r = .53$ with ratings of managerial potential and $r = .36$ with measures of managerial job performance have been reported (Gatewood & Feild, 1994). Descriptions of procedures for developing interactive work samples are reported elsewhere (Schippmann, Hughes, & Prien, 1987).

Reference Checks.   The reference checking activity is seldom performed by assessors as part of the individual assessment activity. However, we are aware of a few practice settings where this is done. It seems intuitively obvious that a person's prior track record of accomplishments would be a valuable predictor of future performance, if in fact the person has a work history. The idea is that information from those knowledgeable about the candidate in the past will be able to improve the prediction equation for future performance. Certainly, it is common practice in employment settings to ask a candidate to provide references (e.g., former employers, colleagues, teachers). Despite the fact that reference checking is a close second to the interview in terms of frequency of use as an employment screen (Morgan & Smith, 1996), there are very few research studies on the subject. The few studies that do exist report far from stellar validities, ranging from $r = .16$ for predicting promotions to $r = .26$ for ratings of job performance (Hunter & Hunter, 1984). For the most part, reference checks tend to focus on:

- confirming dates of employment;
- confirming job titles and work experiences;
- description of most recent work activities and performance evaluations;
- description of candidate's personality; and
- determination of whether the referring individual would hire (or re-hire) the candidate.

Of course, the common refusal of companies to provide meaningful reference information in fear of litigation further limits the value of conducting these checks. Still, there appears to be a slow pendulum shift occurring. Over the past 10 years, 19 of 50 states have enacted laws that provide employers immunity from legal liability when providing job references to other employers. Similar laws are under consideration in nine other states (Baker, 1996).

A spin-off of the reference check procedure is the assessment of potential applicants using minimum qualifications. This approach is both time and cost efficient as a way of qualifying potential applicants in a way that is unobtrusive and provides a minimum-threshold screening procedure. Whereas the reference check is intrusive, in that an uninvited contact is made, the assessment of a qualifications document, which is willingly submitted and provided by the potential applicant, avoids any third-party involvement. However, although the veracity of the document submitted is open to question, the prudent approach is to simply assume that the applicant will conscientiously put his or her best foot forward simply as a matter of understandable impression management. There is, of course, no means to establish validity of this approach when the applicant presents false documents that are downright lies and fabrications but, by and large, information presented by the applicant can be accepted at face value until otherwise challenged.

Nevertheless, evaluation of minimum qualifications where the focus is on an individual's training and education record is accepted practice and its usefulness has been demonstrated (Ash, 1983; Ash & Levine, 1985; Lavigna, 1992; Levine, Maye, Ulm, & Gordon, 1997; Lyons, 1989). Assessing candidate minimum qualifications or training and education is best approached through the use of a scoring system and can be implemented using a minimum screen/pass–fail standard or standard grading procedure that produces an overall scoring metric. In this way, the data become one more piece of information to be combined with results of other measurements (e.g., test scores, interview ratings, interactive exercise ratings, etc.) as part of a comprehensive multirater–multimethod approach. Good descriptions of methods for developing and validating minimum qualifications are available (Ash, Johnson, Levine, & McDaniel, 1989; Gibson & Prien, 1977; Hough, 1984; Levine et al., 1997; Meritt-Haston & Wexley, 1983; Wooten, Summerlin, & Prien, in press).

Biographical Inventories.   Another potential source of input to an assessment is the biographical inventory, also known as the weighted application blank, personality assessment, or, most commonly, biodata (Guion, 1998; Stokes, Mumford, & Owens, 1994; Super, 1960). Unlike other assessment tools, which have been used on a fairly continuous basis (other than personality testing), biodata has swung in and out of popularity. The technique was developed in the 1920s, refined in the 1940s, and popular again in the 1960s. The 1990s have seen a resurgence of interest in the use of biodata measurement as a predictor of work success.

Biodata is the collection and the objective scoring of events from an individual's prior history related to the question "what kind of person is this?" Based on the age-old assumption that the best predictor of future behavior is one's past behavior, biodata questionnaires ask an individual about his or her past activities (for a complete discussion of the characteristics of biodata items, see Mael, 1991). Typical items ask about an individual's work or educational experiences, or their extracurricular, social, and leisure activities. Items are written (or chosen from prior inventories) based on a conceptual linkage to the constructs of interest. For example, Mael and Hirsch (1993) used questions about outdoor sports to assess military candidates. Demographic items, such as parents' occupation or birth order, are also included and have a history of validity, although the logical or theoretical rationale for these items is less obvious. Items are objectively scored, using a variety of response formats (e.g., multiple choice, yes–no) and different weighting schemes, as discussed by Owens (1976).

Biodata forms can have validities comparable to those of standardized tests. In fact, there is research indicating that the addition of biodata to ability and personality measures can contribute incremental predictive power

(Mount, Witt, & Barrick, 2000). Unfortunately, though, biodata forms have traditionally been one of the "black boxes" of selection research. That is, a biodata form will differentiate between criterion groups (such as successful and less successful managers), but with no clear rationale or articulation as to why. The most recent round of research on biodata (e.g., Mael & Hirsch, 1993) has attempted to provide a theoretical—or, at least what Mael and Hirsch label a "quasi-rational"—foundation for biodata's validity, most commonly drawing on personality constructs as the foundation. Other biodata research relies on statistical methods, using factor analytic techniques to derive interpretable dimensions from biodata questionnaires (Hough & Paullin, 1994; Schoenfeldt & Mendoza, 1994).

Overall, biodata assessment can be a worthwhile addition to the assessor's inventory of potential tests, adding a very different type of data to the multitrait-multimethod matrix of information about the individual. Note too that there is a certain amount of overlap between biodata and the concept of minimum qualifications. Both methods ask about an assessee's past and, for both techiques, similar issues arise regarding scoring and weighting. However, biodata focuses more on the measurement of job-related constructs, whereas the minimum qualification approach has a more direct and closer linkage to specific job skills.

The same issues of validity and job-relatedness apply as with other types of ability and personality tests. We would, however, add one caution to the practitioner, which is that a biodata questionnaire should make minimal use of items that have little obvious connection to job requirements, in the interests of applicants' perception of the assessment as a fair process (Elkins & Phillips, 2000).

360° Ratings. The 360° feedback approach has gained a great deal of popularity in developmental contexts in recent years. The idea is to provide individuals with boss, peer, direct report, and perhaps even customer feedback, and to juxtapose these inputs with self ratings on the same set of work-related dimensions (Bracken, 1994; Bracken, Timmreck, & Church, 2001; Church, 1995; Hazucha, Hezlett, & Schneider, 1993; Waldman, Atwater, & Antonioni, 1998). Although the vast majority of 360° feedback tools target management populations, the approach is increasingly being used for supervisory and various technical and individual contributor segments of the workforce. Despite their popularity and the prevalence of practice, 360° research is still in its infancy stage, and there are more questions than answers (DeNisi & Kluger, 2000; Ghorpade, 2000). Although research (Church, Rogelberg, & Waclawski, 2000) and reviews (Dalessio, 1998; Kluger & DeNisi, 1996) are being conducted and reported, many questions about the psychometric quality of the data remain unaddressed. Regardless, we are aware of more and more internal assessment programs using 360° ratings as part of the input data for promotion assessments.

Selecting Relevant Tests

As stated at the beginning of this section, the second line of research support at this stage of the individual assessment process involves the ability of psychologists to estimate the validity of tests with reference to the requirements of a target job. Unfortunately, there have been only a limited number of studies that directly examine the ability of psychologists to estimate the validity of tests based on a description of target job requirements. Parry (1968) found little agreement among 10 "test experts" concerning their estimated validity coefficients for a number of test and job combinations. In addition, she found little convergence between the experts' estimated validities and obtained validity coefficients. However, a reanalysis of this data by Schmidt and Hunter (1976) using a special *chi*-square statistic found that there was no significant difference between estimated values and actual sample validities.

Next, a study by Schmidt, Hunter, Croll, and McKenzie (1983), using 20 psychologists, samples of over 3,000 subjects for each of nine jobs, and 54 job-test combinations, found that the "experts" tended to slightly underestimate the true validities obtained from empirical research. These authors concluded that expert judgments may provide more accurate estimates than local criterion-related validation studies. A follow-up study reported 3 years later involved 28 recent PhDs in industrial psychology providing estimated validities for the same 54 job-test combinations used by Schmidt et al. The results indicate that these less experienced judges provided estimates of significantly poorer quality than the original 20 experts (Hirsh, Schmidt, & Hunter, 1986). However, the averages of estimates of several less experienced judges were found to be as accurate as those obtained from small-sample empirical studies.

In yet another study, the focus was on how measures of predictor constructs have predictably different patterns of correlations with different criteria (Pulakos, Borman, & Hough, 1988). The first part of this two-part study involved navy recruiters ($n = 267$); the second part involved army soldiers ($n = 8,642$). For the first study, estimates of the predictive magnitudes of the relations between the predictor and criterion constructs were made by seven personnel psychologists who were unfamiliar with the empirical results. In addition, these judges did not participate in the predictor or criterion development efforts. Judges independently estimated the true correlation between each predictor and criterion. The reliability of the expert judges' estimates of the predictor criterion relationships were "reasonably high." Individual judge-by-judge correlations of their 33 estimates (11 predictors and 3 criteria) ranged from .69 to .94, with a median of .81. The second part of the study involved the estimated and empirical correlations between predictor and criterion measures for army-enlisted personnel. The same seven personnel psychologists provided estimates and the judge-by-judge correlations for the 24 estimates ranged from .55 to .96, with a median of .76. Thus, in both studies, although the relationship between the estimated and observed validities was not reported, there was reasonably good agreement between the expert judges.

Finally, although Peterson et al. (1990) did not report obtained validities, a sample of 35 personnel psychologists estimated the true (i.e., corrected) validities of 53 predictor variables for 72 criterion variables as a part of the Army Selection and Classification Project (Project A). The means of the predictor-criterion validity judgments (i.e., cell means in the predictor-criterion matrix) were highly reliable (.96).

An additional line of evidence, one step removed from a direct evaluation of experts' ability to estimate test validities, comes from the work of McCormick and his colleagues in using the Position Analysis Questionnaire (PAQ) to predict attribute or competency profiles (Marquardt & McCormick, 1972; Mecham & McCormick, 1969). Many readers may be familiar with the PAQ as a standardized questionnaire used to define the work activity dimensions associated with different jobs (Jeanneret, 1987; Jeanneret & McCormick, 1969). However, a somewhat less well-known methodology using the PAQ involves predicting the mental ability, perceptual ability, temperament, interest, and psychomotor ability (i.e., competencies) associated with different work activity profiles.

The underlying activity–attribute linkages were compiled from judgments submitted by rating experts (between 8 and 18) with backgrounds in industrial psychology and human resources. The reliabilities of these ratings in the two primary reports of the research were high, generally in excess of .85 (Marquardt & McCormick, 1972; Mecham & McCormick, 1969).

Of greater interest is the efficacy of the PAQ in predicting empirical validities (McCormick, DeNisi, & Shaw, 1979; McCormick, Jeanneret, & Mecham, 1972). Although there have been few efforts to examine this question, the work that has been done suggests that the PAQ does generate conservative estimates of the validity coefficients likely to be obtained in local validation research (Carter & Biersner, 1987; Hoffman & McPhail, 1998; Holden, 1992; Jeanneret, 1992; McCormick, Mecham, & Jeanneret, 1989; McPhail, 1995; Robertson & Trent, 1983; Sparrow, Patrick, Spurgeon, & Barnwell, 1982). In summary, these findings support the practice of estimating the nature and level of certain individual difference constructs that would be characteristic of incumbents in various jobs.

Yet another indirect line of evidence for evaluating the judgments of psychologists serving as test experts, three steps removed from a direct evaluation, comes from the scale construction literature. There are three primary strategies for producing scales, or sets of similar items: making use of judgment (i.e., the rational-theoretical approach), using techniques to group items by internal consistency (usually using factor analysis), and employing group comparisons to identify items (i.e., criterion group or criterion comparison). Furthermore, test theorists and investigators such as Loevinger (1957), Wiggins (1973), and Jackson (1970) have given judgmental activity an important place in selecting items aimed at measuring constructs.

However, there have been several attempts to compare these three strategies to see which one works the best. Hase and Goldberg (1967) and Goldberg

(1972) carried out a series of sophisticated investigations using several methods to produce several different scales. They found that scales produced by
four specific techniques (the first two of which are judgment based)—rational, theoretical, factor-analytic, and criterion group—were equally effective
in predicting external criteria. Our rationale for presenting this information
here is that, if psychologists can accurately select scale items for measuring
specific constructs, the implication is that psychologists might also do a good
job at a similar activity: selecting completed scales/tests appropriate for measuring specific constructs in an employment context. Although this line of
reasoning yields only indirect evidence, it is evidence worth considering.

      Collectively, the results reported in this section suggest that, in the absence
of empirical data to guide test or scale selection, a trained and experienced
psychologist can derive job requirements and provide comparable estimates
of test validity in specific applications. This is a very important supporting link
for the practice of individual assessment. As discussed previously, individual
assessments are typically conducted for jobs with few positions and few candidates. The attractiveness of individual assessment in this situation is predicated on the psychologist's ability to select an array of tests that accurately
mirror the target job's requirements. If job modeling procedures have been
used to characterize and differentiate job activities and competencies that
constitute the target for the assessment, then compelling evidence of the base
rate of validity of various kinds of measurement procedures (tests) requires
only an incidental leap of faith to reach the conclusion that individual assessments are valid and useful predictors of performance. If there is a fault in this
process, it is simply attributable to the fact that individual assessment is an individualized practice and there is relatively little motivation or impetus to
conduct evaluative research. Unfortunately, individual practitioners are not
likely to band together or to share information and results; they generally consider their peers to be competitors who are more interested in displacement
selling than in collaborative undertakings.

PRACTICE EXAMPLES

Continuing with the practice examples introduced in chapter 2, we now
work these examples beyond the modeling step to actually develop the assessment protocol and tailor the mix of tests to the situation. Again, the first
example concerns Linda Jones, a sales associate candidate with Computer
City. The second example involves the assessment being worked up for Peter Martin, an internal candidate for a department manager job with Barnes
Stores. The third example concerns Hector Dantos, an external candidate
for a division president job with Natural Foods World Wide.

Example 1: Sales Associate Assessment

Because of the large number of employees in sales associate jobs at Computer City, the up-front modeling work was more extensive. As a result, the

level of descriptive rigor in this situation approximates the level of review often seen in the development of more conventional, high-volume selection systems. As discussed in the "Practice Examples" section in chapter 2, the organization assessment and job assessment focus group and interview input was used to create a job modeling questionnaire that was administered to 14 store managers. Using a 5-point scale of importance, these managers provided judgments that were used to prioritize the components of the sales associate job. The results of this $n = 14$ job modeling work appears in Fig. 3.1 (work activities) and Fig. 3.2 (competencies).

The critical work activities include selling products and services, public and customer relations, and receiving and disbursing cash. The competencies judged to be most important for job success include the following (hurdle for assessment specifications set at 4.0 level):

- Public and customer relations
- Communications skills
- Merchandising
- Oral communication skills
- Work/organization skills
- Research and evaluation
- Computer skills

Based on this prioritization of what is most important for successful job performance, the protocol worksheet for the sales associate assessment was prepared (see Fig. 3.3). This worksheet outlines the *a priori* decisions about the most relevant tests linked to the competency dimensions to be assessed. Q1 through Q4 in the first column of this worksheet indicate competency dimensions tapped by specific interview questions. The specific tests listed in the second and third columns are identified using the shorthand designations from Table 3.1. For example, "GPPI" refers to the Gordan Personal Profile Inventory. Furthermore, for those tests with multiple measurement scales, the specific scale(s) considered to be particularly relevant are abbreviated in lower case type. For example, GPPI-*p* refers to the personal relations scale in the "Customer Relations" row of Table 3.1. The shorthand designations for specific scales subsumed in a particular multiscale test may also be identified by reviewing the "Description" column of Table 3.1. The fact that there are no entries in the fourth column of Fig. 3.3 indicates that no simulations will be used in the assessment. As a quick reference, the specific tests and scales referenced in Fig. 3.3 include the following:

Cognitive Tests

- Advanced Mental Ability Test (AMAT)
- Numerical Computation Test (NCT)

FIG. 3.1.   Work activity profile for sales associate (Example 1).

76

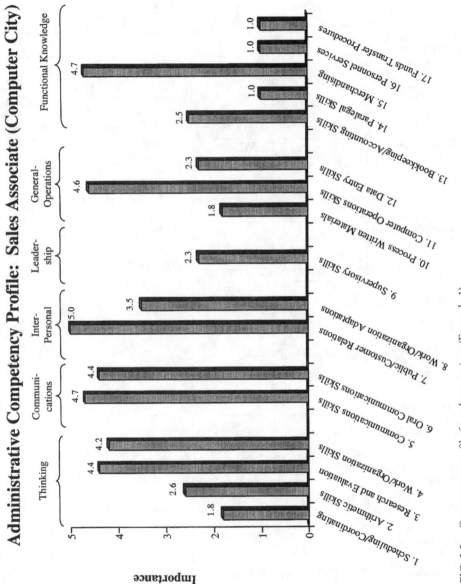

FIG. 3.2. Competency profile for sales associate (Example 1).

77

	Interview and Background Information	Cognitive Tests	Personality, Interest, and Work Style Tests	Simulations
THINKING				
1. Research and evaluation		AMAT NCT	GPPI-e GPPI-o GPPI-r GSDI-r GSDI-int GSDI-dec	
2. Work / Organization skills	Q1	AMAT	GPPI-r GPPI-a GPPI-v GSDI-init GSDI-nach	
COMMUNICATIONS				
3. Communication skills	Q2		GPPI-s GPPI-p GPPI-a GSDI-sa	
4. Oral communications	Q1 – Q5		GPPI-s GPPI-p GPPI-a GSDI-sa	
INTERPERSONAL				
5. Public customer relations	Q3		GPPI-p GPPI-a CSI	
LEADERSHIP X. None				
GENERAL OPERATIONS 6. Computer skills	Q5			
FUNCTIONAL KNOWLEDGE 7. Merchandising skills	Q4	SAT		

FIG. 3.3.   Protocol worksheet for sales associate (Example 1).

- Sales Ability Test (SAT)
  Personality, Interest, and Work Style Tests
- Gordon Personal Profile Inventory (GPPI)
    - emotional stability (e)
    - original thinking (o)
    - responsibility (r)
    - ascendancy (a)
    - vigor (v)
    - sociability (s)
    - personal relations (p)
- Ghiselli Self-Description Inventory (GSDI)
    - intelligence (int)
    - decisiveness (dec)
    - initiative (init)
    - need for achievement (nach)
    - self-assurance (sa)
- Customer Service Inventory (CSI)

Example 2: Department Manager Assessment

This assessment situation illustrates how the job modeling work is conducted and updated on an ongoing basis for a long-term assessment client. In this case, a sample of store managers and job incumbents (i.e., department managers) completed a questionnaire that contained the updated job model for department manager. In all, 22 individuals completed the job modeling questionnaire to identify the work activities (Fig. 3.4) and competencies (Fig. 3.5) that contribute most to successful job performance.

In terms of work activities, the People Management aspects of the job are clearly most important. The specific dimensions that are most critical for job success are Staffing followed by Supervise People. From the General Operations Management section, the dimension of Supervise Work Operations was also critical for successful job performance.

The competencies that explain different degrees of successful performance in the work activities are profiled in Fig. 3.5. As this figure illustrates, the following competencies are important at the 4.0 level or higher:

- Management of performance quality
- Verbal communications
- Supervisory skills
- Work/organization adaptation
- Business relationships
- Project planning
- Analytical ability

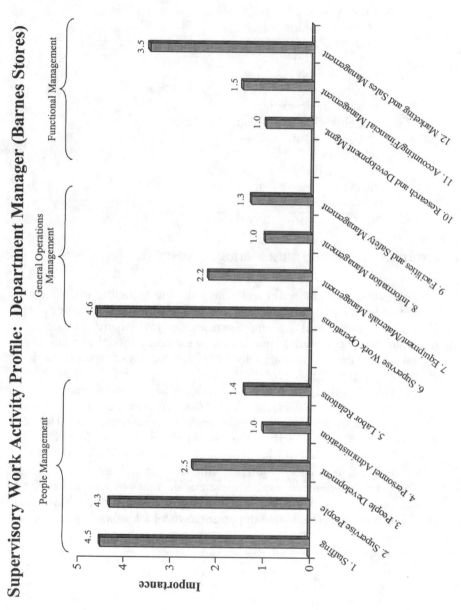

FIG. 3.4. Work activity profile for department manager (Example 2).

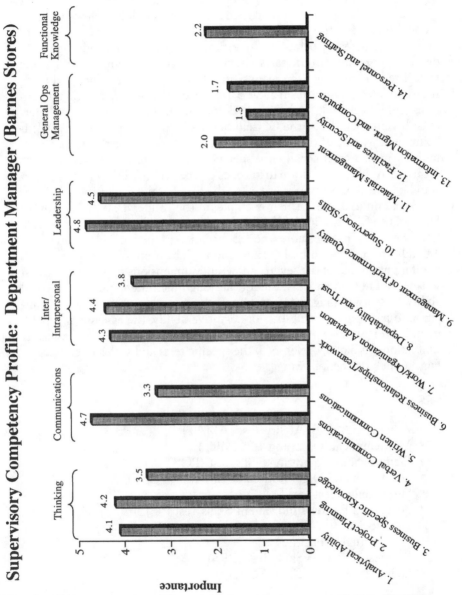

FIG. 3.5. Competency profile for department manager (Example 2).

81

Using the job modeling results as a foundation, the assessment protocol worksheet for the Barnes Stores department manager job was completed (see Fig. 3.6). In this case, because of the ongoing assessment relationship with the client, this work simply confirmed that there were no significant changes to the assessment protocol since the last modeling review. With reference to Fig. 3.6, the Q1 through Q5 notations indicate competency dimensions targeted by behavioral questions in the assessment interview. As discussed previously in the sales associate assessment example, the specific tests listed in Fig. 3.6 in the second and third columns are identified using shorthand designations from Table 3.1. For example, in the "Personality, Interest, and Work Style" column, in addition to the Gordon Personal Preference Inventory (GPPI), the Ghiselli Self-Description Inventory (GSDI) is being used as part of the assessment protocol. Again, for those tests with multiple measurement scales, the specific scale(s) considered to be relevant are listed in abbreviated form in lower case type, where the legend for understanding the abbreviation is linked to the list of scales under the "Description" column in Table 3.1. For example, in the "Supervisory Skills" row of Fig. 3.6, the GSDI-*sa* in the third column refers to the self-assurance scale from the GSDI. Furthermore, the "IB" notation in the fourth column of Fig. 3.6 indicates that an in-basket simulation will be used to provide measurement input on four of the seven competency dimensions targeted by this assessment. Thus, in this assessment, although measurements of analytical ability (first row in Fig. 3.6) can be most accurately measured using standardized paper-and-pencil tests of cognitive ability, the assessor is supplementing this input with problem-solving demonstrations in an in-basket simulation. As a quick reference, the specific tests and scales referenced in Fig. 3.6 include the following:

Cognitive Tests

- Advanced Mental Ability Test (AMAT)
- Mathematical Reasoning Test (MRT)
- Planning and Organizing Skills Test (POST)
- Teamwork and Organizational Skills Test (TOST)
- Sales Ability Test (SAT)
- Social and Business Judgement Skills Test (SBJS)
    - social
    - factual or business
- Business Relations Skills Test (BRS)
- Elements of Supervision (EOS)

Personality, Interest, and Work Style Tests

- Gordon Personal Profile Inventory (GPPI)
    - original thinking (o)

	Interview and Background Information	Cognitive Tests	Personality, Interest, and Work Style Tests	Simulations
THINKING				
1. Analytical ability		AMAT MRT POST SBJS-f	GPPI-o GPPI-r	IB
2. Project planning	Q1	AMAT MRT TOST SBJS-f	GPPI-o GPPI-r GPPI-v	IB
COMMUNICATIONS				
3. Verbal communications	Q1 – Q5	SAT		
INTERPERSONAL				
4. Business relationships	Q2	SBJS-s BRST	GPPI-a GPPI-s GPPI-p	IB
5. Work organization adaptation	Q3		GPPI-r GPPI-v GPPI-c	
LEADERSHIP				
6. Performance quality	Q4	EOS SAT TOST SBJS-f	GPPI-r GPPI-v GPPI-c LOQ-c LOQ-s	
7. Supervisory skills	Q5	EOS TOST SBJS-s	GPPI-a GPPI-r GPPI-v LOQ-c LOQ-s	IB
FUNCTIONAL KNOWLEDGE (not assessed)				
X. None				

FIG. 3.6.   Protocol worksheet for department manager (Example 2).

- responsibility (r)
- vigor (v)
- ascendancy (a)
- sociability (s)
- personal relations (p)
- cautiousness (c)
- Leadership Opinion Questionnaire
  - consideration
  - structure

Example 3: Division President Assessment

The assessor responsible for the eventual assessment completed a management and executive modeling questionnaire (comprised of the work activity and competency items from Appendix A) after interviewing the CFO
and the SVP of HR (see "Practice Examples" from chap. 2). In addition, the
SVP of HR completed the same modeling questionnaire. The results of this
$n = 2$ job modeling work appears in Fig. 3.7 (work activities) and Fig. 3.8
(competencies). In terms of work activities, the People Management aspects of the job are paramount, with the dimensions of External Relations
and Staffing being judged as most critical. Specific activities in the Marketing and Sales Management dimension were also critically important,
closely followed by Accounting and Financial Management and Research
and Development Management.

From the vantage point of competencies, 14 dimensions were important at
the 4.0 level or higher. Based on discussions with the client, it was determined
that the structured interviews by Natural Foods executives would focus much
attention on functional business knowledge and related experiences. For this
reason, competencies having to do with business-specific knowledge or functional expertise ($n = 4$) were excluded from attention in the assessment protocol. This left 10 dimensions to target in the assessment process:

- Analytical ability
- Influencing skills
- Creativity
- Strategic thinking
- Business relationships
- Decisiveness
- Short-term planning
- Verbal communications
- Motivation skills

These 10 dimensions, which span the four broad factors of Thinking,
Communications, Interpersonal, and Leadership, were built into a pro-

Executive Work Activity Profile: Div. President (Natural Foods WW)

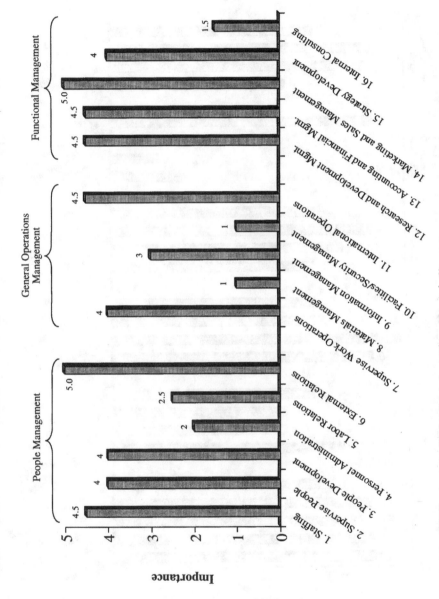

FIG. 3.7.   Work activity profile for division president (Example 3).

85

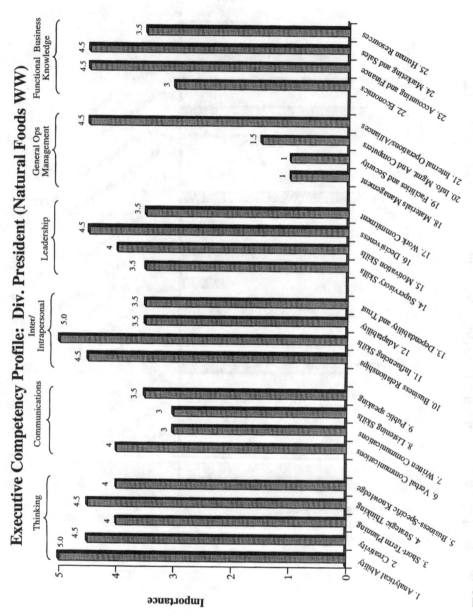

FIG. 3.8. Competency profile for division president (Example 3).

tocol worksheet that could look something like the array of information in Fig. 3.9. As in the previous two examples, in this display, a priori decisions about the most relevant test used to tap aspects of a competency are mapped out. The same shorthand designations and cross-reference links to specific scales in Table 3.1 apply in this assessment protocol worksheet. The one difference is the addition of a role play ("RP") in the fourth column of Fig. 3.9. The role play in this case was a small group presentation, with the assessee delivering a portion of a recent actual presentation to a group of peers: the assessor, an assessment colleague, and the test administrator. As a quick reference, the specific tests and scales referenced in Fig. 3.9 include the following:

Cognitive Tests

- Watson Glaser Critical Thinking Appraisal (WGCT)
- Critical Thinking Test (CTT)
    - verbal reasoning (v)
    - numeric reasoning (n)
- Planning and Organizing Skills Test (POST)
- Sales Ability Test (SAT)

Personality, Interest, and Work Style Tests

- California Psychological Inventory (CPI)
    - intellectual efficiency (ie)
    - flexibility (fx)
    - achievement via independence (ai)
    - independence (in)
    - dominance (do)
    - responsibility (re)
    - sociability (sy)
    - social presence (sp)
    - empathy (em)
- Edwards Personal Preference Schedule (EPPS)
    - change (ch)
    - achievement (ac)
    - order (or)
    - intraception (int)
    - affiliation (af)
    - endurance (end)
    - autonomy (au)

	Interview and Background Information	Cognitive Tests	Personality, Interest, and Work Style Tests	Simulations
THINKING				
1. Analytical ability		WGCT CTT-v CTT-n POST	CPI-ie	IB
2. Creativity	Q1		CPI-fx CPI-ai CPI-in EPPS-ch EPPS-ac	IB
3. Short-term planning	Q2	WGCT CTT-n POST	CPI-do CPI-re CPI-fx EPPS-or	IB
4. Strategic thinking	Q3	WGCT	CPI-fx EPPS-ac EPPS-or EPPS-int	RP
COMMNICATIONS				
5. Verbal communications	Q1 – Q7	CTT-v	CPI-do CPI-sy CPI-sp CPI-em EPPS-af EPPS-int	
INTERPERSONAL				
6. Business relationships	Q4		CPI-do CPI-sy CPI-sp CPI-em EPPS-af EPPS-int	RP
7. Influencing skills	Q5	SAT	CPI-ai CPI-sp CPI-re EPPS-end	RP
LEADERSHIP				
8. Motivation skills	Q6		CPI-ai CPI-sp CPI-re EPPS-end	
9. Decisiveness	Q7	WGCT CTT-v CTT-n	CPPI-do CPI-ai CPI-in EPPS-au	
FUNCTIONAL/GENERAL OPERATIONS KNOWLEDGE (not assessed)				
X. None				

FIG. 3.9. Protocol worksheet for division president (Example 3).

REFERENCES

Arvey, R. D., & Campion, J. E. (1982). The employment interview: A summary and review of recent research. *Personnel Psychology, 35,* 281–322.

Ash, R. A. (1983). The behavioral consistency method of training and experience evaluations: Content validity issues and completion rate problems. *Public Personnel Management Journal, 12,* 115–127.

Ash, R. A., Johnson, J. C., Levine, E. L., & McDaniel, M. A. (1989). Job applicant training and work experience evaluation in personnel selection. *Research in Personnel and Human Resources Management, 7,* 183–226.

Ash, R. A., & Levine, E. L. (1985). Job applicant training and work experience evaluation: An empirical comparison of four methods. *Journal of Applied Psychology, 70*(3), 572–576.

Baker, T. G. (1996). Practice network. *The Industrial-Organizational Psychologist, 34,* 44–53.

Bracken, D. W. (1994). Straight talk about multirater feedback. *Training and Development, 48*(9), 44–51.

Bracken, D. W., Timmreck, C. W., & Church, A. H. (2001). *The handbook of multisource feedback.* San Francisco: Jossey-Bass.

Bray, D. W., & Grant, D. L. (1966). The assessment center in the measurement of potential for business management. *Psychological Monographs, 80* (Whole No. 17).

Campion, M. A., Palmer, D. K., & Campion, J. E. (1997). A review of structure in the selection interview. *Personnel Psychology, 50,* 655–693.

Carter, R. C., & Biersner, R. J. (1987). Job requirements derived from the Position Analysis Questionnaire and validated using military aptitude test scores. *Journal of Occupational Psychology, 60,* 311–321.

Christiansen, N. D., Goffin, R. D., Johnston, N. G., & Rothstein, M. G. (1994). Correcting the 16PF for faking: Effects on criterion-related validity and individual hiring decisions. *Personnel Psychology, 47,* 847–860.

Church, A. H. (1995). First-rate multirater feedback. *Training and Development, 49*(8), 42–43.

Church, A. H., Rogelberg, S. G., & Waclawski, J. (2000). Since when is no news good news? The relationship between performance and response rates in multirater feedback. *Personnel Psychology, 53,* 435–451.

Conway, J. M., Jako, R. A., & Goodman, D. F. (1995). A meta-analysis of interrater and internal consistency reliability of selection interviews. *Journal of Applied Psychology, 80,* 565–579.

Cronbach, L. J. (1990). *Essentials of psychological testing* (5th ed.). New York: Harper Collins.

Crooks, L. A. (1971). *The in-basket study: A pilot study of MBA candidate performance on a test of administrative skills as related to selection and achievement in graduate business school* (Brief No. 4, ATGSB Research and Development Committee). Princeton, NJ: Educational Testing Service.

Crooks, L. A., & Mahoney, M. H. (1971). *Prediction of job performance for Black, Mexican-American and Caucasian inventory management specialists* (PR No. 71–23). Princeton, NJ: Educational Testing Service.

Dalessio, A. T. (1998). Using multisource feedback for employee feedback and personnel decisions. In J. W. Smith (Ed.), *Performance appraisal: State of the art in practice* (pp. 278–330). San Francisco: Jossey-Bass.

Day, D. A., & Silverman, S. B. (1989). Personality and job performance: Evidence of incremental validity. *Personnel Psychology, 42,* 25–36.

DeNisi, A. S., & Kluger, A. N. (2000). Feedback effectiveness: Can 360–degree appraisals be improved? *Academy of Management Executive, 14*(1), 129–139.

Elkins, T. J., & Phillips, J. S. (2000). Job context, selection decision outcome, and the perceived fairness of selection tests: Biodata as an illustrative case. *Journal of Applied Psychology, 85,* 479–484.

Fleishman, E. A. (1975). Toward a taxonomy of human performance. *American Psychologist, 30*(12), 1127–1149.

Fleishman, E. A. (1982). Systems for describing human tasks. *American Psychologist, 37*(7), 821–834.

Fleishman, E. A. (1988). Some new frontiers in personnel selection research. *Personnel Psychology, 41*(4), 679–701.

Fleishman, E. A. (1992). *Fleishman Job Analysis Survey (F-JAS).* Potomac, MD: Management Research Institute.

Fleishman, E. A., & Mumford, M. D. (1991). Evaluating classifications of job behavior: A construct validation of the Ability Requirement Scales. *Personnel Psychology, 44*(3), 523–575.

Fleishman, E. A., & Quaintance, M. K. (1984). *Taxonomies of human performance: The description of human tasks.* Orlando, FL: Academic Press.

Fleishman, E. A., & Reilly, M. E. (1992a). *Administrators' guide for the Fleishman Job Analysis Survey (F-JAS).* Potomac, MD: Management Research Institute.

Fleishman, E. A., & Reilly, M. E. (1992b). *Handbook of human abilities: Definitions, measurements, and job task requirements.* Potomac, MD: Management Research Institute.

Gatewood, R. D., & Feild, H. S. (1994). *Human resource selection.* Orlando, FL: Harcourt Brace.

Gaugler, B. B., Rosenthal, D. B., Thornton, G. C., & Benson, C. (1987). Meta-analysis of assessment center validity. *Journal of Applied Psychology, 72,* 493–511.

Gebhardt, D. L., & Schemmer, F. M. (1985). *Development and validation of selection tests for long shoreman and marine clerks* (Tech. Rep. No. 3113). Bethesda, MD: Advanced Research Resources Organization.

Gellatly, I. R., Paunonen, S. V., Meyer, J. P., Jackson, D. N., & Goffin, R. D. (1991). Personality, vocational interests, and cognitive predictors of managerial job performance and satisfaction. *Personality and Individual Differences, 12,* 221–231.

Ghiselli, E. E. (1966). *The validity of occupational aptitude tests.* New York: Wiley.

Ghorpade, J. (2000). Managing five paradoxes of 360–degree feedback. *Academy of Management Executive, 14*(1), 140–150.

Gibson, J. W., & Prien, E. P. (1977). Validation of minimum qualifications. *Public Personnel Management, 6,* 447–456.

Goffin, R. D., Rothstein, M. G., & Johnston, N. G. (1996). Personality testing and the assessment center: Incremental validity for managerial selection. *Journal of Applied Psychology, 81,* 746–756.

Goldberg, L. R. (1972). Parameters of personality inventory construction and utilization: A comparison of prediction strategies and tactics. *Multivariate Behavioral Research Monographs, 7*(2).

Guion, R. M. (1979). *Principles of work sample testing* (Contract DAHC No. 19-77-C-0007. Washington, DC: U.S. Army Research Institute.

Guion, R. M. (1998). *Assessment, measurement, and prediction for personnel decisions.* Mahwah, NJ: Lawrence Erlbaum Associates.

Guion, R. M., & Gottier, R. F. (1965). Validity of personality measures in personnel selection. *Personnel Psychology, 18,* 135–164.

Harris, M. M. (1989). Reconsidering the employment interview: A review of recent literature and suggestions for future research. *Personnel Psychology, 42,* 691–726.

Hase, H. D., & Goldberg, L. R. (1967). The comparative validity of different strategies of deriving personality inventory scales. *Psychological Bulletin, 67,* 231–248.

Hazucha, J. F., Hezlett, S. A., & Schneider, R. J. (1993). The impact of 360–degree feedback on management skills development. *Human Resource Management, 32,* 325–351.

Hirsh, H. R., Schmidt, F. L., & Hunter, J. E. (1986). Estimation of employment validities by less experienced judges. *Personnel Psychology, 39,* 337–344.

Hoffman, C. C., & McPhail, S. M. (1998). Exploring options for supporting test use in situations precluding local validation. *Personnel Psychology, 51,* 987–1002.

Hogan, J. C., Ogden, G. D., & Fleishman, E. A. (1979). *The development and validation of tests for the order selector job at Certified Grocers of California, Ltd.* (Tech. Rep. No. 3029). Bethesda, MD: Advanced Research Resources Organization.

Holden, L. M. (1992). *Job analysis and validity study for the distribution planning office technical progression* (Unpublished Tech. Rep.). Los Angeles: Southern California Gas Company.

Hough, L. M. (1984). Development and evaluation of the "Accomplishment Record" method of selecting and promoting professionals. *Journal of Applied Psychology, 69,* 135–146.

Hough, L. M., Eaton, H. K., Dunnette, M. D., Kamp, J. D., & McCloy, R. A. (1990). Criterion-related validities of personality constructs and the effect of response distortion on those validities. *Journal of Applied Psychology, 75,* 581–595.

Hough, L. M., & Paullin, C. (1994). Construct-oriented scale construction: The rational approach. In G. S. Stokes, M. D. Mumford, & W. A. Owens (Eds.), *Biodata handbook: Theory, research, and use of biographical information in selection and performance prediction* (pp. 109–145). Palo Alto, CA: Consulting Psychologists Press.

House, R. J., Shane, S. A., & Herold, D. M. (1996). Rumors of the death of dispositional research are vastly exaggerated. *Academy of Management Review, 21,* 203–224.

Huffcutt, A. I., & Arthur, W., Jr. (1994). Hunter & Hunter (1984) revisited: Interview validity for entry-level jobs. *Journal of Applied Psychology, 79,* 184–190.

Hunter, J. E. (1986). Cognitive ability, cognitive aptitudes, job knowledge, and job performance. *Journal of Vocational Behavior, 29,* 340–362.

Hunter, J. E., & Hunter, R. F. (1984). Validity and utility of alternative predictors of job performance. *Psychological Bulletin, 96,* 72–98.

Hunter, J. E., & Schmidt, F. L. (1996). Intelligence and job performance: Economic and social implications. *Psychology, Public Policy, & Law, 2,* 447–472.

Impara, J. C., & Plake, B. S. (1998). *Mental measurements yearbook* (13th ed.). Lincoln, NE: The Buros Institute of Mental Measurements.

Jackson, D. N. (1970). *A sequential system for personality scale development: Current topics in clinical and community psychology.* New York: Academic Press.

Janz, T. (1982). Initial comparisons of patterned behavior description interviews versus unstructured interviews. *Journal of Applied Psychology, 67,* 577–580.

Jeanneret, P. R. (1987, April). Future directions in the application of job analysis data. In M. D. Hakel (Chair), *The dimensionality of work: Future directions, applications and instrumentation.* Symposium conducted at the Annual Convention of the Society of Industrial and Organization Psychology, Atlanta, GA.

Jeanneret, P. R. (1992). Applications of job component/synthetic validity to construct validity. *Human Performance, 5*(1&2), 81–96.

Jeanneret, P. R., & McCormick, E. J. (1969). *The job dimensions of "worker oriented" job variables and of their attribute profiles as based on data from the Position Analysis Questionnaire* (Tech. Rep. No. 2). West Lafayette, IN: Purdue University, Occupational Research Center.

Judge, T. A., Higgins, C. A., & Cable, D. M. (2000). The employment interview: A review of recent research and recommendations for future research. *Human Resource Management Review, 10*(4), 383–406.

Kluger, A. N., & DeNisi, A. (1996). The effects of feedback interventions on performance: A historical review, a meta-analysis and a preliminary feedback intervention theory. *Psychological Bulletin, 119,* 254–284.

Lavigna, R. J. (1992). Predicting job performance from background characteristics: More evidence from the public sector. *Public Personnel Management, 21*(3), 347–361.

Levine, E. L., Maye, D. M., Ulm, R. A., Gordon, T. R. (1997). A methodology for developing and validating minimum qualifications (MQs). *Personnel Psychology, 50,* 1009–1023.

Loevinger, J. (1957). Objective tests as instruments of psychological theory. *Psychological Reports, 3,* 635–694.

Lopez, F. (1966). *Evaluating executive decision making: The in-basket technique.* (AMA Research Study No. 75). New York: American Management Association.

Lyons, T. (1989). *Validity of education and experience measures in traditional rating schedule procedures: A review of the literature* (Rep. No. OPRD-89-2). Washington, DC: U.S. Office of Personnel Management, Office of Personnel Research and Development.

Mael, F. A. (1991). A conceptual rationale for the domain and attributes of biodata items. *Personnel Psychology, 44,* 763–792.

Mael, F. A., & Hirsch, A. C. (1993). Rainforest empiricism and quasi-rationality: Two approaches to objective biodata. *Personnel Psychology, 46,* 719–738.

Marquardt, L. D., & McCormick, E. J. (1972). *Attribute ratings and profiles of the job elements of the Position Analysis Questionnaire* (Tech. Rep. No. 1). West Lafayette, IN: Purdue University, Department of Psychological Sciences.

McCormick, E. J., DeNisi, A. S., & Shaw, J. B. (1979). Use of the Position Analysis Questionnaire for establishing the job component validity of tests. *Journal of Applied Psychology, 64,* 51–56.

McCormick, E. J., Jeanneret, P. R., & Mecham, R. C. (1972). A study of job characteristics and job dimensions as based on the Position Analysis Questionnaire (PAQ) [Monograph]. *Journal of Applied Psychology, 56,* 347–368.

McCormick, E. J., Mecham, R. C., & Jeanneret, P. R. (1989). *Technical manual for the Position Analysis Questionnaire* (2nd ed.). Logan, UT: PAQ Services. (Available from Consulting Psychologists Press, Palo Alto, CA)

McDaniel, M. A., Whetzel, D. L., Schmidt, F. L., & Maurer, S. D. (1994). The validity of employment interviews: A comprehensive review and meta-analysis. *Journal of Applied Psychology, 79,* 599–616.

McHenry, J. J., Hough, L. M., Toquam, J. L., Hanson, M. A. & Ashworth, S. (1990). The relationship between predictor and criterion domains. *Personnel Psychology, 43,* 335–354.

McManus, M. A., & Kelly, M. L. (1999). Personality measures and biodata: Evidence regarding their incremental predictive value in the life insurance industry. *Personnel Psychology, 52,* 137–148.

McPhail, S. M. (1995, May). Job component validity predictions compared to empirical validities. In C. C. Hoffman (Chair), *Current innovations in PAQ-based research and practice.* Symposium conducted at the annual conference of the Society for Industrial and Organizational Psychology, Orlando, FL.

Mecham, R. C., & McCormick, E. J. (1969). *The use of data based on the Position Analysis Questionnaire in developing synthetically derived attribute requirements of jobs* (Tech. Rep. No. 4). West Lafayette, IN: Purdue University, Occupational Research Center.

Meritt-Haston, R., & Wexley, K. N. (1983). Educational requirements: Legality and validity. *Personnel Psychology, 36,* 743–753.

Morgan, R. B., & Smith, J. E. (1996). *Staffing the new workplace: Selecting and promoting for quality improvement.* Milwaukee, WI: ASQC Quality Press.

Mount, M. K., & Barrick, M. R. (1995). The big five personality dimensions: Implications for research and practice in human resources management. In G. Ferris (Ed.), *Research in personnel and human resources management* (Vol. 13, pp. 143–200). Greenwich, CT: JAI Press.

Mount, M. K., Witt, L. A., & Barrick, M. R. (2000). Incremental validity of empirically keyed biodata scales over GMA and the Five Factor personality constructs. *Personnel Psychology, 53,* 299–324.

Murphy, L. L., Impara, J. C., & Plake, B. S. (1999). *Tests in print (V).* Lincoln, NE: The Buros Institute of Mental Measurements.

Myers, D. C., Gebhardt, D. L., Price, S. J., & Fleishman, E. A. (1981). *Development of physical performance standards for Army jobs: Validation of the physical abilities analysis methodology* (Final Report No. 3045). Bethesda, MD: Advanced Research Resources Organization.

Owens, W. A. (1976). Background data. In M. D. Dunnette (Ed.), *Handbook of industrial and organizational psychology* (pp. 609–644). Chicago: Rand-McNally.

Parry, M. E. (1968). Ability of psychologists to estimate validities of personnel tests. *Personnel Psychology, 21,* 139–147.

Peterson, N. G., Hough, L. M., Dunnette, M. D., Rosse, R. L., Houston, J. S., Toquam, J. L., & Wing, H. (1990). Project A: Specification of the predictor domain and development of new selection/classification tests. *Personnel Psychology, 43,* 247–276.

Peterson, N. G., Mumford, M. D., Borman, W. C., Jeanneret, P. R., & Fleishman, E. A. (Eds.). (1999). *An occupational information system for the 21st century: The development of O*Net.* Washington, DC: American Psychological Association.

Pulakos, E. C., Borman, W. C., & Hough, L. M. (1988). Test validation for scientific understanding: Two demonstrations of an approach to studying predictor-criterion linkages. *Personnel Psychology, 41,* 703–716.

Ree, M. J., & Earles, J. A. (1991). Predicting training success: Not much more than g. *Personnel Psychology, 44,* 321–332.

Reilly, R. R., & Chao, G. T. (1982). Validity and fairness of some alternative employee selection procedures. *Personnel Psychology, 35,* 1–62.

Robertson, D. W., & Trent, T. T. (1983, August). *Predicting muscularly demanding job performance in Navy occupations.* Paper presented at the Annual Convention of the American Psychological Association, Anaheim, CA.

Ryan, A. M., & Sackett, P. R. (1987). A survey of individual assessment practices by I/O psychologists. *Personnel Psychology, 40,* 455–488.

Sackett, P. R., Gruys, M. L., & Ellingson, J. E. (1998). Ability-personality interactions when predicting job performance. *Journal of Applied Psychology, 83,* 545–556.

Schippmann, J. S. (1995). *Individual assessment in a consumer electronics company.* Unpublished manuscript.

Schippmann, J. S., Hughes, G. L., & Prien, E. P. (1987). The use of structured multi-domain job analysis for the construction of assessment center methods and procedures. *Journal of Business and Psychology, 1,* 353–366.

Schippmann, J. S., & Prien, E. P. (1989). An assessment of the contributions of general mental ability and personality characteristics to management success. *Journal of Business and Psychology, 3,* 423–437.

Schippmann, J. S., Prien, E. P., & Katz, J. A. (1990). The in-basket test: A review of research and opinion. *Personnel Psychology, 43,* 837–859.

Schmidt, F. L., & Hunter, J. E. (1976). Rational estimation of employment test validities. Washington, DC: Personnel Research and Development Center, U.S. Office of Personnel Management.

Schmidt, F. L., & Hunter, J. E. (1981). Employment testing: Old theories and new research findings. *American Psychologist, 36,* 1128–1137.

Schmidt, F. L., & Hunter, J. E. (1998). The validity and utility of selection methods in personnel psychology: Practical and theoretical implications of 85 years of research findings. *Psychological Bulletin, 124*(2), 262–274.

Schmidt, F. L., Hunter, J. E., Croll, P. R., & McKenzie, R. C. (1983). Estimation of employment test validities by expert judgment. *Journal of Applied Psychology, 68,* 590–601.

Schmidt, F. L., & Rader, M. (1999). Exploring the boundary conditions for interview validity: Meta-analytic validity findings for a new interview type. *Personnel Psychology, 52,* 445–463.

Schmidt, N., Gooding, R. Z., Noe, R. A., & Kirsch, M. (1984). Metaanalysis of validity studies published between 1964 and 1982 and the investigation of study characteristics. *Personnel Psychology, 37,* 407–422.

Schmitt, N. (1976). Social and situational determinants of interview decisions: Implications for the employment interview. *Personnel Psychology, 29,* 79–101.

Schoenfeldt, L. S., & Mendoza, J. L. (1994). Developing and using factorially derived biographical scales. In G. S. Stokes, M. D. Mumford, & W. A. Owens (Eds.), *Biodata handbook: Theory, research, and use of biographical information in selection and performance prediction* (pp. 147–169). Palo Alto, CA: Consulting Psychologists Press.

Sparrow, J., Patrick, J., Spurgeon, P., & Barnwell, F. (1982). The use of job component analysis and related aptitudes in personnel selection. *Journal of Occupational Psychology, 55,* 157–164.

Stokes, G. S., Mumford, M. D., & Owens, W. A. (1994). *Biodata handbook: Theory, research, and use of biographical information in selection and performance prediction.* Palo Alto, CA: Consulting Psychologists Press.

Super, D. E. (1960). The biographical inventory as a method for describing adjustment and predicting success. *Bulletin of the International Association of Applied Psychology, 9,* 18–39.

Tett, R. P., Jackson, D. N., & Rothstein, M. (1991). Personality measures as predictors of job performance: A meta-analytic review. *Personnel Psychology, 44,* 703–742.

Thornton, G. C., & Byham, W. C. (1982). *Assessment centers and managerial performance.* New York: Academic Press.

Ulrich, L., & Trumbo, D. (1965). The selection interview since 1949. *Psychological Bulletin, 63,* 100–116.

U. S. Department of Labor. (1970). *Manual for the General Aptitude Test battery.* Washington, DC: Author.

Vinchur, A. J., Schippmann, J. S., Switzer, F. S., & Roth, P. L. (1998). A meta-analytic review of predictors of sales performance for sales people. *Journal of Applied Psychology, 83,* 586–597.

Wagner, R. (1949). The employment interview: A critical summary. *Personnel Psychology, 2,* 17–46.

Waldman, D. A., Atwater, L. E., & Antonioni, D. (1998). Has 360–degree feedback gone amok? *Academy of Management Executive, 12,* 86–94.

Ward, L. B. (1959). *The business in-basket test: A method of assessing certain administrative skills* (Research Bulletin RB-59-8). Princeton, NJ: Educational Testing Service.

Wiesner, W. H., & Cronshaw, S. F. (1988). A meta-analytic investigation of the impact of interview format and degree of structure on the validity of the employment interview. *Journal of Occupational Psychology, 61,* 275–290.

Wiggins, J. S. (1973). *Personality and prediction: Principles of personality assessment.* Reading, MA: Addison-Wesley.

Wooten, W., Summerlin, W., & Prien, E. P. (2002). *Synthesizing minimum qualifications using an occupational area job analysis questionnaire.* Unpublished manuscript. Available from the first author, Department of Psychology, University of Central Florida, Orlando, FL 32816.

Wright, P. M., Lichtenfels, P. A., & Pursell, E. D. (1989). The structured interview: Additional studies and a meta-analysis. *Journal of Occupational Psychology, 62,* 191–199.

4

Conducting the Assessment

In most cases, a good bit of anxiety, mistrust, misperception, and even sub-dued hostility walks in the door with the assessees on the day of the assess-ment. This is not going to be a normal day for them. On the other hand, the assessor wants assessees to be comfortable, at ease, and acting normal in or-der to get a clear read on what they are really like and so that they can focus and perform up to their true capabilities. The personal interaction with the assessee can either make the assessor's job easier or even more difficult than it already is. Therefore, in addition to doing and saying the right things dur-ing the orientation, testing, and assessment interview, the assessor must consider how these things are done and said.

In fact, it makes a lot of sense to treat every assessee as a potential future client or buyer of assessment services. As such, assessors must work to greet, orient, educate, and deliver service to the assessee as they would any other prospective customer (internal or external). Make sure they are oriented and comfortable. Introduce the assessee to any individuals who will be working with them throughout the day (e.g., test administrator). See if there are any questions about the introductory or preparatory materials sent to them prior to their arrival; see Fig. 4.1 for a sample *Introduction to Your Indi-vidual Assessment* brochure. Collect prework materials (e.g., background questionnaires, interest inventories), if any. Explain the approach to accom-modations with reference to the Americans With Disabilities Act (1990) and have the assessee complete an assessment agreement form (see Fig. 4.2 for a sample). Provide an overview of the assessment day, including a brief blurb about the kinds of tests or exercises that will be encountered, a sense of
96

Introduction to Your Individual Assessment

You have been selected to participate in an individual assessment process. The purpose of the process is to provide information to an organization, and to an individual employee or job candidate (i.e., you!) about job-related competencies. Knowledge about your degree of possession of these competencies will be valuable to both the organization and you.

Background

There are three information-gathering steps in the individual assessment process:

- Learning about the organization and work setting
- Learning about the job's requirements
- Assessing a person's strengths and weaknesses relative to the first two steps

During the course of the assessment, these three sources of information are combined and synthesized to answer a number of questions about you and your fit with the job and with the company. No characteristic about you is a strength or a weakness, except in relation to the company and the job that you might perform in the future.

The Process

The individual assessment process is designed to give you plenty of opportunity to provide information about you, your interests, and specific job-related competencies. This information is collected in a variety of ways, including:

- Paper-and-pencil tests targeting specific cognitive, personality, and interest characteristics

- An interview, during which you have the opportunity to provide more details about yourself and to ask any questions you may have about the process

- Perhaps an interactive exercise or job simulation or two

The Outcome

At the conclusion of the assessment process, we will provide you with an overview of the results. You will work hard during the assessment and you deserve to learn what we have learned about you. If, for any reason, we are unable to provide you with feedback on the day of the assessment, we will work with you to schedule another mutually convenient time.

We will also provide feedback to the sponsoring organization. This feedback will be the same information, though somewhat more detailed, that we provide to you. In other words, you (as the participant in the process) and the organization will hear a consistent message.

FIG. 4.1.   Introductory description for assessee.   (continued on next page)

Introduction to Your Individual Assessment
(cont'd)

Preparation

Other than simply completing the prework materials that we have sent to you (if any), there is nothing you should do to try to study for the assessment. You obviously have a number of job-related strengths that are responsible for your success to date. We want you to be yourself on the day of the assessment and give us a chance to learn more about how and why you have succeeded. Thus, the best way to prepare is to go to sleep a little earlier than usual the night before and come in rested and ready to work on assessment day.

Our Commitment to You

We realize that participating in an assessment process is somewhat stressful. Be assured that we will do everything possible to make your visit as comfortable and pleasant as possible. Our goal is to give you every opportunity to demonstrate your job-related strengths. Knowledge of your degree of possession of certain competencies will enable you to be more selective in your pursuit of career opportunities and provide you with a basis for creating an individual development strategy.

How To Find Us

(Provide directions to the assessment location and contact numbers.)

Time and Date of Your Assessment

We look forward to meeting you on the day of your assessment:

(Write in date of assessment.)

Please arrive promptly at our office at:

(Write in time assessment is to begin.)

FIG. 4.1.   *(continued)*

Assessment Agreement Form

You are about to participate in an individual assessment program. The purpose of this assessment is to obtain job-related information about your abilities and interests with reference to a target job. You will spend several hours taking paper-and-pencil tests, some of which are timed, selected because they yield information that is related to performance in the target job. You will also participate in an interview and perhaps one or two job simulations or interactive exercises. When finished, you will have the opportunity to comment on the assessment process and you will receive a verbal summary of the results.

In summary, we want to learn about you. Our goal is to provide an environment in which you can do your best. If you have questions about the test instructions, have concerns about noise or distractions during the testing process, or need to take a break at some point during the day, let us know.

In addition, if you have a disability or condition that would make it difficult for you to complete the tests in their usual formats, in the allowable time limits, or in the testing location, we will make every attempt to accommodate you.

Do you have any disabilities or conditions that will interfere with your taking these tests or prevent you from completing the testing procedure?

     NO _____

     YES _____

1. If yes, please describe the nature and extent of the disability or condition.

     _____

     _____

2. If yes, please describe the accommodation you require.

     _____

     _____

3. Have you received sufficient information about the testing and interview procedure to answer your questions and satisfy your interests?

     NO _____

     YES _____

4. If you answered "yes" to the previous question, do you give your informed consent to participate and complete the procedure?

     NO _____

     YES _____

NAME _____ DATE _____

FIG. 4.2. Assessment agreement form.

when breaks will occur, and other general housekeeping matters (e.g., location of lunch and restroom facilities).

Throughout the orientation, reinforce the point that assessees should "be themselves." They would not be in front of the assessor on assessment day if they did not have significant job-related strengths. The purpose of the assessment is to gain a better understanding of how and why they have achieved the success they have and this is best accomplished if they demonstrate the competencies that come naturally. Trying to second guess the tests or trying to be someone else in the interview seldom works out to anyone's benefit.

In terms of the schedule for the day, we prefer to administer the tests and exercises first and close out the day with the interview. Specifically, we frequently start with an untimed interest or personality measure, something fairly nonchallenging and with some face validity. This serves as a warm-up to focus the assessee's attention and to minimize apprehension or any kind of resistance. Then, once the testing ice has been broken, we follow up with the timed and maximum performance tests and measures of cognitive ability while the assessee is still fresh early in the day. We also like to mix the timed versus untimed and the personality versus cognitive ability (maximum performance) measures simply to provide variety and alternate the pace during the assessment procedure. However, this brief interaction will also provide the opportunity for the assessor (or test administrator) to observe and note behaviors and reactions during the course of the day. Finally, we tend to position the comprehensive assessment interview toward the end of the process so we can open the file and give feedback on the specific tests and exercises to close out the interview and the assessment itself. As the assessment day closes, there will occasionally be an opportunity or the necessity to resolve and reconcile conflicts or discrepancies in test results and propose or suggest some additional testing to explore a questionable result that may have reflected a misunderstanding of test instructions or directions.

At this point in the process, there should also be an opportunity to provide the assessee with some documentation of the assessment protocol in terms of the job model that has controlling influence on the assessment process and procedure. This degree of specification need not be elaborate, but can simply consist of a summary of work activity categories with a check mark in the margin to communicate the composition of the position for which the candidate is an applicant. There is a danger, however, in providing too much detail, because this might well overwhelm the assessee. A summary form that captures the elements of the assessment specification can serve a very useful purpose and should be considered.

CONDUCTING THE INTERVIEW

As strange as it may sound, most assessment interviews are best conducted as a partnership with the assessee—even selection assessments. The assessor's goal is to get the straight scoop. Conversely, as the assessee, the tug to consciously put the best foot forward and manage impressions is often over-whelming. Nevertheless, in the long run, even the assessee's interests are best served by providing clear, accurate information, as uncluttered as pos-sible by verbal legerdemain, white lies, and outright falsehoods. In our view, creating an environment where the assessee feels comfortable and under-stood promotes this sense of partnership, with the assessor all the while be-ing absolutely clear with the assessee about the purpose of the assessment and how the information will be used.

Thus, the assessment interview should not be viewed as a battlefield be-ing maneuvered upon by two wily combatants. Instead, the assessor should consider viewing it as a chance to get to know a genuinely interesting human being who, because of the assessment context, is probably already feeling a little stressed and intimidated. As such, when meeting the candidate for the first time, asessors should be sure to do the things they would normally do when greeting a friendly acquaintance:

- Smile:
  Nothing takes the tension out of a situation like a smile. After introducing yourself, ask if the candidate is getting bored with all your tests!

- Shake hands:
  The physical contact of a handshake helps put two people on an equal plane. It is more difficult to be intimidated by someone you have touched.

- Demonstrate empathy:
  More than anything, you want candidates to feel they have been listened to, understood, and treated fairly. Nod your head and murmur something appropriate when the candidate comments about the process (e.g., complains about one of the tests or exercises that proved particularly vexing).

- Make small talk:
  It is easier for people to speak up and talk once they have already said something, so make it easy for the candidate to talk in the first 2 to 3 minutes. It will grease the rails of the discussion track you want to take later in the interview. If the candidate came to town the previous night, ask about the accommodations. If it is starting to snow outside, comment on the weather. But, keep the small talk focused on general topics. If you try to engage in conversation that is too spe-cific (e.g., the baseball game the night before), you run the risk of spending time backing out of verbal cul-de-sacs (e.g., when the candidate an-

swers, "No. I hate baseball."), rather than building rapport and getting the candidate
comfortable talking.

A clear signal that the assessor is ready to direct the focus of the discussion back to the matters at hand is to say something like: "Have you been
through any kind of assessment before?" This statement suggests back to
business and gives the assessor a chance to understand any preconceptions
that may exist. If the candidate has been through a previous assessment, find
out if it was a good or bad experience and compare and contrast what he or
she experienced before with what he or she will encounter in the current assessment. If the individual has no previous exposure to assessment, the assessor might ask how what candidates have encountered so far is similar to,
or different from, their expectations.

Now it is time to start framing some expectations for the candidate. Be
sure that the candidate is clear about the purpose of the assessment and
about the assessor's relationship with the sponsoring organization. In a selection situation, the assessor might say something along the lines of:

- The ABC Company realizes that people hired into the company are critical assets that will, hopefully, be around for a long time. As such, they
  are serious about doing everything possible to make sure there is a good
  fit between a person's qualifications and the interests and the needs of
  the company. I've worked with the ABC Company for the past X years
  to help provide one source of input into these hiring decisions.

The purpose of this introduction to the interview is to give the assessor a
chance to soft sell the ABC Company, underscore the central role people
will play in the company's plans for the future, highlight the care and attention paid to matching people to the company, and introduce the fact that
the assessment is just one component factored into the hiring decision. One
might follow the previous statement with something like:

- With respect to the XYZ job for which you are a candidate, I've spoken at
  length with (mention the person or persons from the sponsoring organization that provided responses to the job modeling questions) about the requirements of the job and the specific competencies needed to perform
  effectively in the role. I've used this information to guide the kinds of tests,
  exercises, and interview questions used in your assessment.

The purpose of this statement is to make it clear to the candidate that
there is a clear picture of what success looks like in the target job and of the
kinds of competencies required to achieve success. Although the phrase
"job-related" may not mean much to the candidate, at a minimum the assessor should drive home the point that the kinds of tests and questions that

will be encountered during the assessment were not selected at random. To continue making this point, one might say:

- Given this understanding about the requirements of the XYZ job, the best thing for us to do would be to follow you around in your current job for a month or so so that we could see your competencies and skills in action, and from those observations make a judgment about the level of fit with the new job. Since we can't do that, we've done the next best thing by pulling together those tests and exercises that give us a chance to look at your competencies in action. While taking some of these tests, you may have noticed a few questions that seemed a little odd or off-the-wall. The fact is, most of the tests measure multiple things, but to get a measurement of the piece that is relevant, we have to administer the entire test. Be assured, we will use only those pieces of information related to job performance when pulling the information together and preparing the final report.

This statement does a couple of things. First, it continues to hammer on the job-relatedness nail. Second, it provides a pressure relief valve for some of the useful, though not particularly face-valid, content assessees will see as they slog through a typical assessment day. The next statement will vary depending on the parameters set up with the sponsoring client, but something along the lines of the following needs to be covered, even if it was stated in prework materials sent to the candidate previously:

- When we finish your assessment, I will prepare a report describing your job-related strengths and relative weaker areas with reference to the XYZ job. The information from this report will be blended in with the results of your other interviews and your work history information collected by the ABC Company to help guide their decision. You will not get a copy of the report but you do deserve to know what we've learned about you during the day. So, what you can count on is getting feedback from me on the key messages that will be contained in the report. You and the ABC Company will hear the same message, but their message will be a little more detailed.

What is being accomplished in the previous comments is a clear statement of who gets what. Furthermore, the point has been made a second time that the assessment process is not the hurdle, but part of a mix of data points to be used in the eventual selection decision. Moreover, a burning question in the minds of most assessees is: "Will I know if I passed or failed by the end of the day?" The assessor needs to attempt to douse this question. Assessors work with client organizations to make sure they do not simply use the assessment report as a thumbs-up or thumbs-down indicator and should do what they can to make sure that the assessee realizes this as well. The report will describe the full array of strengths and relative weaker points the candidate brings to a job. The final decision is based, in part, on other predictive indicators, such as the relative performance of other candidates, the time-to-fill schedule of the client organization, and so forth. Furthermore, the ultimate personnel action (i.e., decision) is the responsibility of the clients.

Some assessors prefer to make many of the previous statements as part of the beginning of the assessment day orientation, as opposed to the lead-in to the interview at the end of the assessment day. There are reasonable rationales for positioning these statements near the beginning or near the end of the day—assessors should let their own experience and personal preference be their guide.

The assessor might also include a reference here to the unlikely contingency of an applicant/candidate confessing that he or she has falsified any aspect of the assessment procedure. Assessees do make an attempt to put their best foot forward and will very adroitly make nebulous or misleading statements about their educational status, their work experience, or other factual data by providing vague responses. One survey of HR managers indicated that as many as one third of resumes contain misleading or actually falsified information (Bachler, 1995). The extreme example is the case of an assessee who confessed during the interview that he had never completed college (he was an applicant for an engineer position), but had only attended part of one semester and then developed his own self-study program in order to fake the credentials. This applicant confessed near the end of the full day's assessment testing and was informed that, because of his admission, we had no choice but to report this finding to the client. He agreed that we indeed were obliged to report this fabrication to the client, but, nonetheless, we completed the assessment and wrote the full assessment report.

It so happened that this applicant had carried the masquerade through two previous positions and had learned enough during those practice years to perform quite well. The ruse was uncovered and, when the client then went back in the record, it was discovered that there were, indeed, some blank spots and weaknesses in the previous employer's record and that the candidate left those two previous positions because of apprehension about being discovered. Nevertheless, two previous employers and the assessee on this occasion had created a very credible record and he was offered the opportunity to make good on the falsified credentials.

The more likely scenario is represented by somewhere between 5% and 10% of applicants, who often state in a resume the name of the institution and then indicate they attended it for 4 years, without specifying the degree granted. This goes all the way to the extent of simply using the term "attended" to cover anywhere from 2 to 4 years of the time period, as if the applicant had achieved some terminal point. In a review of more than 750 vitas and resumes of applicants for management and information technology (IT) positions, where a recruiter prepared the documents, fully 20% of the applicants for positions that nominally require a college degree had built-in escape clause language for what can only be construed as flagrant impression management.

At this juncture the assessor is ready to move firmly into interview mode and can make this transition by saying:

- The interview is the part of the assessment process where you get to put the pencil down, sit back, and just talk. I want to learn about you in your own words. You obviously have a number of job-related strengths. I want to learn, from your perspective, all about those strengths and how you have leveraged them to achieve job success in the past. So, while I am going to lead the conversation for the next X hours (allotted time, usually between 1 and 2 hours), I want you to do most of the talking.

This statement makes the point that the assessor is going to set the direction for the meeting, focus on strengths, and expect the candidate to contribute most of the words because the interest is in what he or she has to say to round out the picture that is being developed. The assessor has also established the time frame. Consider following up this statement with:

- Over the next X hours (restate the allotted time), I want to accomplish a number of different things. (Note, for an entry-level screening assessment, a half-hour of interviewing is sufficient. Any more time spent at this level is unlikely to be cost effective.) To begin, I will start at a very broad level and hear about your background, your education, and your job history. Then I will drill down with a number of very specific questions about work-related experiences and accomplishments. My role is to keep our discussion focused and moving forward; your role is to do most of the talking.

This statement reiterates that time is important, and that the interview is not a blue-sky discussion, but is goal oriented. It makes the point that the assessor needs to gather a lot of information in a limited amount of time and will work to keep the interview focused and moving, and that when the assessor steps in to do so, the candidate should not be put off or embarrassed, but should simply recognize the time constraint and follow the lead. At some point during this introduction, the assessor needs to state something on the order of:

- I want you to know that the interview process is very straightforward. There are no trick questions. Simply put, I want to understand what is behind your career success to date and I want to determine how we can use those same characteristics to make you successful in the XYZ job. You also need to understand that this is not a confidential process. What we talk about becomes a matter of record for consideration in the final selection decision. As we proceed, I believe you will find that we will not cover any ground that gives you pause. However, if we do hit upon something you do not want the ABC Company to know about, you need to tell me that you do not wish to speak to me about it. Any questions about this?

The intent of this statement is to make it clear that this conversation is not going to be mysterious, with 14 layers of intent behind each question. The assessor is going to ask about what he or she wants to know about, pure and simple. Of course, the second half of the previous statement is going to get the candidates' attention, and perhaps put them back on edge—there is no way around this. The assessee needs to understand that what follows is not a confidential or privileged discussion. The assessor is going to be considerate, professional, and fair in his or her treatment of the candidate, but at the end of the day has some objective judgments to make and the person being assessed needs to understand what is and is not considered in the field of play. It is just about time to get into the meat of the interview, but before that, a couple of additional thoughts need to be communicated:

- I am going to take notes during the interview to help me remember what we talked about when I sit down later to prepare my report. Don't feel like you need to moderate the speed of our conversation for me to write; I'm using my own shorthand to capture the major themes as we go along. If I need to catch up at some point, I'll let you know.

Notes should be taken, and without creating a barrier in the interview. Most assessors do develop their own shorthand and absolutely do not try to transcribe the entire conversation. While notes will be needed to guide subsequent evaluation, the assessor needs to continue to build rapport with candidates throughout the interview to promote their ease and comfort while talking. Therefore, eyes should be kept on the person who is speaking, and not on a note pad. Maintain a relaxed posture and lean forward once in a while to demonstrate interest in what is being said. Offer approving nods of the head and verbal confirmations like "Yes, I see" or "mm-hmm" on occasion to keep the connection with the candidate. All of this is tough (impossible?) to do if one is furiously scribbling on a note pad. The following is the wrap-up of the introduction:

- Once we are finished with my questions, I'll make sure we have time at the end of the interview for you to elaborate on one of our discussion points or tell me something we haven't covered, if you feel that doing so will help me understand you or your job strengths. Do you have a question for me before we begin?

This statement lets candidates know they will have a chance to contribute what they think is important at some point during the interview. Assessors have enough of a challenge accomplishing everything they want to in the al-lotted time without having the candidates repeatedly trying to pull them down a path of their own choosing. Let them know they will have their chance and that their opportunity occurs at the end of the session. In addition, give the assessee a chance to ask a clarifying question before beginning. Our sug-gestion is to put a boundary on the up-front questioning by saying that "a" (i.e., singular) question will be answered at this point. Avoid getting further behind schedule by responding to a slew of miscellaneous questions before re-ally even beginning, particularly considering that most assessees will find their questions are answered throughout the course of the interview itself. An ex-ception should be made for assessees who are participating in a developmental assessment. The assessor will be spending much more time in feedback mode with these individuals and it is often useful to be able to connect the dots be-fore and after the assessment on several issues to see how things have played out. Consider giving this group of assessees a chance to talk about:

- Their greatest hope or expectation of the process?
- Their greatest worry or concern about the process?
- Looking back on their careers to date, which characteristics are re-sponsible for their success (i.e., candidate's view of own job strengths)?
- Which characteristics will be important for them to improve upon to achieve their future career goals (i.e., candidate's view of own relative weaker areas)?

Now it is time to get into the meat of the interview. The following is a sample introduction:

- Let's get started. I would like to start off in a fairly general way and let you lead me through a description of your background, but I will move us pretty quickly forward to a series of very specific questions about your work-related experiences.

At this point it is important to gather contextual information about the assessee. Without going overboard, it is useful to understand something about their:

- Background
- Current job
- Goals

The reader should take a look at the Interview Worksheet in Fig. 4.3 to re-view sample questions related to these three areas. The questions in Fig. 4.3 are designed to provide insight as to what is important to the person being assessed, in terms of life events, work style, development history, and hopes for the future. Despite being one or two steps removed from questions about

Interview Worksheet

**Positioning
Statement:** This is the part of the process where you get to put the pencil down, sit back, and just talk. In fact, I want you to do most of the talking. I would like to start off in a fairly general way and let you lead me through a description of your background, but I will move us pretty quickly forward to a series of very specific questions about your work-related experiences.

Background: ■ Let's take 10 or 15 minutes and give you a chance to tell me about your background. Obviously we will only have time to cover the highlights. Start anywhere you want, you pick the highlight reels to share with me, but bring me up to your current job and do so in less than 10 minutes.

Current Job: ■ Tell me briefly about your responsibilities in your current job. Who do you report to? Who reports to you?

■ What parts of your job do you enjoy the most? Least?

Goals: ■ What is your plan for your career? What do you want to be doing 5 years down the road? 10? How does the job for which you are being assessed fit into that plan?

■ What competencies need to be developed, or what experiences need to take place, to carry you down this career path? What is your plan for developing these competencies or accruing these experiences?

**Job-Related
Competencies:** Insert the interview questions and follow-up probes linked to each of the identified competencies (factor- or dimension-level); for example:

■ Creativity – describe the most creative or innovative idea you have generated and implemented within the past 2 years. What made it so unique? What was the genesis of the idea? What opportunity did it address? What has been the impact or result of implementing the idea?

FIG. 4.3.   Interview worksheet.

108

specific work activities, this contextual information can yield rich insight into understanding future job performance.

However, the assessor should not delve too long in these areas because the richest source of information does come from more direct examinations of assessee work activities through the behavioral interview questions. It is trite, but true, that the best predictor of future behavior is past behavior. Therefore, if the target job requires a great deal of creativity and ingenuity, then assessees should be asked to describe a past experience when they demonstrated this competency (see Fig. 4.3).

As a final checklist in Table 4.1, we have prepared a brief list of important *dos* and *don'ts* in assessment interviewing. We are not recommending that you tape these up on the refrigerator, but there is a lot going on concurrently in a good assessment interview and it never hurts to review the basics once in a while.

TABLE 4.1

Dos and Don'ts in Assessment Interviewing

- Before starting an interview, review the selection specifications and draft the hypothetical questions for the situational interview.

- Do not tell the applicant what you want to hear and do not ask questions that can be answered "yes" or "no." Instead, take the time to listen and learn.

- Keep the interview moving but in the direction of your choice; do not wander from topic to topic.

- Do not make evaluative judgments during the interview and especially avoid making judgmental statements.

- When in doubt about something the candidate has said, probe. Do not assume that you have understood what the candidate has said.

- Record data during the interview. Do not rely on memory. Record both the positive and the negative observations.

- Expect, recognize and learn to handle likability, forcefulness, glitter, personal impact, and the safe answers.

- Use open-ended questions to obtain comprehensive information (e.g., "Tell me more about _____ ").

- Do not ask illegal questions about race, gender issues, age, disabilities or medical conditions, sexual preference, marital status, children or child care options, religion, military discharge, or financial status.

- Stick with your interview plan.

EVALUATING INTERVIEW DATA

The interview is not finished until the assessor provides a rating of the responses received for each behavioral question. In other words, each assessment dimension that is being evaluated based on interview input should be followed by an objective rating. We use a 5-point rating scale (see Fig. 4.4). Essentially, this is a set of categories representing different degrees of possession of one of the assessment dimensions or the degree of competence in functioning in the defined area. This is a generic scale with relative level properties. In other words, it is a one-size-fits-all instrument that may be applied with reference to different assessment populations (e.g., administrative, supervisory, executive). The following category definitions are recommended:

- Rating of 1:   A rating at this level indicates no, or a small degree of, possession of the competency. An individual may have passing familiarity with the knowledge or have marginal limited proficiency in the area. Generally, this is not adequate for compensated work in the area.

- Rating of 2:   A rating at this level indicates a borderline degree of possession of the competency. An individual at this level can work, but some deficiencies in performance would be expected.

1	2	3	4	5
Significantly below average	Somewhat below average	Average	Somewhat above average	Significantly above average
There is clear and convincing evidence that the candidate does not have, or has a very limited possession of, the competency.		The evidence is mixed and indicates that the candidate has adequate possession of the competency. This rating indicates presence versus superiority.		There is clear and convincing evidence that the applicant possesses the competency at a superior or mastery level.

FIG. 4.4.   Rating scale used to assess degree of possession.

- Rating of 3:   A rating at this level represents an adequate degree of possession of the competency. Adequate represents just enough for functioning in a job that requires that particular skill.

- Rating of 4:   A rating at this level represents an advanced possession of the competency. At this level, the individual would be considered to have journeyman-level proficiency or competence and could function when required in an independent and unsupervised way.

- Rating of 5:   A rating at this level indicates mastery or almost complete possession of the competency. When an individual is rated 5, the display would be considered a model for other employees and an organization resource.

When making evaluations of the interview data, assessors should keep in mind the seven deadly sins of assessment evaluation described in Table 4.2. These sins are nefarious because they are easy to succumb to and, if they are, the asessor has just poured sugar into the gas tank of the assessment process, with the result that final inferences are going to get sticky and gummed up. Of course, this same rating scale may be applied to evaluate information from other sources, such as reference materials or scored work sampled. Furthermore, as will be seen later in this chapter, a variant of this scale is used to assess degree of possession of each competency in the final assessment evaluation.

RESEARCH CONTEXT

As we noted in chapter 3, corrected validities for unstructured interviews range from .14 to .30 and the validities for structured interviews range from .35 to .62 (Huffcutt & Arthur, 1994; Hunter & Hunter, 1984; McDaniel, Whetzel, Schmidt, & Maurer, 1994; Schmidt & Hunter, 1998; Schmidt & Rader, 1999; Wiesner & Cronshaw, 1988; Wright, Lichtenfels, & Pursell, 1989). The research evidence clearly supports using a structured interview format similar to the one proposed in this chapter as part of the individual assessment process.

Furthermore, there is some research suggesting that past behavior types of questions (Janz, 1982; e.g., "Within the past 2 years, describe a specific instance when you developed and delivered a major sales presentation. What was the outcome?") are superior to hypothetical, what-if, situational types of questions (Latham, Saari, Pursell, & Campion, 1980; e.g., "Suppose you were giving an important sales presentation and someone in the audience was visibly not buying in to what you were saying, what would you do?").

TABLE 4.2

The Seven Deadly Sins in Assessment Evaluation

- Contrast Errors: occur in assessments when you observe several candidates who have exceptional qualifications for the job and then interview one who is only average or, conversely, when you are working with interview and assessment results from one or more marginal candidates, and then work with an assessee who is average. In either case, the average applicant will suffer or benefit relative to their competition. To avoid this contrast effect, compare each candidate to your clearly defined competency requirements rather than to each other.

- First Impression Errors: refer to the tendency for the assessor to form an initial favorable, or unfavorable, judgment about the applicant based on early information. Any information the applicant gives after that is either ignored or distorted so as to support the initial impression. To control this error, discipline yourself to postpone any evaluation until all the assessment results are in.

- Halo Errors: are the result of overgeneralizations. Occasionally, the assessor can be so influenced by one striking quality of an individual that the assessee's other qualities and characteristics are ignored or diluted in comparison. Again, the key to avoiding halo errors is discipline. Refuse to make any evaluative judgments until all the assessment results have been accumulated. Then review each item of information only with reference to the defined competency requirements.

- Stereotyping Errors: are as common in the assessment observation as in the outside world. Germans are industrious, the British are stuffy, women are good secretaries but not management material, disabled persons are absent more frequently, and so forth. It is extremely important not to let personal biases get in the way of objective applicant evaluation. The solution? Stick to comparing an individual's assessment performance to the job requirements rather than to stereotypical images.

- "Similar-to-Me" Errors: may occur when the assessor shares a common interest or background with the assessee. This communality can influence the interpretation of the assessment results simply because of the dynamic relationship. Work hard to establish a trusting work relationship with all assessees, regardless of superficial similarities, and keep a laser beam focus on, you guessed it, the competency requirements of the target job.

- Central Tendency Errors: are committed by the assessor who wants to play it safe or who simply is not sure how to rate a candidate and minimizes their chances of being wrong and sticks to the middle of the assessment rating scale. By avoiding any extreme judgment, either favorable or unfavorable, the interviewer has chosen to avoid an error should the applicant turn out to be a winner or a loser. A better alternative is to simply skip the rating in this particular competency area. A rating in the middle of the degree of possession distribution is a meaningful data point; do not undercut its value by using it as a dumping ground for namby-pamby ratings.

- Negative and Positive Leniency Errors: are committed by the assessor who is either too hard or too easy in rating a candidate's degree of possession of a competency. This means that qualified candidates are being rejected or unqualified candidates are being hired. To guard against this error, look for opportunities to calibrate your judgments with other assessors if possible. It not, periodically follow up on the job performance for a sample of assessees you have worked with over the past 12 to 18 months and, as always, stick closely to the assessment rating scale definitions when evaluating a candidate's competencies.

(See also Campion, Campion, & Hudson, 1994; Judge, Higgins, & Cable, 2000; Pulakos & Schmitt, 1995.) Although research on topics such as taking notes during the interview (Burnett, Fan, Motowidlo, & Degroot, 1998; Macan & Dipboye, 1994; Schuh, 1980) and using an anchored rating scale to guide assessor evaluations (Maas, 1965; Vance, Kuhnert, & Farr, 1978) is far from complete, there is enough evidence in our view to support these practices in assessment practice.

In this context, it is also worth noting the importance of a well-developed rating scale for evaluating an assessee's degree of possession of specific competencies. We presented the 5-point scale in Fig. 4.4 because (a) we think it is pretty good and (b) we have grown accustomed to using it. However, it is only a suggestion. There is some evidence that the most useful number of response categories in a rating scale is between five and nine (Bendig, 1952, 1953, 1954; Finn, 1972). Having fewer than five categories is likely to result in a failure to capture meaningful variability in the final evaluation. On the other hand, having more than nine categories is likely to force the assessor to try to make finer distinctions than can be reliably made. From this perspective, having too many response categories can have a negative effect on the quality of the assessment data.

In addition, the words and phrases that anchor the response categories can influence the meaningfulness of the assessment ratings. There is some research that strongly suggests that different expressions of amount (e.g., all, some, or none) or frequency (e.g., always, sometimes, or never) have different meanings and interpretability relative to other expressions of amount or frequency (Bass, Cascio, & O'Connor, 1974; Jones & Thurstone, 1955; Lodge, Cross, Tursky, & Tanenhaus, 1975; Lodge & Turskey, 1981; Reagan, Mosteller, & Youtz, 1989; Spector, 1976). Whether using or modifying an existing rating scale, such as the one presented in this chapter, or building your own, the reader should keep in mind the importance of a well-developed scale in the assessment process.

PRACTICE EXAMPLES

The Practice Example section of this chapter is abbreviated because the entire chapter has a strong practice perspective. Therefore, rather than reproducing the equivalent of an entire transcribed interview, we present just the results from one question (and follow-up probes) for each of the three case examples.

Example 1: Sales Associate Assessment

One area of particular interest in the Linda Jones assessment was demonstrated competence in the area of customer relations. The way the interviewing assessor ("I") pursued and probed for an understanding of Linda's (the assessee or "A") degree of possession of customer relations was as fol-

lows: Specific positive ("+") and negative ("−") indicators that occur in
the assessment interviewer's notes are presented in boxes as part of the
flow of the interview. These are evaluative indicators made by the assessor
in the interview notes in part during the course of the interview and then
supplemented during the overall evaluation postinterview.

I: Tell me about a recent occasion when you've had to explain a particular
     computer program or piece of hardware to a novice or inexperienced user.

A: Last week a friend of my Mom's asked me to show her how to attach photo-
     graphs to an e-mail. The problem was, she had an envelope with the pic-
     tures. I couldn't believe it!

+ engaging, humorous quality to story; not snide or sarcastic	− non work environment example

I: So, how did you start?

A: Well, I was tempted to just take the pictures with me, scan them and e-mail
     them for her, but, if I do that, she'll call me every time the e-mail won't work.
     I asked if she had ever scanned anything. I saw she had a scanner, but I'd
     guessed from her question that she had never used it.

+ wants to build self-sufficiency

I: Were you surprised at how little she knew?

A: Not really—lots of folks aren't experts. Anyway, I showed her how to scan,
     then I let her loose to scan the rest of the pictures. She wasn't real comfort-
     able at first, but I explained to her that she really couldn't break anything.
     After the pictures were all scanned I asked her to start her e-mail message,
     then told her where to click and point to attach the pictures.

+ patient
+ reassuring
+ took extra time up front to educate and avert questions or problems later

I: Were there any problems after that?

A: Depends on what you mean by problems. She e-mailed me a bunch of pic-
     tures last week with a message asking me if I can come over and show her
     how to erase her neighbor from pictures at the church picnic!

> + expressive
> + ready smile
> + sense of humor

Example 2: Department Manager Assessment

One area that was targeted for measurement in the interview with Peter Martin was staffing. The assessor's sequence of questions and probes around staffing are presented, with the positive ("+") and negative ("–") indicators that occur in the assessment interviewer's notes presented in boxes throughout the flow of questions and responses.

I: One problem many managers face today is finding employees with the necessary skills, even for entry-level jobs. Is this a problem that you've faced and, if so, what is your solution?

A: Well, in my current store, which is in the suburbs, that really isn't an issue. My problem there is working around the kids' schedules for school, sports, and their social lives.

I: So, then, has this ever been a problem for you?

A: Oh, yes. In my last store it seemed as though three quarters of the applicants could barely write their name on the application, much less work with any of our forms and reports. I really reached the point where I hated to see anyone walk up to the service desk to ask for an application, because it was just so discouraging to have to tell these kids "no"—they wanted to work.

+ eventually recognized the situation had changed and he recognized the opportunity to act	– initial response was negative, but he accepted the status as an obstacle and thus did not produce an effect

I: So, what was your solution?

A: Well, we were putting a sign in the window when we needed to hire someone, so I started to think about other ways of finding people. First thing I tried was the high school in the neighborhood. One of the guidance counselors stopped in the store and I stopped her one day. I explained the situation to her and asked if she could help. What she offered to do was to send students down to apply who she knew had the skills to do the job.

I: And, how did that work?

A: Very well. I couldn't hire everyone she sent me, but it wasn't because they couldn't read. That gave me an idea though and I went to the church down the street. I asked the reverend if he could organize something similar through his Sunday school or youth groups, and that's turned out just great. The applicants Reverend Jones refers to us have the skills and work ethic we need. Plus, after this had been going on for a month or so, the church switched their buying over to us—they also have a daycare center, so it really added up.

+ recognized the opportunity and responded conscientiously	− took the initiative but without a clear objective or goal in mind − took what was offered and just ran with it − overextended the opportunity and, as a result, had to turn applicants away

A second and related area targeted was that of supervisory skills. In this area, planning and managing to achieve high quality operations performance was critical.

I: What would you do if one of the new hires repeatedly ignored maintaining sanitary conditions?
A: I believe that the best teacher is experience and most of these little problems will take care of themselves if we just wait. We really need to get the work done, get the product on the shelf and out the door.

+ is easygoing and not likely to offend or abuse subordinates	− follow-through and attention to detail will lead to defaults; his awareness to customer relations is sorely lacking and he will let things slide and absorb the negative consequences

I: So, how would you expect the customers to react?
A: In a busy store, a little slippage isn't all that important and most people are in enough of a hurry so that they don't mind it when the produce display is a little messy as long as the customer can get the produce and get out of the store.

+ he is responsive to customers but essentially to simply keep them out of his way	− his understanding of customer relations is almost an embarrassing weakness; he is easy-going and will let things slide just to get by

I: How would you propose to answer the complaints?

A: Well, as I told you, these little problems will go away and once they're gone, no one remembers. If you keep fussing over the produce and the display, I think you will wind up spinning your wheels when you don't really have to work that hard.

> – lacks the initiative to follow through, lacks conscientiousness
> – careless and inattentive about details
> – knows what to do but fails to respond appropriately; ignores the obvious cues

Example 3: Division President Assessment

Influencing skills was a critical component of the division president job and an area that the assessor probed extensively during the interview with Hector Dantos. A paraphrased rendition of the questions, answers, and the chronology of the exchange between the assessment interviewer ("I") and Hector the assessee ("A") are presented. Again, specific positive ("+") and negative ("–") indicators that occurred in the assessment interviewer's notes are presented in boxes as part of the flow of the interview. In part, these are evaluative indicators made by the assessor during the interview itself and in part they represent evaluative comments made after the interview as part of the final evaluation of interviewee responses.

I: Tell me about the most difficult proposal or idea you tried to sell or introduce to your current organization in the last 2 years.

A: Well, I may be wrong, but it seems to me that being able to sell your ideas is absolutely essential. Good ideas that never get implemented don't mean squat. That's why I always take the time to try and figure out what the hooks are for the person I am trying to influence. In other words, I try to figure out what's in it for them.

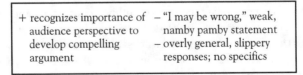

> + recognizes importance of audience perspective to develop compelling argument
> – "I may be wrong," weak, namby pamby statement
> – overly general, slippery responses; no specifics

I: Hector, that is a good description of your philosophy when it comes to selling an idea or initiative. However, I want you to pick one specific instance when you did so and tell me the details. What was the last big idea or concept you really had to work at developing a base of support around?

A: The last big one? Hmm. ...

I: That's O.K. Take a moment to think of a specific example you are particu-
     larly proud of from the past 2 years.

A: O.K. I've got one. It was about 2 years ago. I had been division president
     for the European cookies and biscuits business for about 1 year at that
     point and the business was in its fifth straight year of below plan perfor-
     mance. We had squeezed all the cost out of production and distribution
     as we could, and at the same time were facing increased competition
     from new local and regional entrants to the market. My idea was to com-
     pletely rethink who we were selling to and why. Though everybody on my
     leadership team was under the gun to make their numbers, I succeeded in
     selling them on working with me to conduct a detailed assessment of
     consumer needs and completely rethink our packaging and promotional
     agenda. I plotted our volume, share, and profit numbers for the past 5
     years, and overlayed the demographic changes in our markets for the
     same period and projected out to 2005. By building a logical, fact-based
     case, and presenting the numbers to everyone on the team one on one, I
     was able to sell everyone on the conclusion that just doing more of the
     same would only get us more of what we've currently got—declining re-
     sults. This is another example of my efforts to master complexity in a role.
     Everyone would end up being supportive of the need to rethink the stra-
     tegic agenda of the business.

+ critical thinking skills to define problem	− speaks slowly and softly
+ developed sound, fact-based rationale to support ideas	− comes across as a bit restrained when talking about his big idea
+ gained initial support using data and numbers	− decent eye contact but little extra body language to convey enthusiasm
+ customer and con- sumer focused	

I: What did you conclude? What happened next?

A: After a series of off-site, 2-day meetings, we, the leadership team for Europe,
     put together a detailed report that outlined our recommendations, includ-
     ing refocusing our marketing to kids, revamping our packaging system to ad-
     dress the growing quick snack business and move away from what had been,
     for us, an exclusively big bag business, rethink our competitive cost struc-
     ture, and aggressively pursue cross-promotional partnerships. All of these
     ideas were, however, 180° off the traditional path for what has historically
     been a huge, conservatively run, family-owned business.

+ innovative and willing to take risks	– very matter-of-fact reponses
+ speaks fluently	– no effort to highlight points with examples/ stories or analogies about his big idea
+ good vocabulary and articulation	– still hasn't clearly stated what happened!

I: So what happened? How is the business operating differently today because of your recommendations?

A: Well, to tell you the truth we hit a wall. I submitted our report to the CEO, CFO, and SVP for Strategy prior to our annual planning meeting. I also took two people from my team with me to New York to make the pitch for changes as part of our business update and the presentation of our annual operating plan. I walked everybody through the numbers, presented what I felt was irrefutable logic and a data-based call for change, and just literally hit a wall. These are very bright people, but they just couldn't see the future in the data we presented, no matter how we cut it. As a result, our report has been shelved and nothing has changed.

+ involved others in New York presentation	– idea of being compelling is to repackage "the data"
	– recommendations not implemented
	– submitted report without first building pull for the conclusions from those at the top
	– all-or-none proposition, not sell in one or two components
	– no attempt to build path for getting from A to B

I: In retrospect, what would you do differently to have achieved a more favorable outcome?

A: The only thing that could have made a difference in the outcome would be to change the players in the room. As I said, it is a private, family-owned business, with a history of going at the market in the same way year after year, and making the numbers by squeezing every last bit of cost and excess out of the system. With that kind of thinking in the room, there was nothing I could do.

+ did build strong intellectual case of support	− no effort to reflect and learn from experience
	− comes across as low energy and a bit flat even when describing a huge disappointment
	− appears to have backed off when told "no" versus taking another run at the issue or selling pieces of ideas into system over time

REFERENCES

Americans with Disabilities Act of 1990. 42 U.S.C. 12101 *et seq.*

Bachler, C. J. (1995). Resume fraud: Lies, omissions and exaggerations. *Personnel Journal, 20,* 50–60.

Bass, B. M., Cascio, W. F., & O'Connor, E. J. (1974). Magnitude estimations of expressions of frequency and amount. *Journal of Applied Psychology, 59,* 313–320.

Bendig, A. W. (1952). A statistical report on a revision of the Miami instructor rating sheet. *Journal of Educational Psychology, 43,* 423–429.

Bendig, A. W. (1953). The reliability of self-ratings as a function of the amount of verbal anchoring and the number of categories on the scale. *Journal of Applied Psychology, 37,* 38–41.

Bendig, A. W. (1954). Reliability and number of rating scale categories. *Journal of Applied Psychology, 38,* 38–40.

Burnett, J. R., Fan, C., Motowidlo, S. J., & Degroot, T. (1998). Interview notes and validity. *Personnel Psychology, 51,* 375–396.

Campion, M. A., Campion, J. E., & Hudson, J. P., Jr. (1994). Structured interviewing: A note on incremental validity and alternative question types. *Journal of Applied Psychology, 79,* 998–1002.

Finn, R. H. (1972). Effects of some variations in rating scale characteristics on the means and reliabilities of ratings. *Educational and Psychological Measurement, 32,* 255–265.

Huffcutt, A. I., & Arthur, W., Jr. (1994). Hunter and Hunter revisited: Interview validity for entry-level jobs. *Journal of Applied Psychology, 79,* 184–190.

Hunter, J. E., & Hunter, R. F. (1984). Validity and utility of alternative predictors of job performance. *Psychological Bulletin, 96,* 72–98.

Janz, T. (1982). Initial comparisons of patterned behavior description interviews versus unstructured interviews. *Journal of Applied Psychology, 67,* 577–580.

Jones, L. V., & Thurstone, L. L. (1955). The psychophysics of semantics: An experimental investigation. *Journal of Applied Psychology, 39,* 31–36.

Judge, T. A., Higgins, C. A., & Cable, D. M. (2000). The employment interview: A review of recent research and recommendations for future research. *Human Resource Management Review, 10*(4), 383–406.

Latham, G. P., Saari, L. M., Pursell, E. D., & Campion, M. A. (1980). The situational interview. *Journal of Applied Psychology, 65,* 422–427.

Lodge, M., Cross, D., Tursky, B., & Tanenhaus, J. (1975). The psychophysical scaling and validation of a political support scale. *American Journal of Political Science, 19*, 611–649.

Lodge, M., & Tursky, B. (1981). The social psychophysical scaling of political opinion. In B. Wegener (Ed.), *Social attitudes and psychophysical measurement* (pp. 123–141). Hillsdale, NJ: Lawrence Erlbaum Associates.

Maas, J. B. (1965). Patterned scaled expectation interview: Reliability studies on a new technique. *Journal of Applied Psychology, 49*, 431–433.

Macan, T. H., & Dipboye, R. L. (1994). The effects of the application on processing of information from the employment interview. *Journal of Applied Social Psychology, 24*, 1291–1314.

McDaniel, M. A., Whetzel, D. L., Schmidt, F. L., & Maurer, S. D. (1994). The validity of employment interviews: A comprehensive review and meta-analysis. *Journal of Applied Psychology, 79*, 599–616.

Pulakos, E. D., & Schmitt, N. (1995). Experience-based and situational interview questions: Studies of validity. *Personnel Psychology, 48*, 289–308.

Reagan, R. T., Mosteller, F., & Youtz, C. (1989). Quantitative meanings of verbal probability expressions. *Journal of Applied Psychology, 74*, 433–442.

Schmidt, F. L., & Hunter, J. E. (1998). The validity and utility of selection methods in personnel psychology: Practical and theoretical implications of 85 years of research findings. *Psychological Bulletin, 124*(2), 262–274.

Schmidt, F. L., & Rader, M. (1999). Exploring the boundary conditions for interview validity: Meta-analytic findings for a new interview type. *Personnel Psychology, 52*, 445–463.

Schuh, A. J. (1980). Verbal listening skill in the interview and personal characteristics of the listeners. *Bulletin of the Psychonomic Society, 15*, 125–127.

Spector, P. E. (1976). Choosing response categories for summated rating scales. *Journal of Applied Psychology, 61*, 374–375.

Vance, R. J., Kuhnert, K. W., & Farr, J. L. (1978). Interview judgments: Using external criteria to compare behavioral and graphic scale ratings. *Organizational Behavior and Human Performance, 22*, 279–294.

Wiesner, W. H., & Cronshaw, S. F. (1988). A meta-analytic investigation of the impact of interview format and degree of structure on the validity of the employment interview. *Journal of Occupational Psychology, 61*, 275–290.

Wright, P. M., Lichtenfels, P. A., & Pursell, E. D. (1989). The structured interview: Additional studies and a meta-analysis. *Journal of Occupational Psychology, 62*, 191–199.

5

Integration
and Interpretation

Human judgment in general, and expert judgment in particular, requires the integration of numerous pieces of complex information to arrive at a final judgment about expected outcomes. To begin, consider an example that illustrates how human judgment works in everyday life. Assume you make plans to meet a friend at the front gate of a baseball park to watch a game. At the prearranged meeting time you are waiting at the front gate, but your friend is not there. As you reason through the situation, you will consider a range of information input that will guide your decision about the course of action most likely to result in finding your friend. If your friend is chronically late, you might stay at the front gate for some indeterminate grace period while waiting for him or her to show up. On the other hand, if your friend has a history of never being late, you might consider that one of you got your wires crossed about the designated meeting place and go to search for him or her at one of the other entrances to the ballpark. Then again, still assuming your friend has a history of never being late, you might factor in the information from the morning news about a major road construction project starting up today between your friend's house and the ballpark. In this situation, you might stick by the front gate after all, under the assumption that he or she was caught up in traffic and, for once, will be late. Clearly, these kinds of judgments, based on the integration and differential weighting of multiple sources of input data, make up a major portion of your everyday life (Wiggins, 1980).

Of course, in the context of individual assessment, the assessor is presented with a multiplicity of these kinds of decisions, compounded by the fact that the assessor has no personal history with the assessee from which to draw predictive information. Consequently, the assessor must, for the most part, rely on data input generated at the time of the assessment, both quantitative and qualitative.

Furthermore, the integration and interpretation of the assessment results for multiple candidates for a single position, with a single set of job requirements, can be very different. In other words, three candidates for the same job may receive good, or poor, assessment evaluations in the same competency dimension for three different reasons. For example, consider the following three candidates for a shop supervisor position:

- Candidate A: Has a poor understanding of the supervisory role and poor knowledge of supervisory practices. Thus, this candidate simply does not understand what a supervisor does, or recognize how and when to monitor, intervene, and otherwise manage a group of people in a goal-oriented manner.
- Candidate B: Has a strong knowledge of what should be done as a supervisor, but lacks the personal forcefulness and strength to take charge and be firm when necessary. This candidate will have difficulty actively implementing what he or she knows to control the work group's efforts, particularly in the face of any opposition.
- Candidate C: Also has a good understanding of the basics of supervision, but has a very poorly developed sense of personal responsibility. This individual will have trouble keeping his or her own work efforts goal oriented, not to mention trying to manage and keep other people's work focused on performance goals.

The previous examples highlight the nonlinear geometry involved in the integration and interpretation of predictor data. That process is the hallmark of the individual assessment practice and very clearly constitutes an idiosyncratic strategy for the process and procedure. There are, of course, various specific tactics for producing the final outcome (the final recommendation) as illustrated in the preceding examples, where an item of quantitative or qualitative information is incorporated and uniquely weighted in the assessment process. Numerous examples in case data occur in which a single item of information, hopefully with confirmation, can and does have compelling influence on the final recommendation. Ideally, when a significantly divergent score is identified, the assessor will seek confirmation by administering a parallel form of the test or a test that assesses the same measurement dimension. Alternatively, during the process of providing feedback to the assessee, the assessor will provide an opportunity for clarification through direct questions. Furthermore, although the initial focus may be on objective data, there is also the need to consider subjective information. Objective measurement, or *mechanically collected* data, is absolutely essential, but subjective measurement, or *clinically collected* data, becomes an important factor, because it facilitates understanding and interpretation of test data and, ultimately, enhanced meaning about the person.

At this point in the assessment process, it is essential to consider and acknowledge the function of measurement data. Different tests have different characteristics and properties that must be considered and incorporated in the assessment process. There are two types of measurement in assessment. One type of measurement is based on absolute scores. The second type of test is based on ipsative scoring procedures. In absolute measurement, a score is interpreted in a standardized form and has absolute meaning. The frame of reference for score interpretation is the normative database, which may be as broad as employed workers across the occupational spectrum or as specific as a comparison group of experienced computer programmers with 3 to 5 years of specific experience.

In the ipsative scoring measurement procedure, a pair comparison model is used where items are presented with pairs of statements (e.g., Item A/Item B). The examinee chooses A or B. In addition, the text consists of a fixed number of those pairs of statements where the examinee chooses A or B. An ipsative test may consist of two or more scoring dimensions, such that, for example, there are 20 pairs of dimension A, 24 of dimension B, and so on. The score on each dimension then is determined by the number of A or B responses within that dimension and, thus, the procedure distributes qualified data among a fixed set of categories. Thus, while absolute scores are to be interpreted at face value, ipsative scoring procedures yield results which are specific to the sampling procedure. Similar ipsative scores may have different meanings for different populations.

Both mechanically and clinically collected data become an important part of the characterization of the individual and require considerable care and caution in score interpretation depending on the test measurement properties. In order to appreciate the interpretation of test results, the assessor must consider the source of measurement data. In general, test scores have a normative property and the interpretation is that a score means exactly what it is intended to represent. However, in the assessment process, there are a variety of references that must be considered when interpreting the scores with reference to job requirements. Some test scoring procedures may require a population reference for meaningful interpretation. For example, tests designed for administration to groups that are considered marginal manpower would not be appropriate for administration to a population of gifted persons, even though the two groups may fall into the same age group.

Competent test score interpretation requires knowledge and understanding of different subgroups of individuals and appropriate selection of tests for the intended purpose. In general, in the working population, there may be several different levels of performance represented in test score distributions for the same test, although some score distributions may be significantly skewed. For some test measures, the score distributions may be represented by a single score distribution, even though the test may be administered to individuals with fairly significant differences in job-related training or experience. In any case, in the individual assessment process the interpretation of test results is based on the experience and training of the assessor and, thus, may have an impact on the quality of the assessment process.

This process of test score interpretation in the context of individual assessment is much more extensive than is usually the case in paper-and-pencil testing, where the quality of the measurement is determined by the originator of the testing procedure. In this case, it is the process of handling the data that involves the skill of the assessor and becomes critical.

At this point in the process, attention is shifted to a dynamic interpretation of the test data to take into account the nature of the interaction of various test scores and measurement data. This interpretation and integration is idiosyncratic, in that a single test score will have a particular, unique meaning within a set of scores and, often, in reference to a particular job. For example, for a candidate for a technical research job, a relatively low score on a scale of caution or deliberate activity, combined with high scores on a test or scale of critical thinking, would be interpreted quite differently from a low score on critical thinking. The inference is that an individual will be able to successfully take chances or risks if he or she has the level of cognitive ability to realistically and fully assess risk and chance. However, if the position is in sales and marketing, where the need for quick, decisive action is greater and the decision-making requirements lower, then a low score on either caution or critical thinking would not have the same implication for future job performance. This is the kind of dynamic interaction of scores in which different combinations of test scores lead to different outcome decisions.

At this juncture, the background for developing a picture of the individual based on psychological assessment data is based on the results from the job modeling process (see chap. 2), including the profile of test scores and any other measurement procedure that provides relevant information. Most of this information is developed in a very systematic way and can be used in absolute measurement terms for characterizing the individual. However, at some point in the process, the competency model for the target job must be compared with the individual assessment picture. At this point in the process, it becomes essential to incorporate the concept of *normative versus relative* comparison of the picture of the person against the relative background of the database.

The score distributions for an entry-level operative position will be quite different from the distribution of scores on the same test for technical/scientific positions. Thus, it is essential that assessees be appropriately positioned in relation to their competition or target. Many tests have score distributions that do not reveal differences in average scores or spread of scores. Other tests, however, show large differences based on such demographics as gender, education, experience, and training. It is essential that the reference group be realistically chosen and firmly linked to the specific competency model being used. An additional caution is the need to consider the ipsative nature of a few test score distributions. These score distributions require extra consideration and caution in the process of interpretation to understand the person in the process of assessment.

At this point, it is appropriate to put considerable emphasis on the description and appropriate characterization of the target individual. We do not apply any decision-making algorithm until the basic descriptive data is established and the interaction of measurement data is processed with the information with reference to a competency model. The desired outcome here is the assembly of a cohesive set of data that allows the assessor to describe and characterize an individual with reference to a competency model.

RESEARCH CONTEXT

Given the assessment professional's role as expert judge, the literature pertaining to decision making and judgment becomes relevant. Actually, there are several pockets of this literature base that underpin different areas of practice in the integration phase of assessment work. First of all, in any complex decision-making environment, the person making the decision puts him- or herself in a position to decide correctly by focusing on reliable information that is relevant to the decision. As discussed in chapter 3, there are a wide range of psychometrically sound tools that may be used to provide input to improve assessor judgments. These instruments provide reliable data with demonstrated relationships to different measures of individual difference characteristics. A line-extension concept not covered in chapter 3 is the fact that decision makers can improve the quality of the decision if they can reduce the amount of information they must process, and one way to do so is to rely on relevant inputs and ignore information from other sources (MacCrimmon & Taylor, 1976).

Continuing this line of reasoning, the relevant connection to the decision in individual assessment is made primarily through the results of the job modeling process. The competency components identified as important for the target job (whether factor, dimension, or item-level descriptors), when used as the basis for setting the assessment specifications, serve to screen out irrelevant information. This comes into play even after the selection protocol has been set, the tests have been administered, and the results are in. For example, most personality instruments provide measures of multiple aspects of personality. For an assessor to obtain measures for the three or four aspects judged to be linked to competency requirements, the entire instrument, including all the subscales, must be administered. Consequently, even after the assessment, the assessor must stay focused on the assessment target and ignore information from irrelevant sources (i.e., scales).

Specific to the point of the assessment procedure, the assessment center literature includes the topic of information overload and the limitations in handling data. From a variety of sources, we find that there is an inherent limitation in the information processing capability of individuals (assessors) that seems to be on the order of "Rule of 7" (Miller, 1956), reflected in the number of scale intervals that can be used in performance appraisal. This is similar to the situation for the number of data points that can be differentiated in the assessment process and, also specific in this context, the number of dimensions that are identified as a result of factor analysis of assessment-center judgments, individual assessment test batteries of test score dimensions (Klimoski & Brickner, 1987; Sackett, 1987; Sackett & Dreher, 1982; Shore, Thornton, & Shore, 1990; Turnage & Muchinsky, 1982).

The competency components at the heart of the assessment protocol serve another useful purpose as well. There is a line of research that suggests that a strategy of "chunking" helps a decision maker to impose meaning on a broad field of stimuli by effectively organizing the information and thereby reducing the cognitive demands on the decision maker (Simon, 1969). By chunking pieces of information into categories and arranging them in order of importance, the decision maker can increase his or her information processing capability in the face of a virtual information assault (Posner, 1963). Interestingly enough, supporting evidence comes directly from the individual assessment literature, where it has been shown that assessment reports that contain voluminous amounts of information cloud the judgments of eventual users of the reports. The practical description of how the assessor applies this methodology is described in the Practice Examples section of this chapter.

Of course, one of the strongest findings in the decision-making literature is that, when the information inputs are quantitative in form, their mechanical combination (e.g., weighting the inputs based on known statistical relationships) provides predictions superior to those of clinical interpretation and combination of the inputs (Meehl, 1954, 1986; Sawyer, 1966). The underlying view is that people are not particularly efficient when it comes to integrating information (Dawes, 1988). However, as others have recently noted (Ganzach, Kluger, & Klayman, 2000), the evidence in support of this conclusion is usually indirect and based on findings showing that human information integration is fraught with inconsistencies, misweightings, and heuristic thinking (Kahneman, Slovic, & Tversky, 1988; Nisbett & Ross, 1990). Direct evidence of the superiority of mechanical combination over clinical judgment is rare.

From a somewhat different perspective, if one is to conclude that the clinical combination of information inputs adds something to the predictive equation, then an underlying predicate must be that clinical judgments are nonlinear. In other words, the rules governing the combination of these judgments must be different from the rules that support the linear combination of data. It follows, therefore, that it must be possible to examine the degree to which the decision making of novices is different from that of experts. This difference is often described in terms of linearity and configurality. Linear rules are compensatory, where a person's final decision is based on a weighted average of the values associated with different sources of information. Configural rules are those that vary in weight based on the weightings of one or more other sources of information. In other words, the weighting of input information a is contingent on the final weight associated with input b.

From this perspective, it can be argued that the decisions of novices are likely to be based on simple linear strategies, whereas experts are likely to employ more complex configural strategies that let the weightings of different information inputs change as a function of the weightings of other variables in the predictive mix (Camerer & Johnson, 1991). Although a number of research efforts have shown that the decisions of experts are based on nonlinear rules (Chase & Simon, 1973; Ericson & Polson, 1988; Johnson, Hasserbrook, Duran, & Moller, 1982), only a handful have shown configurality in the outcome of expert decisions (Einhorn, Kleinmuntz, & Kleinmuntz, 1979; Ganzach, 1994; Hitt & Barr, 1989)—until recently, that is. Using improved nonlinear models, Yoav Ganzach has been reporting a series of studies that do show that these new versions give better fit to the data than the linear model (Ganzach, 1995, 1997; Ganzach et al., 2000).

In summary, one of the unfortunate facts of life is that it is difficult, if not impossible, to conduct a follow-up validation and evaluation study of the individual assessment practitioner model without making some substantive assumptions about the nature of the different databases. An individual assessment practitioner is confronted with an extraordinarily dynamic and constantly moving target. Hypothetically and practically, the individual assessment practitioner works at the case level and, thus, today might be assessing a candidate for a position as a branch bank president, tomorrow an applicant for design engineer in a manufacturing operation, and then, on the next day, an applicant for sales merchandiser, a position in consumer electronics retail. For an active practice, it is quite possible for an individual assessment practitioner to have 10, 15, or more applicants per month where each target position is unique. It is quite conceivable that, even clustering these positions in a very active practice, the annual sample size could top out at a maximum of 10 or 20 cases. Over that span of time, economic conditions and circumstances and the nature of client businesses might be evolving, dynamic and in flux, changing so that any particular algorithm, no matter how carefully developed, could be obsolete.

A real-life example may help bring this point home. Two years ago, a new client requested service to design and develop a selection procedure for positions in the information technology field. The owner and president of the company had been a senior vice president in another organization and started a new business. During the first year of operations, individual assessments were conducted for approximately 100 positions, resulting in the hiring of approximately 20 new employees. Assessment, selection, and hiring accelerated sharply during the next year, resulting in the company growing from that start-up to over 250 employees. Obviously, although the company remained in the same general business, evolving over 2 or more years from start-up to maturity, the nature of the business, the character of the organization, and all of the attendant potential forces changed quite dramatically and the target jobs and selection decision making changed radically as well.

These cases are far from the hypothetical ideal represented in the studies of pilot selection in World War II, where validities ranged up to .70 for multiple correlations for the final selection procedure (Flanagan, 1948). It should be noted also, in that context, that the procedures that have been most used in the military include multiple cutoffs and clinical evaluations. In this sense, clinical evaluations were based on determining whether a man was qualified by examining the complete array of test scores until one was found on which he was disqualified. This is the basic algorithm in which "the classification officer examines all of the test scores and presumably carries out in his head the application of various procedures such as multiple cutoffs, the use of information regarding the pattern of abilities, and compensations of scores on one trait or those found on another" (Flanagan, 1948, p. 66). The point here is that the individual assessment paradigm simply does not fit neatly into the personnel research and development and validation research model. The continuously changing and dynamic nature of the different aspects of the problem simply defy a final solution and always will defy a final solution.

PRACTICE EXAMPLES

This installment of the practice example discussion follows the assessor through the integration and interpretation stage of the process for Ms. Jones, Mr. Martin, and Mr. Dantos.

Example 1: Sales Associate Assessment

Figure 5.1 presents the integration worksheet for Ms. Jones, who is being assessed for an entry-level sales associate job with Computer City. What follows is background and contextual information for the assessment and some of the thinking behind the final set of ratings provided on the integration worksheet.

Ms. Jones' appointment in our offices was at 1:00 p.m.; she arrived at 12:45 p.m. and sat in the waiting room, chatting with the receptionist (Mrs. Sutherland) for a few minutes until we were ready to begin the assessment testing. Mrs. Sutherland reports that Ms. Jones asked a few questions about the testing and assessment process in a friendly and pleasant manner. Also, Ms. Jones allowed the conversation to come to a halt when it was obvious that Mrs. Sutherland had other work to do. At first, this behavior does not appear to be consistent with Ms. Jones' test scores: She scored only at the av-

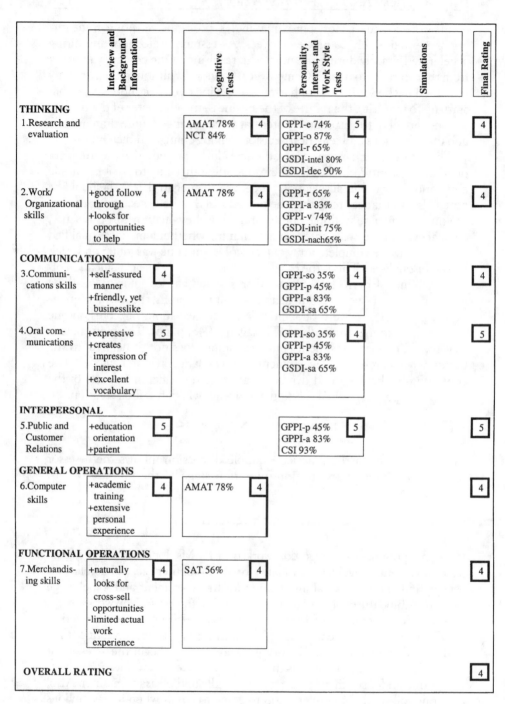

	Interview and Background Information	Cognitive Tests	Personality, Interest, and Work Style Tests	Simulations	Final Rating
THINKING					
1.Research and evaluation		AMAT 78% [4] NCT 84%	GPPI-e 74% [5] GPPI-o 87% GPPI-r 65% GSDI-intel 80% GSDI-dec 90%		[4]
2.Work/ Organizational skills	+good follow [4] through +looks for opportunities to help	AMAT 78% [4]	GPPI-r 65% [4] GPPI-a 83% GPPI-v 74% GSDI-init 75% GSDI-nach65%		[4]
COMMUNICATIONS					
3.Communi- cations skills	+self-assured [4] manner +friendly, yet businesslike		GPPI-so 35% [4] GPPI-p 45% GPPI-a 83% GSDI-sa 65%		[4]
4.Oral com- munications	+expressive [5] +creates impression of interest +excellent vocabulary		GPPI-so 35% [4] GPPI-p 45% GPPI-a 83% GSDI-sa 65%		[5]
INTERPERSONAL					
5.Public and Customer Relations	+education [5] orientation +patient		GPPI-p 45% [5] GPPI-a 83% CSI 93%		[5]
GENERAL OPERATIONS					
6.Computer skills	+academic [4] training +extensive personal experience	AMAT 78% [4]			[4]
FUNCTIONAL OPERATIONS					
7.Merchandis- ing skills	+naturally [4] looks for cross-sell opportunities -limited actual work experience	SAT 56% [4]			[4]
OVERALL RATING					[4]

FIG. 5.1. Integration worksheet for the sales associate assessment (Example 1).

erage level on measures of sociability and agreeableness. However, a look at Ms. Jones' other test scores clears up this apparent inconsistency; she is quite assertive and reasonably confident and self-assured. Ms. Jones also scored high on various measures of interpersonal skill. Ms. Jones' behaviors in the waiting room—asking questions, letting the conversation die down—also indicate a high degree of practical judgment or common sense. Note, too, that Ms. Jones is above average on conscientiousness.

Ms. Jones was dressed neatly and professionally, in a skirt and blazer, and her hair was neatly and conservatively arranged. Unlike some other Computer City applicants, Ms. Jones did not have any obvious piercings or tattoos. The immediate inference from Ms. Jones' appearance is a confirmation of Ms. Jones' social judgement, as reflected in the test scores. In addition, the fact that Ms. Jones was dressed in a business-like manner suggests that she is a mature individual and is motivated to succeed in the business setting.

During the assessment testing, Ms. Jones appeared to be alert and conscientious. When the test administrator gave the instructions, Ms. Jones repeated them back, to be sure that she had understood them correctly. She took one short break during the testing process, but moved quickly through the tests. Again, this behavior is consistent with the high sense of responsibility and high level of assertiveness later shown on Ms. Jones' test scores. In addition, Ms. Jones' behavior and demeanor were all intended to make a favorable impression. Finally, Ms. Jones' pace of work was consistent with the high levels of energy and decisiveness from the test scores.

During the interview, the assessor asked Ms. Jones about her academic work, activities outside of school, and her long-term career plans. During the interview, Ms. Jones presented herself in a calm, self-assured manner. She responded to questions fully and expansively. Again, as discussed previously, Ms. Jones' behavior and test scores are consistent and indicate that she is outgoing and confident and has the social skills necessary to create and sustain a favorable impression.

Ms. Jones is a college student, a senior majoring in business administration. She attends a small local college with an excellent business school and is strongly recommended by one of her professors (who has recommended strong candidates to us in the past). Ms. Jones has taken several courses in IT, going beyond the requirements for her general business major, and has received mostly As in these classes (to date, she has a 3.80 GPA). During the interview, Ms. Jones was asked why she had chosen a general business major, rather than a more demanding course of study. Her response was that she did not want to be limited to a purely technical role, but wanted to advance in sales or management. Although she enjoyed working with computers, the less technical major allowed her to take classes in marketing and management, which would be valuable to her as she progressed in her career.

Ms. Jones' educational achievements are consistent with her level of ability. However, given her ability (well above average in comparison with her peers), as well as her strong level of conscientiousness (c), vigor (v), and intellectual curiosity (intel), as shown on both the GSDI and GPPI, it was a bit surprising that she did not choose a more demanding course of study (such as computer science). Ms. Jones' explanation for this, though, is consistent with other aspects of her personality and motivational picture. She wants to learn and increase her knowledge and she has a strong need to achieve, both qualities that are consistent with her choice of the general business major. Note, also, that Ms. Jones' score on the test of good sales practices is about average in comparison with the experienced working population, consistent with her academic achievement and lack of practical experience.

During the interview, Ms. Jones indicated that she anticipates graduating in the spring. Ms. Jones also said that she would be interested in pursuing an MBA in the future, but that, at the present time, she was more interested in gaining practical work experience. Ms. Jones' statements about her plans for an MBA are consistent with her scores on measures of intellectual curiosity and need for achievement. Her plan to delay the MBA until she has gained work experience is additional confirmation of her strong practical judgment. In addition, Ms. Jones is an energetic, ambitious individual, as shown by her test scores and her responses during the interview, and it is not surprising that she would want to start on her career, rather than spending another 2 to 3 years in school.

Ms. Jones is also active in a local computer users' group, a group designed for women in the IT area. She maintains the group's web page. Ms. Jones also has a personal web page focused on her upcoming wedding. The content of this page is very sophisticated and Ms. Jones appears to be managing a major wedding (her own) almost completely online.

To begin with, this level of outside activity confirms that Ms. Jones is an energetic, active individual. In addition, her participation in a professional group confirms prior indications that she understands impression management, that is, the effect of her participation on future employers. Finally, this is additional confirmation of Ms. Jones' career orientation—taking the opportunity to make contacts with professionals in the area and to discuss real-world issues. Normally, there would be some question as to how well an individual with only academic and personal experience will be able to translate his or her knowledge to the work setting. However, the type of experience that Ms. Jones reports—working with other people, as she has done with the users' group, and creating a web site that is useful (as opposed to being a showcase for programming tricks)—supports an inference that she will be able to effectively use her knowledge and skills working with other people in the real world. Again, this confirms the test scores showing a high level of common sense, or practical judgment.

At the close of the interview, Ms. Jones had several questions of her own, primarily about long-term career prospects with Computer City. Her questions about long-term career prospects reflected her high level of motivation and may also have represented an attempt at influence management. Ms. Jones consistently worked to create a favorable impression during the interview. Specifically, it appeared that Ms. Jones was looking for a long-term career with Computer City, rather than just a short-term or temporary job. This behavior reflects both her competence in interpersonal relations and her high level of motivation; Ms. Jones' test scores show a high need for achievement in comparison with the normative group and an unusually high need for achievement (GSDI, need for achievement, 86%; not shown in Fig. 5.1) for the typical young Computer City applicant.

Example 2: Department Manager Assessment

Figure 5.2 presents the integration worksheet for Mr. Martin, who is being assessed for the department manager job with Barnes Stores. For the record, Pete Martin had an appointment for the assessment testing at 8:15 a.m. on June 15, but he called stating that he would be late because his car broke down and that he would have to find alternative transportation. He finally appeared at 9:30 a.m., expressed a reluctant apology, and was then given the preliminary briefing and instructions for completing the assessment testing. Mr. Martin was dressed casually in a shirt and slacks with a generally disheveled appearance. His hair was down the back of his neck and was put up in a brief ponytail. He had a short, straggly beard. Mr. Martin was a tall and lanky 31-year-old White male who completed high school and then went to work at various unskilled jobs.

In the interview, Mr. Martin stated that he is currently operating his own business. This is a continuation of the work he has done during periods when he was between jobs. He picked up spending money by cleaning cars, but did not develop anything representing a business during the previous 10 to 12 years. Most jobs during the period lasted for a year or less, with periods of unemployment when he was between jobs. His most recent position was as a bulk merchandiser for a soft drink distributor, which essentially involved route sales and servicing retail customers. He was fired for being outspoken and overly critical of his supervisor and employer. At that point, he was unable to find employment, so he set up his own business, called Classical Auto Reconditioning Service, in the garage at the rear of his home. By his comments, he is slowly starving to death and his wife issued an ultimatum that he either get a job or get out.

During the interview, Mr. Martin was initially skeptical and somewhat defensive and tried to give short answers to open-ended questions. In describing his past employment, he indicated that he works as a matter of necessity, but he usually did not fit in very well and really did not care to work for other people. He stated that he never worried about the direction he was going in and, basically, he expected people to essentially accept him for what he was. Because he did not have any particular occupational or career goal in mind, he worked at what he was told to do for those periods that he was employed.

As the interview continued, Mr. Martin became less defensive and somewhat more expressive in his responses to questions. In describing his most

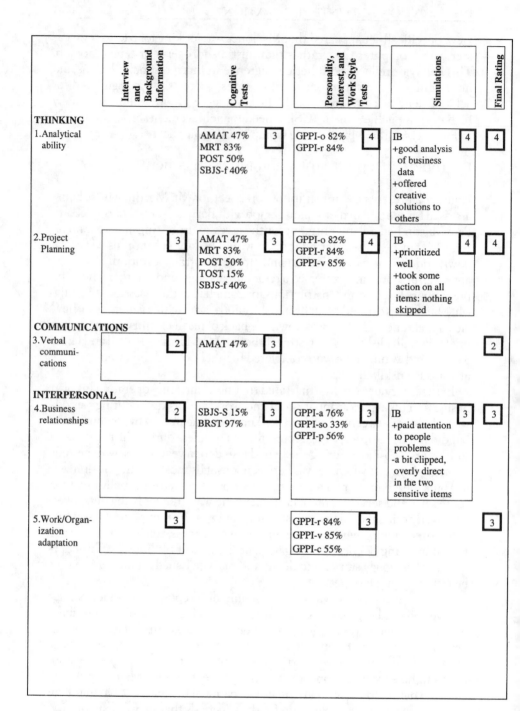

	Interview and Background Information	Cognitive Tests	Personality, Interest, and Work Style Tests	Simulations	Final Rating
THINKING					
1. Analytical ability		AMAT 47% MRT 83% POST 50% SBJS-f 40%	3	GPPI-o 82% GPPI-r 84%	4	IB +good analysis of business data +offered creative solutions to others	4	4
2. Project Planning	3	AMAT 47% MRT 83% POST 50% TOST 15% SBJS-f 40%	3	GPPI-o 82% GPPI-r 84% GPPI-v 85%	4	IB +prioritized well +took some action on all items: nothing skipped	4	4
COMMUNICATIONS					
3. Verbal communications	2	AMAT 47%	3			2
INTERPERSONAL					
4. Business relationships	2	SBJS-S 15% BRST 97%	3	GPPI-a 76% GPPI-so 33% GPPI-p 56%	3	IB +paid attention to people problems -a bit clipped, overly direct in the two sensitive items	3	3
5. Work/Organization adaptation	3			GPPI-r 84% GPPI-v 85% GPPI-c 55%	3		3

FIG. 5.2.   Integration worksheet for the department manager assessment (Example 1).

(continued on next page)

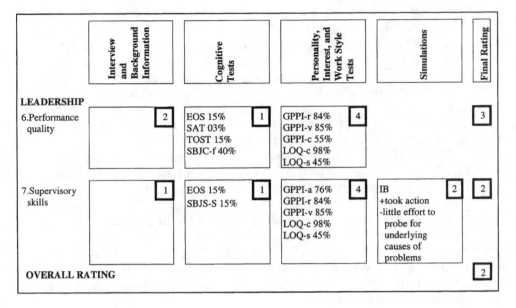

	Interview and Background Information	Cognitive Tests	Personality, Interest, and Work Style Tests	Simulations	Final Rating
LEADERSHIP					
6.Performance quality	2	EOS 15% · 1 SAT 03% TOST 15% SBJC-f 40%	GPPI-r 84% · 4 GPPI-v 85% GPPI-c 55% LOQ-c 98% LOQ-s 45%		3
7.Supervisory skills	1	EOS 15% · 1 SBJS-S 15%	GPPI-a 76% · 4 GPPI-r 84% GPPI-v 85% LOQ-c 98% LOQ-s 45%	IB · 2 +took action -little effort to probe for underlying causes of problems	2
OVERALL RATING					2

FIG 5.2.   *(continued)*

recent job, he indicated that he learned relatively little about retail sales operations because that was not his business, but that he did learn how to push products because of the potential bonus. Unfortunately, he did not approve of some business practices that required extra effort on his part and expressed his dissatisfaction too bluntly and as a result was fired.

At the completion of testing, the assessor indicated that Mr. Martin was entitled to feedback and, at that point, he spontaneously offered the comment that he "didn't believe in tests." During the feedback, Mr. Martin paid closer attention and then spontaneously commented that he was very surprised at the accuracy of the feedback in terms of his own self-assessment. His only question concerned his opportunities for employment in view of his very unstable work history and in view of his rather unconventional personal and organization-related behaviors.

A careful review of the test score protocol indicates a number of points that warrant mention. First of all, cognitive test scores indicate that his abilities are generally above the average of his competitors who are similarly situated and that he has basic verbal and quantitative thinking skills. What jumps out, however, is that test scores reflecting the extent to which he utilizes his abilities are considerably lower (specifically, TOST, EOS, and SAT). These are tests that involve experiential learning and development and strongly suggest that Pete Martin does not or has not profited from work-related experience.

In this case, the key is the discrepancy between the core cognitive competency and the experience-based competency, but the client then accepted the risk of hiring Pete, who was gone 2 weeks later. Pete was not fired; he left of his own accord, but his departure might have been encouraged. A possible explanation is that the personality and affective expression-type tests also indicate that, although he is reasonably outgoing and expansive, it is not to the point that he could be characterized as assertive. However, again, the relatively low score on SBJT, which linked to applied problem solving, is well below average. In contrast, note the higher scores on BRST, the consideration scale (c) of the LOQ, and the responsibility scale (r) of the GPPI, indicating that he is a very action-oriented and otherwise very responsible producer.

Overall, the test score profile reveals some anomalies and, when combined with the interview protocol, is cause for concern about Pete's future prospects and longevity. The striking disparity is that there is a consistency between leadership competencies (TOST and EOS) and his past history that comes close to having compelling influence on the outcome of the assessment in terms of his prospects. Note that Pete has apparently not acclimated himself to the constraints of a structured organization with rules and procedures. The recommendation also reflected that, at the time of his employment, new employees were not easily recruited and management was willing to take risks in new hiring.

However, sometime later management prepared a mission statement that emphasized quality of performance, which would have mitigated the tendency to staff on demand. The organization was known for its responsiveness to customer relations, but the message had not come through clearly to all management.

Example 3: Division President Assessment

Figure 5.3 presents the integration worksheet for Mr. Dantos, who is being assessed for the division president job with Natural Foods World Wide. What follows is background and contextual information for the assessment and some of the thinking behind the final set of ratings provided on the integration worksheet.

As arranged, Mr. Dantos flew into town the night before the assessment and was at our office promptly at 7:30 a.m., as scheduled. Despite being encouraged in the scheduling correspondence to come dressed in business casual style, he arrived looking like he was ready for a boardroom presentation. Even when encouraged to lose the tie, he politely but flatly refused. His current role as an executive, combined with a high capacity for status score and somewhat elevated good impression score from the CPI (not reported in the integration worksheet in Fig. 5.3), helps explain this behavior.

Mrs. Edwards, our test administrator, reported that, throughout the morning of paper-and-pencil testing, Mr. Dantos responded appropriately when spoken to, but otherwise did not engage her in small talk. In fact, Mrs. Edwards stated that he gave the impression of being somewhat put out and somehow above having to be bothered with the trifles of testing. The initial

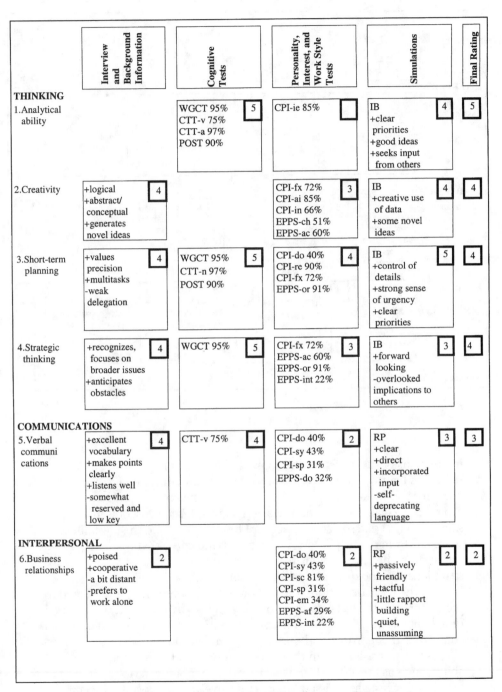

	Interview and Background Information	Cognitive Tests	Personality, Interest, and Work Style Tests	Simulations	Final Rating
THINKING					
1. Analytical ability		WGCT 95% CTT-v 75% CTT-a 97% POST 90% [5]	CPI-ie 85% [ ]	IB +clear priorities +good ideas +seeks input from others [4]	5
2. Creativity	+logical +abstract/conceptual +generates novel ideas [4]		CPI-fx 72% CPI-ai 85% CPI-in 66% EPPS-ch 51% EPPS-ac 60% [3]	IB +creative use of data +some novel ideas [4]	4
3. Short-term planning	+values precision +multitasks -weak delegation [4]	WGCT 95% CTT-n 97% POST 90% [5]	CPI-do 40% CPI-re 90% CPI-fx 72% EPPS-or 91% [4]	IB +control of details +strong sense of urgency +clear priorities [5]	4
4. Strategic thinking	+recognizes, focuses on broader issues +anticipates obstacles [4]	WGCT 95% [5]	CPI-fx 72% EPPS-ac 60% EPPS-or 91% EPPS-int 22% [3]	IB +forward looking -overlooked implications to others [3]	4
COMMUNICATIONS					
5. Verbal communications	+excellent vocabulary +makes points clearly +listens well -somewhat reserved and low key [4]	CTT-v 75% [4]	CPI-do 40% CPI-sy 43% CPI-sp 31% EPPS-do 32% [2]	RP +clear +direct +incorporated input -self-deprecating language [3]	3
INTERPERSONAL					
6. Business relationships	+poised +cooperative -a bit distant -prefers to work alone [2]		CPI-do 40% CPI-sy 43% CPI-sc 81% CPI-sp 31% CPI-em 34% EPPS-af 29% EPPS-int 22% [2]	RP +passively friendly +tactful -little rapport building -quiet, unassuming [2]	2

FIG. 5.3. Integration worksheet for the division president assessment (Example 1).

(continued on next page)

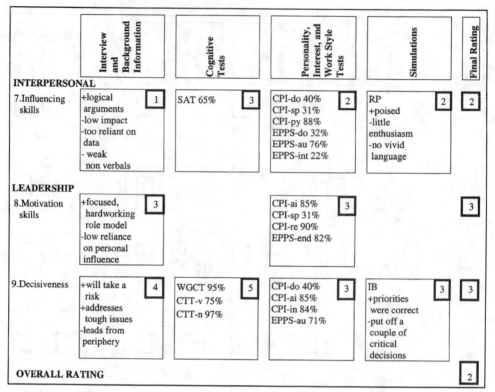

	Interview and Background Information	Cognitive Tests	Personality, Interest, and Work Style Tests	Simulations	Final Rating
INTERPERSONAL					
7. Influencing skills	+logical arguments -low impact -too reliant on data - weak non verbals **1**	SAT 65% **3**	CPI-do 40% CPI-sp 31% CPI-py 88% EPPS-do 32% EPPS-au 76% EPPS-int 22% **2**	RP +poised -little enthusiasm -no vivid language **2**	**2**
LEADERSHIP					
8. Motivation skills	+focused, hardworking role model -low reliance on personal influence **3**		CPI-ai 85% CPI-sp 31% CPI-re 90% EPPS-end 82% **3**		**3**
9. Decisiveness	+will take a risk +addresses tough issues -leads from periphery **4**	WGCT 95% CTT-v 75% CTT-n 97% **5**	CPI-do 40% CPI-ai 85% CPI-in 84% EPPS-au 71% **3**	IB +priorities were correct -put off a couple of critical decisions **3**	**3**
OVERALL RATING					**2**

FIG. 5.3.   (*continued*)

impressions of the assessor, who took Mr. Dantos to lunch, were much the same. Mr. Dantos was not very expressive and uninclined to say much about himself or his feelings (e.g., reactions to the testing process), without a lot of prompting. Again, this is not unexpected given his lower scores in terms of sociability (cy) and social presence (sp) from the CPI and the low affiliation score (af) from the EPPS. Mrs. Edwards also indicated that Mr. Dantos paid attention to her instructions to the tests and proceeded to follow the instructions with no questions, which is something of an anomaly, given that some of the test instructions are convoluted and confusing. He appeared to breeze through the tests, finishing quickly and in advance of the established time limits. He asked for no breaks, though he took one when offered, and completed this portion of the assessment much more quickly than most. This is not surprising, given that his scores on standardized tests of mental ability, such as the WGCT and CTT, were superior. Even on the in-basket test, he addressed more issues, more extensively, than most of his peers. By all accounts, he is one of the most intelligent and focused individuals that has come through the assessment shop in some time.

During the interview it was learned that Mr. Dantos and his three brothers were raised by their father, a small business owner, in Danbury, Connecticut. More so than his siblings, Mr. Dantos was actively involved in his father's business. He recalled how proud he was when his father gave him the responsibility of receiving and stocking inventory. Similarly, he showed some emotion when he told the assessor that his father eventually picked him to keep the company financial books instead of one of the older brothers. His personality profile also describes someone more comfortable dealing with data or things than people. Whereas his brothers were all very sociable and the stars of various high school and college athletic teams, Hector Dantos took a different path. Although something of an athlete in his own right, Mr. Dantos is independent (CPI, independence score of 84% and achievement via independence score of 85%), precision oriented (EPPS, order score of 91%), and, as noted previously, prefers not to be the center of attention. It should be noted that, although Mr. Dantos is clearly not dominant or assertive in behavior, there are plenty of indicators to suggest that he is not submissive.

Once all the assessment data were in, it became clear that Mr. Dantos' stress on objectivity and logic, even in interpersonal relations, contributes to his being perceived as distant and impersonal. He is not the most empathetic person in the world (CPI, empathy score of 34% and EPPS, intraception score of 22%). Furthermore, his CPI-py score (psychological mindedness; not included on the integration worksheet) was 77%; people with high py scores can create the impression that they are more interested in observing than in engaging other people. As indicated in Fig. 5.3, Mr. Dantos also has a tendency towards overcontrol (CPI, self control score of 81%). One of numerous confirming observations in this regard came from the executive presentation role play, where he presented a wonderfully original idea and an exciting business model with about as much energy and passion as a person lounging on a deck chair by a pool.

REFERENCES

Camerer, C. F., & Johnson, E. J. (1991). The process performance paradox in expert judgment. In A. Ericson & J. Smith (Eds.), *Towards a general theory of expertise: Prospects and limits* (pp. 195–215). Cambridge, England: Cambridge University Press.

Chase, W. G., & Simon, H. A. (1973). Perception in chess. *Cognitive Psychology, 4,* 55–81.

Dawes, R. M. (1988). *Rational choice in an uncertain world.* New York: Harcourt Brace Jovanovich.

Einhorn, H. J., Kleinmuntz, D. N., & Kleinmuntz, B. (1979). Linear regression and process tracing models of judgment. *Psychological Review, 86,* 465–485.

Ericson, K. A., & Polson, P. G. (1988). An experimental analysis of the mechanisms of a memory skill. *Journal of Experimental Psychology: Learning, Memory, and Cognition, 14,* 305–316.

Flanagan, J. C. (1948). *The Aviation Psychology Program in the Army Air Forces* (Report No. 1). Washington, DC: U.S. Government Printing Office.

Ganzach, Y. (1994). Theory and configurality in expert and layperson judgment. *Journal of Applied Psychology, 79,* 439–448.

Ganzach, Y. (1995). Nonlinear models of clinical judgment: Meehl's data revisited. *Psychological Bulletin, 118,* 422–429.

Ganzach, Y. (1997). *The weighing of pathological and non-pathological information in clinical judgment.* Manuscript submitted for publication.

Ganzach, Y., Kluger, A. N., & Klayman, N. (2000). Making decisions from an interview: Expert measurement and mechanical combination. *Personnel Psychology, 53,* 1–19.

Hitt, M. A., & Barr, S. H. (1989). Managerial selection decision models: Examination of configural cue processing. *Journal of Applied Psychology, 56,* 130–134.

Johnson, P. E., Hasserbrook, F., Duran, A. S., & Moller, J. (1982). Multimethod study of clinical judgment. *Organizational Behavior and Human Performance, 30,* 201–230.

Kahneman, D., Slovic, P., & Tversky, A. (Eds.). (1988). *Judgment under uncertainty: Heuristics and biases.* London: Cambridge University Press.

Klimoski, R., & Brickner, M. (1987). Why do assessment centers work? The puzzle of assessment center validity. *Personnel Psychology, 40,* 243–260.

MacCrimmon, K. R., & Taylor, R. N. (1976). Decision making and problem solving. In M. D. Dunnette (Ed.), *Handbook of industrial and organizational psychology* (pp. 1397–1453). Chicago: Rand McNally.

Meehl, P. (1954). *Clinical versus statistical prediction: A theoretical analysis and a review of the evidence.* Minneapolis: University of Minnesota Press.

Meehl, P. (1986). Causes and effects of my disturbing little book. *Journal of Personality Assessment, 50,* 370–375.

Miller, G. A. (1956). The magical number seven, plus or minus two: Some limits on our capacity for processing information. *Psychological Review, 63,* 81–97.

Nisbett, R., & Ross, L. (1990). *Human inference: Strategies and shortcomings of social judgment.* Englewood Cliffs, NJ: Prentice-Hall.

Posner, M. I. (1963). Immediate memory in sequential task. *Psychological Bulletin, 60,* 333–349.

Sackett, P. R. (1987). Assessment centers and content validity: Some neglected issues. *Personnel Psychology, 40,* 13–25.

Sackett, P. R., & Dreher, G. F. (1982). Constructs and assessment center dimensions: Some troubling empirical findings. *Journal of Applied Psychology, 67,* 401–410.

Sawyer, J. (1966). Measurement and prediction, clinical and statistical. *Psychological Bulletin, 66,* 178–200.

Shore, T. H., Thornton, G. C., III, & Shore, L. M. (1990). Construct validity of two categories of assessment center dimension ratings. *Personnel Psychology, 43,* 101–116.

Simon, H. A. (1969). *The sciences of the artificial.* Cambridge, MA: MIT Press.

Turnage, J. J., & Muchinsky, P. M. (1982). Transsituational variability in human performance within assessment centers. *Organizational Behavior and Human Performance, 30,* 174–200.

Wiggins, J. S. (1980). *Personality and prediction: Principles of personality assessment.* Menlo Park, CA: Addison-Wesley.

6

Feedback, Reporting,
and Program Evaluation

Oliver Wendell Holmes described the goal of data reduction as finding simplicity on the other side of complexity. A similar sentiment applies to the individual assessment report. The report organizes the massive amount of information (about the organization, the job, and the individual) generated from the assessment process and summarizes and combines it in a way useful to the client's decision makers. This can be as simple as an oral discussion communicating the decision to accept or reject the candidate, or as complex as a 20- or 30-page narrative including charts and graphs. In effect, it is the client who determines the extent of reporting.

In general, assessment results are reported in writing in a standardized report format. A standardized format is essential because it gives the client a standardized frame of reference for understanding the report and the recommendations. The report can be a line graph or bar chart, a computer-generated test score profile, a listing of normative scores, a computer-based report capturing the strategy of an assessor, or a uniquely composed report with both verbal and quantitative content. In the interest of enhancing the utility of assessment reports to the user, it is obvious that some degree of standardization is a minimum requirement. Although both standardization and complete and comprehensive reporting have been emphasized previously in this text, this point cannot be emphasized too often. A certain degree of standardization is necessary if individuals are to be compared to one another. Clients can more easily process information if it is presented in a familiar, standard format. Thus, although format details vary, for the most part, the report will include background information on the assessee and an enumeration of the assessee's relative strengths and weaknesses (hopefully with reference to stated organization and job requirements).

In the selection context, the report normally closes with a clear statement about the candidate's chances for success on the job. The report may also include suggestions on how the manager can best work with the individual to maximize his or her productivity, effectiveness, and impact on the job. A report prepared for development purposes will include the elements just enumerated, as well as a section of specific recommendations and suggestions for addressing opportunities for development. To facilitate writing a narrative report, assessors should think through all of their experiences with the client to determine what the client wants or needs to know about an individual's functioning. Writing a narrative report that represents the integration of all of the assessment data can be used to answer these questions. It is appropriate to go through each of the questions because this list will provide the assessor with what a user wants to know and can use in the report. There is an interaction between the operations that constitute the individual assessment, job modeling, and basic descriptive report of the results of accumulated assessment information. To begin, it is one thing to analyze and evaluate information, but it is another to then begin the process of specific job- and competency-related inference making. Taking that step of integrating job competency information with the interpretative reporting of results requires considerable finesse and expertise. As the assessor begins to expand his or her understanding of the assessment database, the focus shifts to developing an understanding of the individual, both in general and in terms of job competency requirements. In this respect, the results of the assessment can also be viewed in terms of individual development planning. The implication is that the assessment does not end at this point, but is simply one additional step in the employee development process. In effect, this is a transition stage in which the focus includes the assessment, the decision making, and the extension of that action model into the future. In making that transition from the candidate or applicant phase to the recent hired phase, some of the questions with an assessment focus can become considerably more meaningful. When the assessee makes the transition to becoming the employee, the shift to individual development planning opens up an entirely new venue of assessment and evaluation.

When assessors make an endorsement, there is some controversy about whether they should just report and describe or fit themselves into a decision-making role. It is not an uncommon practice for an assessor to have veto power to reject an applicant, but less common to force an acceptance, although all of us have, from time to time, urged a client to "grab this one before he or she gets away." In other situations, the client may simply want a description and some level of discussion of what could be done if the individual was hired or promoted, even with deficiencies or training needs. In still other instances, the job may need to be tailored to match the individual's mode of functioning.

Once the assessment has been conducted and completed and a decision made, there may still be a role for the assessor. The assessor's involvement may be extended when the candidate's reaction to the assessment is unusual; for example, if there is significant evidence that the person is under considerable duress or is distressed. In this instance, some sort of additional follow up is necessary and essential. This can occur in two different situations, one where the assessee is a current employee and is being assessed for either development or for reassignment or, second, where the candidate is from outside the organization and is being considered for selection. The individuals referred to in this context are those who constitute a problem to themselves or who react in a very atypical way, indicating a need for support. There are documented cases where individual assessees responded in a violent way when rejected, challenged the assessor after the fact, or became distraught and commited suicide. In other cases during the process of assessment, the assessee may admit to having committed serious crimes and participated in illegal and fraudulent activities with a previous employer, including fabricating a resume, a history, or a completely different identity. Overall, between 1% and 2% of assessees require more than a simple farewell with a handshake or "have a good day" dismissal. In the case of a distressed individual, it is essential—and an ethical responsibility—that the assessor acknowledge and provide response to those individuals whose behavior indicates that the assessment situation was not simply just another event in their life. If necessary, the assessor as a professional assumes the responsibility to follow up and communicate with another involved authority, such as the manager or executive of the hiring official who authorized the assessment. The assessor may participate in that conference or negotiation, but beyond that closing conversation, caution, or reminder, the results of the assessment are owned by the client.

In the practice of individual assessment, whether the focus is on screening or development, the process requires some degree of closure, simply in order to fulfill the requirements for an individual assessment. Ethical practices, whether in the professional sense or the business sense, require that the individual assessment project be brought to a point of closure that will satisfy the assessee and the client. Basically, the assessee is entitled to some form of feedback, even if it only consists of an overview of the assessee's performance on the test and exercises. The feedback should be descriptive and not evaluative with reference to the target position specifications. In this respect, the feedback should not or, in most cases, must not incorporate or include any reference to the decision made or contemplated by the client reflecting the client's disposition. There will always be the assessee who wants to know or claims a need to know the outcome of the assessment. Some individuals may even go through extensive posturing and impression management to present their position or to influence the outcome of the assessment process. In one instance, a candidate asked what the results would be, then coolly informed the assessor, "My father is a friend of the CEO." Even after a negative report was delivered to the client, the candidate made several calls to our offices, suggesting that we reconsider our recommendation. The appropriate response in this situation was to decline any discussion and to refer the candidate back to the hiring manager. The outcome, incidentally, was that the hiring manager flatly refused to hire the individual, in part because of the original report, but also because of the candidate's blatant attempt to pull strings and apply pressure.

Feedback in a selection decision model is not intended to constitute developmental or guidance emphasis; that is grist for another function, the developmental assessment. At the most, a brief suggestion or two, such as "continue your education," may not be out of place, but once the assessor opens that window, it is quite possible for the assessee to step in and pry open the door.

One of the other difficulties in the assessment procedure is revealed when the assessment process is handled by a single individual. One of the features of the multimethod paradigm is separation of the methods. In order to establish and maintain separation, it is essential to separate, to the extent possible, the various operations in the sequence and move from one method to another. For example, the assessor could conduct a brief interview, then administer a cognitive test, followed by a personality measure, a probing interview, and then an exercise with a constructed response. When at all possible, a single assessor should leave the scoring of the assessment until the very last step in the procedure in order to avoid method contamination. This may result in delaying feedback to the individual in order to maintain some semblance of independence of measurement operations to minimize the effect of the one-person-does-all pitfall.

Given some time interval, it is possible for the assessor to score the majority of the tests during the testing period. This will provide an opportunity for at least partial feedback to individuals before they leave the assessment setting. The ideal setting is when support staff is available to conduct the scoring of the tests and a second assessor can replicate the interviewing to achieve a complete multimethod-multitrait design. The independence of different measures and replication will go a long way toward increasing the accuracy of the assessment and the validity of the results.

However, another problem may occur when multiple assessors participate in the assessment process, but only one assessor produces the final report. For example, in an executive assessment setting, where a senior public service officer was assigned the responsibility of drafting the final report and the two or three companion assessors simply participated in the interview procedure, a factor analysis of the assessor ratings revealed significant differentiation in the ratings of the report writer, in comparison to the observers and raters. When multiple assessors are included, it is essential that the assessment process include some type of discussion, in order to reconcile ratings. Different assessors, with different perspectives and different exposures to the candidate, may arrive at significantly different results. The reconciliation discussions may become rather heated and it may, on occasion, be necessary to agree to disagree.

One final obstacle in the process and procedure is the case when the practitioner is the sole provider of all operations. Although the idea of a multimethod-multitrait assessment is critically important, the fact is that research indicates that individual assessors will develop a practice orientation, a style and strategy that influences the outcome of the assessment. Basically, assessors develop patterns and habits, looking for particular pieces of information that may blind them to the unusual.

Some additional questions that arise are:

1. How does one interpret results when testing indicates a conflict?
2. Do similar tests show similar results?
3. How dos one handle a situation when there is no time or opportunity to collect more data?
4. How does one fill in blank data when the opportunity ceases for additional data collection?
5. What does one do when, at the closing hour, the assessor discovers that some form of manipulation or fabrication occurred and the data is invalid?

These are all very practical considerations that arise in actual practice, often resulting in assessors wringing their hands or simply pleading no contest. The lesson here is that a completely infallible, zero-defect assessment is an unattainable objective.

In the practice of individual assessment, under normal conditions and circumstances, when an assessment is conducted and completed, there are still a number of opportunities for constructive action. The assessor should keep in mind the following points:

1. When conducting an assessment, it is essential to use correct names and titles when communicating with the assessee to prevent undermining the credibility of the report.
2. The assessor should describe how the assessee is likely to perform in the work environment, using behavioral descriptions rather than psychological terms or jargon. The assessee should not be described as "having low levels of stress tolerance and impulse control," but rather "likely to respond under pressure or stress without thinking through the consequences of his actions."
3. Assessors should demonstrate understanding of the organization by describing how the assessee will likely fit with the target job, how he or she relates to jobholders, the boss, and the organization culture. An example statement is: "Mr. Smith is a very introverted, solitary individual who will have difficulty in collaborating and cooperating as a member of a work team."

4. Assessors should use action verbs to make sure the assessee sounds like a living, breathing person, for example, using the pronouns, *he* and *she*. These words speak in action-oriented terms so that assessees know that they are being addressed as real people.

These suggstions will go a long way to establish and maintain credibility with the assessee. It is necessary to keep in mind that the individual candidate could later become the assessor's boss if the assessment is conducted within a particular organization.

Finally, the assessor needs to be very careful and maintain a steady-state level of assessment evaluation, a constant that is not influenced by the difficulties in recruiting. We know that recruiters, when the candidates are scarce, tend to lower their standards, but assessors must not. There may be pressure to pass a candidate, but accepting warm bodies will serve the long-term interests of neither the organization nor the assessor.

At this point we are ready to offer some concrete suggestions for structuring an assessment report. Although there are a number of different formats, we have found it useful to organize reports into three main sections (four if there is a development component).

- Section 1:   Introduction and assessee background.

- Section 2:   Foundations for career success; this section of the report describes the candidate in several broad areas, such as:
  —Social and personal functioning
  —Intellectual functioning
  —Motivation and career aspirations
  The areas covered in this section of the report are often standard regardless of the job because they are fairly broad and are important across jobs.

- Section 3:   Competency evaluation; the assessment report's third section consists of an evaluation of the candidate's degree of possession of specific competencies important for success in the target job.

- Section 4:   Development suggestions; typically only reports conducted for development purposes will have a fourth section.

In conclusion, keep in mind that, although there are variations in format for reporting and certainly individual styles of writing, a good assessment report is one that effectively communicates the results to the client.

ASSESSEE BACKGROUND

The introduction of the report includes information specific to that individual assessment. The typical report data include basic personal information, but exclude the test data and results of other screening procedures such as the results of the medical examination, reference check, and so forth. The specific legitimate questions to address are as follows:

1. What is the individual's full name?
2. What is the source and authority for the request for assessment?
3. What was the purpose of the assessment?
4. Was feedback conducted?
5. What pertinent events or circumstances existed in the assessment activity that the reader needs to know or have recorded?
6. What is the structure of the report?

FOUNDATIONS FOR CAREER SUCCESS

Social and Personal Functioning

Here the individual is described in general terms, with the focus being the person's approach to dealing with other people. Questions to address include:

7. What is the basic social orientation of the individual?
8. What are the dominant characteristics that have controlling influence on this person's relevant social or interpersonal behaviors?
9. What are the dominant characteristics that have controlling influence on the individual's behavior in work or work-related settings?
10. What are the dominant characteristics that have controlling influence over the individual's behavior, relative to other employees or contacts?
11. What are the contingencies regarding organization behavior?
12. Does social and personal functioning affect intellectual functioning?
13. Does social and personal functioning have implications for motivation and aspirations?
14. Are there any overriding considerations that have implications for job or organization behavior?
15. Is the person's social and personal functioning amenable to development?

Intellectual Functioning

Here, the interest is, again, in very general terms, in the candidate's intellectual abilities and approach to problem solving. The questions to address are as follows:

16. What is the individual's general level of intellectual functioning?
17. How does this person think? Is this an analytical thinker? An intuitive thinker? A primitive thinker?
18. What is this individual's general experiential knowledge base?
19. Are there any major influences on intellectual functioning?
20. What is this individual's approach to the work environment in terms of problem identification and problem solving?
21. What is this individual's general approach to work, in terms of detail orientation, level of endurance and persistence, and intellectual curiosity?
22. To what extent has the individual benefited from prior experience?
23. Does this individual have a defined or developed job performance strategy?
24. Are there special considerations that are related to the forecast of this individual's intellectual functioning for specific job content areas?
25. What are the contingencies regarding work style based on social and personal functioning or motivation?

Motivation and Career Aspirations

Here, we are interested in why a person is working and what his or her approach is to getting work done. Questions to focus on include the following:

26. What are the individual's primary motives that influence performance?
27. What motivations influence the individual's future performance?
28. What is the person's level of energy, endurance, and sense of urgency?
29. What are the individual's aspirations; where are they going?
30. How will the individual respond to training or on-the-job coaching?
31. What is this individual's level of personal adjustment, sense of self-sufficiency, and sense of competence?
32. Do the individual's motivations or aspirations constitute contingencies for either personal or social functioning or for intellectual functioning?
33. How will the individual respond to coaching and counseling?
34. Is this a mature individual?
35. What degree of personal insight does this individual have?
36. What is this individual's level of work and organization adaptation?

COMPETENCY EVALUATION

The competencies assessed and evaluated in this section of the report are those determined by the results of the job modeling process described in chapter 2. Thus, there is a direct link between the target job requirements and the specific competencies to be assessed. For example, for a sales management job, the specific competencies assessed and described in this part of the report might include verbal communication, project planning, and supervision competency. On the other hand, for a mid-level management job in a manufacturing company, the specific competencies assessed and evaluated might include direct supervision skills, project planning skills, and problem analysis and decision-making skills.

The specific competencies addressed by the assessment and described in this section of the report will change depending on the unique requirements of the job. Moreover, the actual number of competencies evaluated varies from job to job. Obviously, more complex or higher level jobs will include more, and a wider range of, competencies than simpler or lower level jobs. The constant balancing act involves the desire to evaluate as many relevant competencies as possible. Given typical time constraints, targeting more of the latter (i.e., more competencies) means relying on fewer of the former (i.e., fewer predictors per competency).

Typically (and this approach we strongly prefer), assessment reports will include a numerical rating of the assessee in each competency, in addition to the descriptive narrative, thus empirically comparing the individual to his or her peers (i.e., executive peers, mid-level management peers, manufacturing supervisor peers, administrators, specialists, and so forth). This descriptive narrative is frequently a brief 40- to 50-word statement that summarizes the relevant descriptive data from which an inference is made. In selection contexts, the report will usually also include an overall evaluation of the match between individual competencies and job requirements.

One of the intermediate steps suggested in facilitating or conducting the assessment and achieving a complete and thorough understanding of the individual is to decompose the process and conduct a retranslation of assessment measurements to the assessment model. In our practice, we have attempted a number of different algorithms and generally settle on analyzing the assessment dimension, scanning the results of the assessment measurement (testing), and, finally, selecting those test scores that have meaning with reference to competency dimension for that individual. We do not recommend a mechanical process whereby one particular set of test scores is always the basis for assessment of a particular competency. In some cases, the interaction of scores may be important, requiring the assessor to look at additional test scores. Test scores may indicate that the candidate is an extremely original, innovative thinker, making it necessary to also look at the individual's level of risk tolerance in order to completely and accurately assess problem-solving competency. This process forces the assessor to develop a unique weighting algorithm with reference to each assessment dimension and provides the initiative to consider the unique weighting of each measure.

The unique selection and weighting of scores also comes into play when there is obvious discrepancy between test scores that should be highly correlated. For example, with reference to the problem-solving competency dimension, one measure of general cognitive ability might yield a normative score at the 75th percentile and another test might yield a score at the 30th percentile. Assuming that both tests are appropriately and consistently compared to the appropriate normative standard, then a conflict exists that must be reconciled. For maximum performance measures, this is less of a problem, in that we generally assume that high scores on a maximum performance power test are not accidental. On the other hand, two scores measuring basically the same trait, such as conscientiousness, might be somewhat different and either require some additional testing or, in the case of personality dimensions that are important in the assessment procedure, the use of an average score. One of the anomalies in individual assessment occurs when there are discrepancies, where one set of test scores indicates one outcome and another set of test scores (different tests) suggests a conflicting interpretation. In the case study of Peter Martin (Practice Example 2), conflicting data raises its ugly head; high test scores on business relations skills, the LOQ (on consideration), GPPI (on responsibility), and acquiring information all suggest that Pete is quite a capable individual. These test scores link to several of the important competency dimensions and would generally lead to a positive overall assessment. However, Pete Martin's scores on empathetic judgment, knowledge of good supervisory practices, and teamwork and organization skills are all right at the bottom of the distribution. It was not until the interview notes were reviewed and the personal data questionnaire was examined that it was learned that Pete Martin was a very unconventional individual who had only one previous job (for 1 year) and then a series of jobs as a sole producer. In this role, he made a living of sorts as an automobile detailer (which means cleaning, washing, and waxing automobiles), as a day laborer at a local Manpower, Inc. facility, and other hand-to-mouth kinds of jobs. In essence, over the 10 to 12 years of that type of existence, Peter Martin did not mature. He remained a free spirit without ties to family or any kind of permanent employment. In this particular situation, the organization hired Pete. However, on follow up, we learned that 2 weeks later he left the job without any kind of explanation or excuse. Pete was simply tired of working in an organized setting where he would be expected to follow some rules and procedures and make some effort to fit in to the organization and the job role.

In principle, the objective is to use as much of the information as the assessor is capable of assimilating and integrating. As a general rule, simply giving more redundant tests increases the probability of information overload and of the social consequence of wearing out one's welcome in view of the assessee as well as the client, who consumes the results of the assessment.

DEVELOPMENT SUGGESTIONS

As noted previously, individual assessment is most frequently thought of as part of the selection process. However, it may also be an initial step in individual development planning and succession planning activities. The basic steps and procedures in the individual assessment process remain constant, but the reporting and feedback of results have a somewhat different focus.

To begin with, it is necessary to briefly establish what we mean by *individual development planning* and *succession planning*. Individual development planning is a planned activity for the development of an individual employee or groups of employees for future positions within the organization.

The focus of the development component of an assessment is not normally on specific job-related skills for the individual's current position, but rather on the broader skill set needed for advancement within the organization, either in the entry management ranks or, on a higher level, technical or professional positions. The first step in individual development, as with any training activity, is assessment. In this case, the individual assessment is the needs assessment phase. Succession planning, on the other hand, focuses on the needs of the organization rather than those of the individual. In succession planning, the organization has identified a position or group of positions that will become vacant in the future, either through retirements, individuals leaving the organization, or individuals being promoted to higher level jobs. The purpose of succession planning is to identify, well in advance, the individuals who can be promoted or transferred to these vacant positions so that any necessary developmental activities can be initiated.

In the case of individual development planning, the individual employee is deeply involved in the process. As a result, the individual will receive a copy of the report, which means that the assessor must adopt a different tone and language in preparing the report, as well as focus on different aspects of the data. In the standard individual assessment for selection, the focus is on adequate versus inadequate performance as the individual stands at that time. With individual development assessment, in contrast, the focus is on strengths and weaknesses, as well as possibilities for leveraging strengths and possible methods for dealing with an individual's weaknesses. For example, a report for selection might indicate that an individual's knowledge of planning and organizing activities was below standard for a particular position and go no further. In the development report, this statement would be followed by, first, an indication of how critical this weakness is and, second, suggestions for how this weakness could be addressed (e.g., participation in training or self-development activities). The language employed in the individual development report is also different. First, the report is generally written in the first person, for example, "you have above average ability to define and solve quantitative problems." Second, the language used is somewhat more constructive and tactful. Although an individual may have weaknesses, they should be described in a tactful and constructive manner and, whenever possible, strengths should also be pointed out, for example, "you will have somewhat more difficulty than your peers in solving mathematical problems, but you will compensate by working harder and more persistently on this type of problem."

Another aspect of individual assessment for development is the follow-up. In individual assessment for selection, the individual is or is not hired, and that is generally the end of the process. In contrast, even if the assessor is not involved in the development activities, it is not unlikely that the assessor will be asked to provide extensive verbal feedback to the individual being assessed and possibly to do some follow-up testing and evaluation after an interval to determine how successful development activities have been.

Moreover, the competency model used for individual development assessment will tend to be a more general one, because the individual is being assessed and evaluated not for one specific target position, but for a range of possible positions that the individual may or may not hold in the future.

For succession planning, the assessment can take the character of selection or development, that is, individuals may be assessed for their potential for positions within the organization using the selection model where the promotion will more than likely take place in the short-term future. In this case, the assessment report would follow the selection model described in previous sections of this book. In other cases, the succession planning may include a strong developmental component and the reporting would follow the developmental model described previously.

RESEARCH CONTEXT

Individual assessment is an applied practice that involves conducting and establishing client and customer relationships that meet at least minimum standards as a business practice. In practice, one of the first issues to be addressed involves communication, not only to prospective clients, but also to the recipients of service and to the nebulous and otherwise unidentified observers and critics. When an individual assessment is conducted, there are three additional constituent interests other than the assessor and these are the assessee, the assessment client, and the unidentified location of records that might be assessed by unidentified monitors or evaluators. Individual assessment is a business activity and, as a result, must professionally and legally be conducted as a business. As such, practical issues that need to be addressed include informing the relevant others about the practice.

Pragmatically, from a research standpoint, it is essential to have clearly in mind what kind of information, and how much information, should be provided to the relevant others after the assessment. It is possible to attempt to develop too much information in reporting (and thus cloud key messages to the client) or to err on the side of providing too little information, in terms of quantity or quality or the form in which that information is transmitted. Although relatively little has been written about individual assessment practice uniquely, considerable insight can be gained from the assessment center history (Thornton & Byham, 1982). In summary, there is a balance between too much and too little information and the quality of that information.

One of the very essential concerns here is the degree of utility of the information that is provided; a number of issues relating to this were raised by Messick (1995). Correspondingly, from a slightly different perspective, Helms (1992) raised the entire litany of questions into the consequences with reference to cross-cultural sources of individual assessment information. Similarly, the issue of nontraditional topics for measurement (e.g., Organ & Ryan, 1995; Sternberg, Wagner, Williams, & Horvath, 1995) focuses attention on those nonconventional measures that are involved in the individual assessment practice. By *nontraditional,* we mean topics other than the standardized paper-and-pencil measures. In the individual assessment practice, as the practitioner drifts away from convention and begins to focus on what may be attractive alternatives, the risk of not only getting into unchartered waters but also beginning to focus measurement on trivial pursuits can become hazardous. By *trivial pursuits,* we mean things like cutesy interview questions on the order of: "If you could be any kind of animal, which one would you choose?" or "How would you like to spend your next million dollars?" Many of these cute questions end up being scored according to some homegrown procedures. One of the fundamental precepts in individual assessment is, "If it's a question you wouldn't ask your mother, then don't ask it."

Thus, the essential aspect here is that, in accumulating information, the assessor needs to know as much as is needed to understand the individual and to support inferences (with verification) of the applicant's level of possession of competencies. The description of the search for information and understanding should be reasonably broad and include what we might call "big, deep background" information. Certainly, basic information about job modeling (Schippmann, 1999) provides a comprehensive direction for competency assessment that is not limited to any particular discipline. The ultimate issue, of course, concerns the accuracy of the individual assessment interpretation and then the development of the final product, which is either a decision or a rating of the degree of possession of the job-related competencies that are communicated as a profile or as an overall index to the client. The background includes the research and writing by Meehl (1954), Sawyer (1966), and the accumulated writings of Sam Messick (summarized in Messick, 1995), which are the benchmark foundation of conceptualization regarding validity of psychological assessments. Again, however, no consideration of validity could be complete without those concerns raised by Helms (1992) on cultural equivalents and Organ and Ryan (1995) on citizenship behavior, all of which lead to the conclusion that we basically seem to know what we are doing and that we are doing it fairly well. The question that remains is, if we know what we are doing and we are doing it well, why do we not understand it better, and why can we not describe process and results more effectively with reference to the fundamental nomological net, which supposedly provides the foundation for all of the pragmatic answers?

Two questions in the context of individual assessment that receive relatively little attention are how best to report information to the individual assessee and, the corollary, how that assessment information is used by the assessee. This goes back to the domain of individual development in part, via coaching and counseling, and is interrelated to management training and development using other methods and techniques in training. Regardless, providing feedback to the assessee is an aspect of professional ethical responsibility. In the context of individual assessment, each assessee is entitled to at least an overview or explanation of the results of the assessment in terms of strengths and weaknesses as related to the individual assessment testing battery. In practice, this does not include feedback on the decision reached by the assessor or as interpreted by the assessment client—that is an outcome that must remain under control of the client in terms of the potentially continuing relationship with the assessee. It is safe to assume in this respect that the assessee has a vital and compelling interest in the outcome of the event, but it would be a mistake to assume that the assessor can either simply dismiss the assessee with a curt and superficial comment or that very detailed feedback, including some characterization of the nature of the assessment decision, can be made available to the assessee. Feedback to the assessee must be handled with some delicacy, in view of the fact that the client (regardless of the outcome of the assessment) may choose one or another of the assessment candidates to offer a position to.

The follow-up of the assessment operation in terms of feedback becomes a potential subject for additional counseling if that route is selected by the assessee or the client as part of the continuing practice. In no case should the assessor view the engagement as an opportunity to sell additional services to the assessee, independent of a collaborative request by the client. To promote that kind of business practice would be unquestionably unethical and well beyond the limits of simply being unprofessional.

PRACTICE EXAMPLES

This is the final Practice Example chapter subsection, in which we wrap up our discussion of the Linda Jones, Peter Martin, and Hector Dantos assessments.

Example 1: Sales Associate Assessment

The final assessment report for Linda Jones, an external candidate for a sales associate job with Computer City, is presented in Fig. 6.1. Recall that this assessment is being conducted as an external selection screen for an entry-level job. Both of these reasons help drive the decision to prepare a fairly minimal formal report. Note especially that the report is confined to a discussion and rating of competencies, without the general overview of personal functioning, intellectual functioning, and motivation.

Example 2: Department Manager Assessment

The final assessment report for Peter Martin, an external candidate for a department manager job with Barnes Stores, is presented in Fig. 6.2. This assessment is being conducted as an external selection screen for a supervisory job. The report is more extensive than the sales associate assessment in Example 1 and includes some breakout discussion of social and per-

CONFIDENTIAL ASSESSMENT REPORT

Linda Jones
(March 20, 2001)

Computer City
Memphis, TN 38101

This confidential assessment report is intended for use by client-authorized management personnel only. Statements by the author are based on professional interpretation of interviews, biographical information, psychological tests, and the requirements and standards of the client organization. Such statements would be of limited use to the individual and could be misleading to parties other than the client.

FIG. 6.1. Assessment report for sales associate (Example 1).

(*continued on next page*)

This report summarizes the results of the entry-level screening assessment of Linda Jones, which was conducted on March 20, 2001. The purpose for the assessment was to determine Ms. Jones' strengths and weaknesses for the SALES ASSOCIATE position with Computer City. Following completion of the assessment testing I reviewed the results with Ms. Jones, pointing out areas of general strength and weakness, and provided her a chance to ask questions about the testing. In response Ms. Jones stated that she was, at first, a little intimated by the tests and the situation, though she felt much more at ease after the introduction provided by the test administrator and once things got started. After our assessment debrief, she seemed comfortable and even a bit intrigued by the testing process.

The assessment results for each of the competency areas determined to be most important for successful job performance as a sales associate are described below. This set of job specifications was derived from the completed administrative modeling questionnaire completed by store managers as part of a previous research effort (see Computer City: Sales Associate Job Modeling Report).

1. RESEARCH AND INVESTIGATION:

Ms. Jones has well above average general intellectual skills in comparison to her peer group and she has developed a correspondingly high level of skill in handling quantitative information. In addition, Ms. Jones is an original thinker, who will not hesitate to try new and different approaches to defining and solving problems. Finally, she will stick with an assignment and work through it persistently until she has reached a solution. The implication of this for the work setting is that Ms. Jones will take a proactive approach. She will not be likely to overlook a problem or ignore an issue, hoping it will go away. Her resolution of problems will be high quality, and she is unlikely to make careless errors or mistakes, nor will she overlook details. She will work methodically and carefully, but will not let herself get caught up in irrelevant details. Rating 4.

2. WORK / ORGANIZATION SKILLS:

Ms. Jones is a conscientious, energetic, and diligent worker who will fulfill all job and organizational expectations for performance. She views her position with Computer City as an opportunity to gain work experience for her planned career in sales and will take advantage of opportunities to enhance her skills in this area. In this context, we note that Ms. Jones has had relatively little work experience, although she presents herself in a professional manner. Overall, Ms. Jones can be described as a model organizational citizen. Rating 4.

3. COMMUNICATIONS SKILLS:

Ms. Jones is an assertive yet personable individual who will interact with others in a calm, self-assured manner. She has good understanding of how to adapt her style and approach to different situations. Overall, Ms. Jones will impress others as a mature individual, willing to be helpful and friendly yet business-like. Rating 4.

FIG. 6.1.   (*continued on next page*)

4. **ORAL COMMUNICATIONS:**

Ms. Jones expresses herself fluently and clearly, without any hesitation or awkwardness. She is expressive and creates the impression of a high level of interest and involvement. In conversations with others, Ms. Jones can take charge and direct the exchange, without coming across as domineering or aggressive. Rating 5.

5. **PUBLIC/CUSTOMER RELATIONS:**

Ms. Jones has excellent knowledge of how to interact with other people in the retail sales setting. She wants to help others and be of service, yet she will also remember her employer's interests. Ms. Jones will do what it takes to meet customer expectations, without bending over backwards to the long-term detriment of the organization. Ms. Jones understands that she is representing Computer City to customers and she will conduct herself appropriately, taking the lead in finding and satisfying customer needs and solving problems. Rating 5.

6. **COMPUTER OPERATIONS SKILLS:**

Ms. Jones has relatively little work experience in this area, although she has academic training in PC hardware and software. During the interview, Ms. Jones also indicated extensive personal experience in this area. Her cognitive skills are quite good and she will have no difficulty in acquiring additional knowledge in this area. Rating 4.

7. **MERCHANDISING:**

Ms. Jones has good knowledge of sales practices and techniques, although her actual experience in this area is quite limited. However, Ms. Jones has a high level of practical judgment or common sense, and should encounter little difficulty in transferring her knowledge to practice. In addition, Ms. Jones is an innovative thinker who will look for opportunities for a non-obvious cross-sell. Ms. Jones will not hesitate to suggest additional products or product upgrades, but she will not take an abrasive hard-sell approach. Rating 4.

RECOMMENDATION:

The results of the individual assessment support a strong endorsement of Ms. Jones for the sales associate position. Overall Rating 4. Potential 5.

FIG. 6.1. (*continued*)

CONFIDENTIAL ASSESSMENT REPORT

Peter Martin
(June 12, 2001)

Barnes Stores
3501 S. Saguaro Shadows
Tucson, AZ 85730

FIG. 6.2.   Assessment report for department manager (Example 2).

(*continued on next page*)

This report summarizes the results of the Level I assessment testing of Peter Martin, which was conducted on June 12, 2001. The purpose for the assessment was to determine Mr. Martin's strengths and weaknesses for the **DEPARTMENT MANAGER TRAINEE** position and his potential for development as a **DEPARTMENT MANAGER**. Following completion of the assessment testing, I reviewed the results with Mr. Martin, pointing out areas of general strength and weakness, and provided him with an opportunity to ask questions about the testing. In response, Mr. Martin commented that he had taken the Fire Department Entry Examination on eight occasions and has never been hired and is thus very skeptical about testing and was willing to express his thoughts. In the following discussion, he commented that his tendency to be outspoken had cost him one of his previous jobs. After some discussion, however, he was quite pleased at what the test results revealed and confirmed the accuracy of the feedback.

This report contains two main sections, the first consisting of the three general assessment areas in which Mr. Martin is characterized in general psychological terms. The second section of the report consists of short evaluative statements with a numerical rating for each of the seven job-related competency areas for Level I positions in the Barnes' organization. This set of job specifications was derived from the completed supervisor modeling questionnaire completed by store managers and job incumbents as part of a previous research effort (see Barnes Stores: Department Manager Job Modeling Report).

SOCIAL AND PERSONAL FUNCTIONING

The results of the assessment indicate that Mr. Martin is not a very social person, but that he is very assertive and tends to be a bit outspoken. He is quite comfortable in solitary activities, although when he is with his peers, he can be quite congenial. Mr. Martin is not interested in social leadership and, although he has a good vocabulary and is quite articulate, he is not interested in persuading people or in having social influence. People who know him will describe him as a quiet person who stays to himself and works at those things that personally interest him.

In the work setting, Mr. Martin will stick to business, but he will also feel free to express his thoughts to other people. He is not very sociable, but at the same time, he is not inhibited about what he says and will on occasion rub people the wrong way. He does have superior knowledge of what people expect in the business setting, but he does not always use that information in what he will say or do. Mr. Martin is an unusual individual with unusual personal values and dispositions that will influence his performance in social and work settings. He wants to be independent and not be held to someone else's standards, but, in order to survive, he finds it necessary to attempt to accommodate and conform and fulfill job responsibilities.

INTELLECTUAL FUNCTIONING

The results of the assessment indicate that Mr. Martin has about average intellectual abilities in comparison with the Level I population. However, he does not use his intellectual resources except where it is necessary for his own specific purposes. As a result, he has not developed a uniform level of job skills at his general level of functioning. For example, his

FIG. 6.2.   (*continued on next page*)

skill in handling numerical computations is superior, but his knowledge of sales skills and his knowledge of good supervisory practices are both at the bottom of the score distribution. Although Mr. Martin was skeptical of the testing, there was no indication that he was uncooperative or careless in responding to the tests.

In reviewing Mr. Martin's work history, he has bounced from job to job, but in each case he did learn something. He is generally well informed and not unwilling to learn, but for one reason or another in certain areas, he simply has not developed appreciable levels of competence.

MOTIVATION

Mr. Martin has many of the features of the adolescent free spirit who wants to be independent, unrestricted, undisciplined, and accountable only to himself. When he works, it is important to him that he has a sense of accomplishment and competence, but the conventional features of achievement are relatively unimportant to him. In this sense, Mr. Martin is not a very mature individual and, although he has quite good insight to his personal characteristics and motivations, he is not very adaptable to either work or organization requirements. Mr. Martin is under some pressure at the present time to either get a job or get out of his home (his wife's instructions) and so he is looking for full-time employment.

My evaluation and rating on the job-related competencies are as follows:

1.   **ANALYTICAL ABILITY:**

Mr. Martin has about average abilities in comparison with the Level I population and has developed a very mixed array of job-related skills. It appears that, if something is important to him, he does develop some competency and, if it is not important to him, he virtually ignores it. As a result, he has very limited knowledge of good supervisory practices or of sales skills, but excellent knowledge of numerical computation, planning and organizing skills, and what I generally call social sensitivity. Obviously, the potential is present for him to analyze and solve problems and to develop job-related competencies. Rating 4.

2.   **PROJECT PLANNING:**

Mr. Martin has average knowledge of planning and organizing operations and skills, but he is a very energetic individual with a very strong sense of responsibility. He is also very decisive and has a high level of initiative, but what he actually does will depend upon his interests and motivations. The ability is present, but the actual performance may vary considerably. Rating 4.

3.   **VERBAL COMMUNICATIONS:**

Mr. Martin has a very adequate vocabulary and can express his thoughts clearly, but he tends to be somewhat reserved. He has excellent knowledge of what people expect in the business setting, but he has extremely limited knowledge of sales

FIG. 6.2.   *(continued on next page)*

160

techniques and skills. As a result, doing what comes naturally may or may not be appropriate in contact with customers. Rating 2.

4. BUSINESS RELATIONSHIPS:

Mr. Martin will be a very considerate supervisor who will get along very well with his associates. He has excellent knowledge of what people expect in the work setting and will be generally accommodating except when he expresses his thoughts or observations in a direct or outspoken way. Mr. Martin does not know when to keep his mouth shut or tell a little white lie in order to maintain harmonious relations. In addition, he lacks knowledge and understanding of good supervisory practices so that, although he is willing to assert himself and manage conflict situations, he will not always know what to do. Rating 3.

5. WORK/ORGANIZATION ADAPTATION:

Mr. Martin is an assertive individual who will speak his mind and do so on occasion when he should be quiet. He has excellent knowledge of what people expect in the business setting and, if necessary, will use that information to get along with others, but not necessarily to be persuasive or influential. Rating 3.

6. PERFORMANCE QUALITY:

The results of the assessment indicate that Mr. Martin has a reasonably action-oriented and task-oriented style of leadership, a strong sense of responsibility, and a high level of energy and initiative. In the work setting, he will establish priorities and provide individuals with feedback, which may at times be a bit blunt and direct, but will, nonetheless, result in productivity. Rating 3.

7. SUPERVISORY SKILL:

Mr. Martin has a relatively action-oriented style of leadership, which places considerably stronger emphasis on working with people and being considerate. He will also get along very well with associates by doing what comes naturally. However, his interest in supervisory functions and his disposition toward the supervisor hierarchy is certainly less than desirable. In addition, he has very limited knowledge of good supervisory practices. Rating 2.

RECOMMENDATION:

The results of the assessment support an endorsement of Mr. Martin, but with the caveat that his motivations and disposition are such that he is a poor risk for long-term employment. Mr. Martin may be at a turning point in his life, but at the present time, the best prediction is that he will continue to function as he has in the past and that is to bounce from one job to another. Overall Rating 3.

FIG. 6.2.   (*continued*)

sonal functioning, intellectual functioning, and motivation (in addition to the specific competency dimensions identified by the job modeling work).

Example 3: Division President Assessment

The final assessment report for Hector Dantos, an external candidate for a division president job is presented in Fig. 6.3. This assessment is being conducted as an external selection screen for an executive job. This report also includes a breakout summary discussion of the candidate in terms of social and personal functioning, intellectual functioning, and motivation (i.e., over and above the assessment narrative for each of the competency dimensions identified by the job modeling effort).

CONFIDENTIAL ASSESSMENT REPORT

Hector Dantos

(January 24, 2002)

Natural Foods World Wide
2000 Plaza VII Towers
Minneapolis, MN 55402

FIG. 6.3. Assessment report for division president (Example 3).

(*continued on next page*)

This report summarizes the results of the individual assessment of Hector Dantos, which was conducted on January 24, 2002. The purpose for the assessment was to determine Mr. Dantos' strengths and weaknesses as a candidate for the position of **DIVISION PRESIDENT** of the Natural Candies division of Natural Foods World Wide. On his arrival, I explained the purpose for the testing and the schedule to Mr. Dantos and he commented that he had expected only an hour or perhaps 2 hours of testing and interviewing, which is what he had experienced in some previous pre-employment situations. However, he did not object to staying the full day and worked diligently on all of the testing assignments. However, early on, there was a consistent low-level expression of skepticism, irritation, and impatience with the process. I spent a long lunch with Mr. Dantos, during which I explained in some detail the methodology behind the approach and reiterated the fact that several executives with Natural Foods World Wide helped set the specifications for his assessment. His attitude toward the process continued to become more positive when faced with the interactive assessment exercises (e.g., the executive presentation role play) in the afternoon. By the time we ended our interview and debrief of the assessment results at 6:30 p.m., his attitude had changed 180° and he was actively interested and engaged in the discussion.

This report contains two main sections, the first consisting of the three general assessment areas in which Mr. Dantos is characterized in basic psychological terms with a minimum of evaluative content. The second section of the report consists of evaluative statements with a numerical rating on a 5-point scale for each of the nine job-related competency areas identified as important for the target position. This set of position specifications was derived from the completed Management and Executive modeling questionnaire completed by the Senior Vice President of Human Resources for Natural Foods World Wide and by the assessor after interviewing the company's Chief Financial Officer and Senior Vice President of Human Resources.

SOCIAL AND PERSONAL FUNCTIONING

The results of the assessment along with the simulations, observation, and interview discussions with Mr. Dantos indicate that he is responsible, serious-minded, somewhat reserved, and a bit reluctant to compete for social visibility without a purpose. Though self-assured and poised, he simply prefers to observe, rather than engage, other people. However, he is very smart and is reasonably attuned to social nuances, so he recognizes when circumstances dictate a change in his interpersonal style and tries to adjust accordingly, with mixed success.

In the work setting, Mr. Dantos will operate at the periphery of the social network. Compared to other executives, he simply needs less close, convivial relationships with his colleagues. Although he will be more difficult to get to know than some of his peers, he does care about people, is a straight shooter, and will not undermine others for his own gain. Thus, over time, he will be someone people come to trust. When it comes to shaping the thinking of other people, his understated style will work against him. Furthermore, at times he will become so engrossed in building a compelling intellectual case for an idea or initiative that he will overlook the need to provide the requisite emotional appeal; the facts and data inspire him and he mistakenly assumes that this is all it will take to inspire others.

FIG. 6.3.   (*continued on next page*)

Mr. Dantos possesses an exceptionally strong array of mental abilities. In those areas where standardized tests are available, his scores are in the superior range even with reference to a high-level executive peer group. Similarly, his performance on an in-basket simulation indicates he is a logical, analytical thinker who capably considers multiple perspectives to comprehensively analyze issues.

In his own words, Mr. Dantos "floated" through high school until his junior year. Although he maintained a high B average up to that point, he says he was not particularly challenged and did not apply himself. However, when he quit the various sports he had participated in and dedicated himself to his studies, he maintained an A average from that point on. He decided to go to Hofstra (primarily because none of his three brothers had played football there) and graduated summa cum laude as a business major 4 years later.

MOTIVATION

Mr. Dantos displayed at an early age his drive to achieve. The youngest in a family of four boys, Mr. Dantos admits to being somewhat intimidated by the achievements of his brothers, who were all sports stars in high school and college. Mr. Dantos' energy and goal accomplishment took a different direction and he ran a variety of small businesses with their father (selling firewood, a small but profitable landscaping business, etc.) throughout his high school and college years. Although he acknowledges his strong thinking skills, he really credits his performance in school and business to his ability to "focus like a laser beam" on goals he sets for himself. Furthermore, he sets a high bar for himself (e.g., deciding he was going to graduate from Hofstra University summa cum laude). He will discipline and push himself to meet his own high expectations. In the workplace, he will expect others around him to bring the same degree of drive and focus to their work. In his view, success translates into significant task accomplishment and he is very willing to extend himself to expand his scope of responsibility.

My evaluation and rating on the job-related competencies are as follows:

1. **ANALYTICAL ABILITY:**

    The results of the assessment indicate that Mr. Dantos has excellent critical thinking and analysis abilities in comparison to his peers. Furthermore, he values intellectual matters and pushes himself to his competencies to their fullest when evaluating alternatives and making decisions. He is resourceful and will seek and incorporate input from others before making decisions. At the same time, he is decisive and quickly moves from analysis to action, being very comfortable making inferences or deductions based on incomplete data or information. Mr. Dantos is correct when he notes that his ability to "focus" and "master complexity" is a cornerstone of his career success to date. Rating 5.

FIG. 6.3. (*continued on next page*)

2. **CREATIVITY:**

A logical and analytical thinker, Mr. Dantos is capable of understanding and integrating large amounts of information, and using this information platform to extrapolate beyond the obvious and develop creative solutions to business problems. Able to quickly integrate information on-the-fly and change directions accordingly, he does not value change simply for the sake of change. He complements his creative abilities with a strong results orientation ("a good idea not implemented doesn't mean squat") and the decisiveness and independence to trust his own instincts. Rating 4.

3. **SHORT-TERM PLANNING:**

Mr. Dantos clearly has the competencies necessary to operate in a complex and fast-moving business environment. He is organized, efficient, and dedicated to doing a good job. As a result, he will not miss much or make careless mistakes along the way. He sets priorities as appropriate to drive issues forward and will be viewed as someone who accomplishes a great deal of work. Mr. Dantos does tend to keep himself immersed in too many of the details or hands-on activities when he should be delegating more to the people around him. Rating 4.

4. **STRATEGIC THINKING:**

Mr. Dantos recognizes the importance of, and maintains an appropriate focus on, long-term goals and objectives. In many respects, he is excellent in terms of anticipating problems and potential difficulties such as changes in the market, implications resulting from decisions, and so forth. It should be noted that he may have something of a blind spot when it comes to recognizing the cultural or perceptual impact of some of his decisions. Rating 4.

5. **VERBAL COMMUNICATIONS:**

In this area the results are mixed. Mr. Dantos has an excellent vocabulary and articulates his ideas and thoughts clearly and efficiently. He also has good listening skills. On the other hand, he is somewhat reserved and unwilling to compete for social visibility. In a related vein, his focus on production, combined with his somewhat limited insight to the motives and feelings of others, will result in his missing opportunities to foster open communication with peers. Consequently, there were times during the assessment when his words did not speak as loudly as his convictions. Rating 3.

6. **BUSINESS RELATIONSHIPS:**

Compared to other executives, Mr. Dantos has less need for close, convivial relationships in the workplace. When approached, he will be friendly and responsive; he simply will do less proactive approaching than his peers. He will state his opinions clearly, carefully, and fairly, and will be viewed by colleagues as a straight shooter,

FIG. 6.3. *(continued on next page)*

unwilling to undermine others for his own gain. At the same time, Mr. Dantos will be viewed by colleagues as somewhat distant and uninterested in their affairs. While poised and in control, he does lack some personal forcefulness and will be viewed as tentative in some social contexts, particularly when it is necessary to compete for air time. Rating 2.

7. **INFLUENCING SKILLS:**

Mr. Dantos will typically not compete for social visibility without a purpose. His preference is to operate at the periphery of the social network until he sees events or decisions going down a path counter to his thinking. At this point he will dive bomb right into the middle of the situation and attempt to shape the direction of decisions or thinking by virtue of an irrefutable logic or data-based call for change. Although he has a solid understanding of basic sales skills, numerous indicators throughout the assessment suggest Mr. Dantos overrelies on logic and data to craft a compelling message, and underrelies on the ability of relationships and personal influence to shape outcomes. Rating 2.

8. **MOTIVATION SKILLS:**

Mr. Dantos is a very achievement-oriented individual who will dedicate effort and energy to goal accomplishment without reservation. He is highly motivated toward excellence in his work and places organizational success above his own accomplishments. In many respects, Mr. Dantos will serve as a positive, hard-working role model for others to follow. However, his efforts to serve as a rousing, inspirational leader will be infrequent and the results are likely to be less than awe inspiring. Rating 3.

9. **DECISIVENESS:**

Mr. Dantos is comfortable operating in situations that are unstructured or ambiguous. He is very capable of making sense of complexity and of establishing priorities to guide his actions. He is willing to take a well-thought-out, educated risk if the risk-payoff ratio is favorable. Similarly, once he has decided action is called for, he is willing to step up and confront tough issues. It helps that Mr. Dantos is forward thinking and always planning and, in fact, is always ready for a crisis. Rating 3.

RECOMMENDATION:

In many respects, Mr. Dantos is very talented and would be effective in the target job. In other respects, his position would require a level of competence that he is not yet ready to deliver. A factor to be considered is the fact he has never received detailed feedback of this kind before, he has never participated in any kind of job related assessment or coaching, and he has never attended a formal leadership development program. By the end of our day together, he was clearly energized by the feedback and was making plans for how to further develop some of the weaker areas covered in the assessment debrief. All this is to say that Mr. Dantos would be an ideal number 2 in the Natural Candies Division, or in a role where he

FIG. 6.3.   (*continued on next page*)

could be given a chance to muscle build in a couple of weaker, but imminently developable, areas. Thus, in terms of an overall rating for the position of division president, Natural Candies Division, at this point in time, the Overall Rating is 2. In terms of being a longer term prospect for moving into the role 2 to 3 years out, the rating of Potential is 4.

FIG. 6.3.   *(continued)*

REFERENCES

Helms, J. E. (1992). Why is there no study of cultural equivalence in standardized cognitive ability testing? *American Psychologist, 47,* 1083–1101.

Meehl, P. E. (1954). *Clinical versus statistical prediction: A theoretical analysis and a review of the evidence.* Minneapolis: University of Minnesota Press.

Messick, S. (1995). Validity of psychological assessment: Validation of inferences from persons' responses and performances as scientific inquiry into score meaning. *American Psychologist, 50,* 741–749.

Organ, D. W., & Ryan, K. (1995). A meta-analytic review of attitudinal and dispositional predictors of organizational citizenship behavior. *Personnel Psychology, 48,* 775–802.

Sawyer, J. (1966). Measurement and prediction, clinical and statistical. *Psychological Bulletin, 66,* 178–200.

Schippmann, J. S. (1999). *Strategic job modeling: Working at the core of integrated human resources.* Mahwah, NJ: Lawrence Erlbaum Associates.

Sternberg, R. J., Wagner, R. K., Williams, W. M., & Horvath, J. A. (1995). Testing common sense. *American Psychologist, 50,* 912–927.

Thornton, G. C., III, & Byham, W. C. (1982). *Assessment centers and managerial performance.* New York: Academic.

II

Additional Issues
Affecting Practice

7

Legal, Professional, and Ethical Issues

The practice of individual assessment is not conducted in a vacuum; there are external considerations, such as legal, professional, and ethical guidelines, to consider. This chapter addresses the external issues relevant to the assessment process and, where possible, we offer additional guidance or suggestions that complement, and are consistent with, existing legal standards and published guidelines. In these discussions, we offer ideas, options, and some choices for assessors to consider in their individual assessment practice. Please note that the specific ideas and options presented here are not exhaustive. There may well be other equally appropriate alternatives to consider, of a legal, professional, or ethical nature, within the specific context of each unique assessment delivery situation.

LEGAL ISSUES

From the perspective of the *Uniform Guidelines for Employee Selection Procedures*, (1978), any system that is used for employee selection or promotion, including individual assessment, is considered to be a test. As such, individual assessment is expected to be consistent with federal, state, and local employment laws. Depending on the employer's size, location, and type of business, a variety of laws may apply. Applicable statutes and executive orders include (but are not limited to):

- Civil Rights Act, Title VII (1964)
- Civil Rights Act (1991)
- Executive Order No. 11246 (1978)
- Age Discrimination in Employment Act (1967)
- Rehabilitation Act (1973)
- Americans with Disabilities Act (1990)
- Pregnancy Discrimination Act (1978)

Federal EEOC laws and executive orders apply to the majority of employers. Very small organizations (i.e., less than 15 employees) and religious organizations are exempt under federal law. Federal contractors, including financial institutions, are required to comply with the affirmative action provisions set forth in Executive Order No. 11246 and enforced by the OFCCP. Finally, there are numerous state and local laws that may touch on employee selection.

However, the primary concern for the individual assessment practitioner is federal law. Interpretive guidance for Title VII is found in a federal document, *The Uniform Guidelines on Employee Selection Procedures* (1978). This document addresses issues of test validity, record keeping, and procedure that affect personnel decision making.

The purpose behind all of these laws, regulations, guidelines, executive orders, and court cases is to ensure that employees are selected for their ability to perform the job—not on the basis of extraneous or irrelevant factors such as gender, race, age, national origin, or religion. As discussed in previous chapters of this book, the goal of individual assessment is to identify individuals who can perform a job, without eliminating talented applicants for non-job-related reasons. Thus, a competent individual assessment practitioner should be in legal compliance. However, there may well come a time when the results of an assessment must be legally defended, that is, the practitioner may be required to establish the validity and job relatedness of the assessment process. Remember, not only is the individual assessment process comprised of individual tests, but the process itself—in total—is viewed as a test.

At this point then, the discussion turns to the validity of the process. *Validity* can be defined as the best approximation to the truth or falsity of inferences and predictions based on some application or predictor (Guion, 1998; Schmitt & Landy, 1993). In this instance, validity is established if the assessment process is job related and if the results of assessments predict a criterion such as job performance or other qualified criteria. Furthermore, there are different approaches for investigating and establishing the truth or falsity of inferences from an applicant or predictor. Although an extended discussion of the various approaches for addressing the validity of question is not appropriate here, it is useful to briefly review the three major aspects of validity covered in the *Uniform Guidelines* (1978).

- Criterion validity   Criterion validity is the type of validity that most often comes to mind when people talk about the concept. This approach requires that a test or predictor be significantly associated with a criterion (i.e., job-related work outcomes). Take another look at Fig. 1.1 in chapter 1.

- Content validity   In this approach, the goal is to logically establish that test content completely assesses the skills needed to perform the job and that it closely resembles what a person would actually do on the job.

- Construct validity   Construct validity is more abstract and all encompassing than the previous two approaches. It establishes the usefulness of a predictor in measuring an individual's possession of job-related characteristics or traits. To be valid, the characteristic must be shown to be essential for doing the job effectively.

In the individual assessment practice, the assessor does not make the final decision. Instead, a recommendation is made to the client after the report has been prepared and delivered. However, this by no means absolves practitioners from their obligation to confirm the validity of the assessment process, employing one or another strategy, as discussed in chapters 1 and 3 and reiterated here. In actual practice, the individual assessment process requires a unique and unconventional validation strategy that defies conventional outcome evaluation. This idea was originally introduced in chapter 1 and is expanded on here.

There are multiple lines of evidence that may be used to support the assessment process or respond to a challenge. First, though difficult, it is possible to rely on traditional empirical validation evidence (i.e., criterion-related research). The difficulty stems from the nature of the situation in which individual assessment is typically used (i.e., situations where few people perform the work in question and where the applicant flow is limited). In these situations, it is difficult, if not impossible, to generate the research sample sizes necessary to conduct a conventional criterion-related validation study, although in some settings, this may, over time, be possible (see, e.g., Vinchur, 1993).

In the absence of a solid research effort, the second most important line of evidence comes from a sound job modeling effort. Being able to clearly identify the important job-related work activities and competencies as a result of a logical analysis and modeling process and then using these results to guide the structure of the assessment is the essential basis for establishing the content validity of the assessment process.

A third line of evidence comes from all the research and data available concerning the usefulness of various tests and everything that is known about the base rate of validity for various measures (e.g., Barrick & Mount, 1991; Hunter & Hunter, 1984; Schmitt, Gooding, Noe, & Kirsch, 1984; Tett, Jackson, & Rothstein, 1991). This includes research supporting the use of interview information (e.g., McDaniel et al., 1988) and, specifically, research indicating that employment interviews that involve questions based on a formal review of the job predict future job performance better than interviews that do not (Wiesner & Cronshaw, 1988). As discussed in chapter 3, there is convincing evidence of a significant base rate of validity to paper-and-pencil tests and other measurement procedures in different organizational settings and with different employee groups.

A fourth line of evidence links the second and third lines together. This evidence involves what is known about the ability of an assessment professional to examine the requirements of a job (i.e., construct validity) and make meaningful decisions regarding the tests and scales to be built into the assessment protocol (i.e., drawing on the base-rate validity of the specific measures). Though not extensive, there are both direct and indirect evaluations of this test and scale selection process. As discussed in chapter 3, this research suggests that, in the absence of criterion-related data to guide test selection (i.e., Steps 4 through 8 of Fig. 1.1, which outline the traditional criterion validation strategy), a trained and knowledgeable assessment specialist can provide comparable estimates of test validity in specific situations.

Now, after all this discussion, the fact is that there has been little activity in terms of practice litigation with reference to individual assessment. The exception to this general trend is the legal challenges emanating from the practice of clinical psychologists who are conducting assessment-like activities in the area of police officer selection, where purely clinical tools are being used to make selection decisions. Where Industrial and Organizational (I/O) psychologists are concerned, we are not aware of a single Title VII-based legal suit. This should not lead to the assumption that individual assessment is immune from challenge, just that suits are less likely to occur.

Undoubtedly, one of the factors that has reduced the likelihood of a legal challenge harkens back to the fact that individual assessment is an individualized process. Again, in individual assessment practice, applicants are identified, one at a time, assessed and evaluated, one at a time, and a decision is made at the individual case level. In contrast, in more conventional pre-employment selection procedures, there are often policies and procedures that involve or require identifying multiple candidates for a single position, which could then lead to an order of merit register in which the top candidate is selected first. In the more typical practice, decisions are made one case at a time until the process is completed. The order-of-merit paradigm exists primarily in public service organizations, where there is a historical precedent for competitive selection going back to the early history of the civil service. In recent years, however, there has been increasing acceptance of construct-based selection measures, such as personality tests. This development can also lead to a commingling of the mechanical and clinical procedures.

An additional factor possibly explaining the paucity of legal challenges is the personal nature of the individual assessment process. Candidates typically receive explanations about the process and how is it job related and, often, receive feedback and have the opportunity to ask questions. These factors may contribute to candidates' perception of the fairness of the process, which, in turn, makes it less probable that candidates will look to the legal system for redress (Goldman, 2001).

Of course, by aggregating across numerous individual assessments over time, it is possible to conduct criterion-related research that does mirror a traditional validation approach. As noted in chapter 1, efforts to conduct this type of research are few, dated, and flawed, though generally favorable. Although this base of information does little to support a specific assessment program, it does provide some broad level of support for the practice in general.

In terms of on-the-ground practice, there are a number of specific issues that should be noted. For example, in chapter 4, we presented the *dos* and *don'ts* in assessment interviewing. It is worth mentioning again the need to be responsible in this area. Usually, job-related aspects are safe to explore. Straying too far from the job modeling results, or into areas about family life, health, religion, financial status, and so forth, is asking for trouble.

Similarly, as noted in chapter 6, assessors must not get sloppy with their language in the written report. Actually, they should also be careful about comments in their file notes as well. All these materials are potentially discoverable documents in a legal challenge. As such, it is essential to avoid report comments or assessor notes that refer to family life, health, religion, gender, ethnicity, or age stereotypes. For example, rather than a reference to an assessee's "younger years" in the report, comments could be worded in terms of the person's "early career." Many assessors, when interviewing multiple candidates in a single day, jot down a brief description to later remind themselves of who is who; again, notes would read better as "the individual in the pink golf shirt" than as "the heavy-set middle-aged woman."

Another clear no-no is making adjustments or corrections to test scores or final assessment ratings on the basis of race, religion, gender, or ethnic background. One result of the Civil Rights Act of 1991 was to eliminate the practice of making score adjustments on the basis of protected class status.

PROFESSIONAL ISSUES

Closely aligned with our discussion of legal issues is the presentation of professional practice issues. There are several documents in particular that provide relevant source material for those practicing individual assessment. First and foremost, the *Standards for Educational and Psychological Testing*, published by the American Educational Research Association, American Psychological Association, and the National Council on Measurement in Education (1999), provide detailed criteria for evaluating tests, testing practices, and the measurement of the effects of test use. As such, the *Stan-*

dards provide a frame of reference for identifying and addressing many of the psychometric issues associated with best practice in testing.

The *Principles for the Validation and Use of Personnel Selection Procedures* (1987), published by the Society for Industrial and Organizational Psychology (SIOP), is another important reference document. The *Principles*, which are currently being revised and updated by a SIOP task force, present this professional society's official statement concerning procedures for conducting validation research and employee selection. The *Principles* are intended to be consistent with the APA *Standards* (1999), though there are some confusing disconnects. The much anticipated revision of the *Principles* is designed to eliminate these areas of confusion and to provide a significantly more modern look at best practice in employee decision making related to selection, promotion, placement, and other personnel actions. Nevertheless, these two documents do present a consistent view that testing and assessment interventions should be reliable and valid.

The *Test User Qualifications* (Eyde, Moreland, Robertson, Primoff, & Most, 1988) is a third document frequently consulted by assessment practitioners. These guidelines refer to the combination of knowledge, skills, abilities, training, experience, and practice credentials that the APA recommends for the responsible use of psychological tests. The purpose of the *User Qualifications* is to inform test users, individuals involved in providing training to eventual test users, regulatory and credentialing bodies, and the public about the basic test user qualifications in an effort to promote high professional standards in practice. A useful executive summary of these guidelines has recently been published (Turner, DeMers, Fox, & Reed, 2001).

A final document that may have relevance for some assessors is the Society for Human Resource Management's (SHRM) *Code of Ethical and Professional Standards in Human Resource Management* (SHRM, 2002). Although SHRM does not go as far as either APA or SIOP in providing specific guidelines for ethical conduct, the *Code* is quite clear that SHRM members are expected to collect and use personnel information in an ethical, professionally responsible manner.

This leads us to the concrete question of who is competent to assess. The practice of individual assessment, just as any other job, requires that the practitioner possess a specific array of competencies in order to do the job adequately and responsibly. The view advocated here is that the assessment process can actually be conducted at several levels. It should be apparent that within the broad category of assessment there is a progression ranging from basic and fairly straightforward procedures to the complex assessments requiring higher levels of expertise. Generally, the more complex the assessment operations and activities the assessor plans to use and implement, the greater will be the need for expertise based on education, training, and experience.

Let us expand on this point just a bit. In the process of selection, interpreting a set of test scores to arrive at a final evaluative judgement constitutes, by definition, an individual assessment operation. In specific operational terms, this can be characterized as a sequence in which a single test score leading to an action may constitute a decision-making procedure. When using a comparative frame of reference (norm tables or an expectancy table), a test administered to one individual on one occasion in isolation may constitute an individual assessment practitioner activity. Certainly, when two tests have been administered and a composite score is derived, leading to an action, this might also define an individual assessment practitioner action. The fact is, however, that in both the first and second cases, operations are typically handled in an objective manner that may also constitute a mechanical data collection and data handling procedure. However, when there are two tests and additional information is collected about the individual, leading to a decision about or evaluation of the individual, and a composite rating or score is calculated leading to action, there is definitely an individual assessment.

What was just described is a breakdown of the decision-making algorithm and, from this point forward, it is definitely an individual assessment. As the complexity of the job content and competency models increases, the demand for assessor competency increases as well. In reality, there are many individuals, both in organizations and in private practice, who are conducting individual assessment, using procedures all the way from the simplest to the most complex and exhaustive assessment procedures. For the most part, these individuals have been trained in industrial or organizational psychology or in clinical or counseling psychology and hold the terminal degree (PhD, EdD, or PsychD). Most, though not all, also hold a license (Ryan & Sackett, 1992). Many professionals believe that the practice of individual assessment must be limited to those who hold the PhD (or other terminal degree), preferably in the field of I/O psychology.

However, there are other individuals, often with a terminal degree (PhD or DBA), whose expertise and training is in a field such as management, perhaps specifically in organization behavior or human resource management. These individuals are successfully using the methods and procedures that individual assessment practitioners have developed and are currently using them in their business activities. Thus, we believe that there is a role for practitioners who possess other relevant education, training, and experience. By providing training in the individual assessment methods and procedures for practitioners, it is our view that the capabilities of these individuals can be enhanced so that they are competent to conduct individual assessments. Furthermore, the assumption that only a select elite should and can have access to tests and test scores is simply not supportable. Traditionally, human resource (HR) professionals have been the users of assessment results, making decisions on the basis of these reports, but have not been seen as having the expertise themselves to generate the assessment itself. To this point, many HR professionals hold master's degrees—the degree held by psychological examiners who administer tests and interpret test scores and profiles in the

clinical setting. Moreover, many of these HR professionals hold certification and belong to organizations, such as SHRM, with a prescribed code
of ethical and professional conduct.

In an effort to provide some guidance in this area, we offer the individual
assessment practitioner taxonomy of competencies in Table 7.1. This model
of the competency requirements for individual assessors is derived from the
comprehensive job analysis work conducted under the auspices of SIOP and
reported in a symposium presentation and report (Prien & Macey, 1984).
There is every reason to believe that this model remains relevant and can be
used to guide professional activities today.

In terms of licensing the practice of individual assessment, there are no
simple answers. All things considered, there is no reason to deny or limit responsible and conscientious persons from performing individual assessment
practices as they are broadly described in this text. From a practical standpoint, the assessment of these professional competencies can be used by an
individual or a qualified colleague to guide self-assessment and as a means to
foster individual remedial development.

The issue of some form of certification or licensing control has been
around for many years. Unfortunately, there appears to be no clear-cut, definitive specification of precepts to guide various practitioners. Historically,
SIOP has taken the position that I/O psychologists should not have to be licensed. However, because of concern in recent years about state practice
laws, which have the potential to restrict some of the assessment practices of
SIOP members, the society is reevaluating its current position.

At times in the distant past, a number of barriers were established and
maintained to limit the practice of testing and assessment. One of the methods used to curtail practice was through test publishers who were self-ap-
pointed gate keepers. Some publishers still require users to provide evidence
of general qualifications, but the point-of-sale barrier is no longer practically
feasible. Another, and possibly more potent, vehicle is the copyright provision (although that, too, can be circumvented). The fact is that the only barriers to testing and assessment are the APA professional and ethical
standards, which prohibit—selectively—classes of individual assessor pro-
prietors who advertise service for a fee. Moreover, only the specific title of
"Psychologist" is protected. It seems unlikely that there will be an end to the
conflict anytime soon, particularly in view of the partisan parties at interest
to economic rewards.

Finally, one of the basic and most powerful deterrents to incompetent or
unethical practice is simply the cost associated with failure. Purchasers of
service are the most vocal and demanding critics of service providers, because they have the most to lose in the employment or organization development activity. The purchaser of competently provided service is the user
who gains and profits from the quality of work of the service provider. In the
long run, it is the forces in the marketplace then that provide control of individual assessment practice.

TABLE 7.1

Individual Assessment Competencies

1. Job modeling

    - Skill in inferring specific knowledge, skills, and/or abilities for varying levels of performance for a specific job function

    - Knowledge of techniques used to assess individuals' job-related competencies

    - Knowledge of strengths and weaknesses of alternative job modeling procedures in relation to application purposes

    - Knowledge of techniques used to write work activity descriptors content or behaviorally stated competency descriptors

    - Skill in conducting job modeling research to identify performance standards and behaviors for characterizing job competencies

    - Knowledge of the relationship between job content and the factors used in defining and characterizing job competency content

    - Knowledge of how business is conducted, including organization structure, business functions, and individual job roles

    - Knowledge of business and organization practices, including organization mission, business strategies, business philosophy, and tactics in business development

    - Knowledge and understanding of organization structure and organization philosophy in the business setting as it relates to individual assessment practice and requirements

2. Validity and validation research

    - Skill in judging and evaluating the usefulness of criterion measures

    - Knowledge of the factors involved in or contributing to adverse impact of a personnel decision-making procedure

    - Knowledge of the standards for validation research outlined in the APA *Guidelines* and SIOP *Principles*, the methodologies involved, and their intended applications

    - Knowledge of the limitations of research findings in terms or research design and/or statistical analysis

    - Knowledge of the content, interpretation, and application of the *Uniform Guidelines on Employee Selection Procedures* and other related regulations

    - Knowledge of the techniques involved in conducting validation research

    - Knowledge of performance evaluation criteria and standards for skillled performance

(continued on next page)

TABLE 7.1 *(continued)*
Individual Assessment Competencies

- Knowledge of the sources of individual, group, and organization performance and effectiveness criteria

- Skill in integrating information from several sources and applying the information to research problems and explanatory models

- Knowledge of criterion development methods and processes to use in performance evaluation for management or higher level technical job content

3. Tests and measurement

  - Knowledge of methods for assessing reliability and validity of items within an instrument

  - Knowledge of the procedures and techniques for construction and standardization of tests as selection procedures

  - Skill in applying the design, sampling, and statistical requirements of a validation model in validation research

  - Knowledge of psychometric principles, research results, and practices for the construction, standardization, and evaluation of measurement of individual differences

  - Knowledge of statistical techniques used to assess the reliability and validity of instruments, including inventories, tests, or questionnaires for a specific application

  - Knowledge of physiological, psychomotor, cognitive, and affective individual differences and their measurement properties and problems

  - Knowledge of the characteristics, strengths and weaknesses, and methodologies of scaling techniques used in the measurement of human attitudes, opinions, personality, and so forth

  - Skill in analyzing and evaluating technical problems and issues within the context of legal requirements and regulations

  - Skill in organizing a research study to establish the validity of a decision-making procedure

  - Knowledge of factors in personnel research settings that affect research operations and results

4. Data collection and analysis

  - Skill in analyzing and categorizing information gathered through interviews or surveys

  - Skill in characterizing and sequencing interview questions and techniques to obtain job-related information for applicant decision-making purposes

- Skill in evaluating the practicality, feasibility, and usefulness of interviews, questionnaires, and checklists for data collection

- Knowledge of the factors that affect sampling procedures in the process of collecting data for surveys, normative data, or population statistics

- Skill in recognizing and evaluating the effects of system/situational noise in assessment measurement practices

- Skill in assessing and evaluating the implications of uniqueness in idiosyncratic interpretation of assessment data

5. Occupation information analysis

   - Knowledge of occupation-related education and training practices, resources and individual options for acquiring qualifications

   - Knowledge of the principles of human learning as related to individual and group formal training and on-the-job training

   - Knowledge of the impact of experiential and social learning on human performance behavior in organization/work settings

   - Knowledge of group dynamics and processes that explain individual and group behavior and provide the rational for constructive actions

6. Testing and assessment practice

   - Skill in developing and organizing test administration and scoring procedures

   - Knowledge of assessment instruments available for determining vocational interests, aptitudes, and skills

   - Skill in interpreting results of assessment instruments used to determine vocational interests, aptitudes, and skills

   - Knowledge of techniques and procedures to be used in assessment operations

   - Knowledge of the situational and in situ factors for contingencies that limit or distort assessee performance

   - Knowledge of the alternative options for conducting individual assessment and applying multitrait/multimethod paradigms to evaluate individual assessment validities

   - Knowledge of the in situ factors that contribute to error in judgment in the individual assessment decision-making process

   - Knowledge of the demographic and cultural factors that limit the accuracy of judgement in the individual assessment practice

   - Knowledge and understanding of the evolutionary changes in different work activities and the associative individual difference characteristics that impact individual and group performance

(continued on next page)

TABLE 7.1 (continued)
Individual Assessment Competencies

7. External and professional standards

    •   Skill in identifying and defining the specific behaviors of a psychologist that deviate from professional and ethical standards

    •   Ability to analyze and evaluate the actions and activities of others in relation to the principles and standards of professional ethics

    •   Knowledge of professional standards that may be applied to the practice of Industrial/Organizational Psychology

    •   Knowledge and awareness or appreciation of cross- or multidiscipline conflicts that contaminate individual assessment practice

8. Counseling—ineffective performance

    •   Knowledge of the etiology and manifestations of personal maladjustment as related to individual and group functioning in organization settings

    •   Knowledge of the principles and techniques of employee coaching for effective performance

    •   Knowledge of symptoms displayed by people with marital problems, drug abuse, alcoholism, emotional problems, depression, and psychotic tendencies

    •   Knowledge of the affective and behavioral signs of individual-environmental stress

    •   Skill in sequencing and timing individual interventions to initiate adaptive constructive responses and to mitigate performance deficiencies

    •   Skill in accommodating mitigating conditions or circumstances in the individual assessment process leading to personnel decisions

SPECIFIC ETHICAL ISSUES

Ethical practice in the individual assessment arena is predicated on understanding and finding guidance in the legal and professional guidelines discussed previously. For example, it would clearly be unethical to use tests of dubious psychometric quality in an assessment protocol. However, ethical practice in an assessment does warrant some additional discussion. Why? In short, the answer is that ethical issues in this context are already complex and are becoming even more challenging in an era of global work settings and Internet-everything. Although it is not possible to address every issue, we would like to address a few common ones.

To begin with, there are ethical issues that arise in the course of conducting the assessment—the testing and the interview. First, it is reasonable to expect practitioners to protect assessees' confidentiality. This includes limiting scoring keys, examples, completed tests, reports, and notes to those who have a legitimate need for access, and taking reasonable precautions to ensure that confidential material remains confidential. This is a very basic ethical responsibility, one that is basic to both psychology (Lowman, 1998) and HR management (SHRM, 2001).

Who should do the testing? The vast majority of individual assessments use paper-and-pencil instruments, as opposed to projective instruments. Thus, there is no practical or ethical reason that a member of the office support staff cannot score and perhaps even administer the tests. If this is the case, it is critical that the assessor thoroughly train the individual, focusing on the need for consistency in administration and care in scoring. A trained and experienced clerical test administrator is a valuable resource to the assessment practitioner. Often, especially with lower level assessments, assessees reveal more information to the examiner or behave differently with the examiner than they would with the assessor.

It should be noted that there is some history indicating that the fine line between trained support staff and assessors who are professionally qualified has been crossed on occasion, with disastrous results. In a very busy practice, there are instances known to us where test administration, test scoring, and the interpretation of results have been taken over by otherwise well-intentioned paraprofessionals. Furthermore, we know of instances where students in practicum settings have become quite confident that they can conduct assessments for entry-level positions and, with the approval of the business principal, have done so. These instances represent an unquestionably unethical practice and it becomes particularly troublesome when it is apparent that it is a naive student of the craft who is essentially being conned and led to believe that he or she is competent to perform a full-fledged assessment.

There is no doubt that there are individuals with a bachelor's degree and a major in psychology or business who have a considerable accumulation of information, sufficient to carry the masquerade to the point of being dangerous. There are a number of sources of information, such as texts by Lyman (1971) on test scores and the article by Green (1981) that provide support, albeit superficial, that could lead individuals to engage in practice activities for which they are not qualified. On the other hand, we have conducted validation research projects that led to the development of testing programs in large organizations where we trained individual personnel to administer testing programs, but where the procedure was automated and mechanical decision-making procedures were established.

These are legitimate procedures and should not be confused with the *wannabes* who want to go it on their own.

We should also make a quick note about the importance of an assessment chaperonage. It is wise to have a second person in the office facility during the testing and interviewing in addition to the assessor, especially if the candidate and assessor are of different genders. Although incidents are extremely rare, it is always better to prevent any possibility of misconstruing or misunderstanding the dynamics of the social or business encounter.

In a broader sense, the assessor's ethical responsibility is to ensure that both the client and the assessee are treated fairly and that each party benefits from the assessment. The assessor's job is to help the client get as much use as possible from the assessment, for whatever decision or decisions that the client has to make. The purpose is always to make sure that the client gets maximum value from the assessment process. In any individual assessment, the assessor needs to make sure that the client understands the relevance of assessment information. At the same time, the client needs to understand the nature of the assessment process, including what the individual assessment can and cannot accomplish. It is critical that the assessor be honest with the client, making no guarantees about the assessment results. Some people change over time, others work to make a favorable impression, and yet others lie. The assessment process, no matter how thorough or how skilled the assessor, is not infallible. Moreover, individuals who have been successful in one work setting or position may not be successful in a different work setting or position.

The assessor's responsibilities to the candidate or assessee, though different from responsibilities to the client, are equally important. In the assessment process, decisions affecting the candidate are made and the procedure requires a certain amount of the candidate's time and effort. The assessor should explain the process fully, accurately, and understandably to the candidate. There are several reasons for this. First, it is simply ethical practice to tell candidates what they can expect, especially given that many candidates are apprehensive or even fearful. Second, candidates and clients deserve every chance to perform at their best. Although it is rare, a high degree of stress or apprehension can have quite a strong negative impact on an individual's performance in the assessment setting.

Candidates are entitled to feedback about their assessment, even if they do not receive a copy of the actual report. Finally, candidates need to have an opportunity to ask questions and, if need be, to question, challenge, or add to the assessor's interpretations and judgments.

The comprehensive and overriding *Ethical Principles of Psychologists* and *Code of Conduct* (American Psychological Association, 1992, 2001) pertain to all psychologists in the practice of individual assessment. These principles have compelling influence on applied practices, but do not extend to other professional organizations such as SHRM, whose members have a vested interest in the individual assessment practice. Likewise, there are numerous other professional organizations at the national, state, and local levels whose members have practices that overlap with APA principles. Thus, with reference to ethical principles, no single body can claim sovereign domain rights to the practice of individual assessment.

REFERENCES

American Educational Research Association, American Psychological Association, & National Council on Measurement in Education. (1999). *Standards for educational and psychological testing.* Washington, DC: American Educational Research Association.

American Psychological Association. (1992). Ethical principles of psychologists and code of conduct. *American Psychologist, 47,* 1587–1611.

American Psychological Association. (2001, February). Ethical principles of psychologists and code of conduct: Draft for comment. *The Monitor on Psychology, 32*(2), 77–89.

Barrick, M. R., & Mount, M. K. (1991). The big five personality dimensions and job performance: A meta-analysis. *Personnel Psychology, 44,* 1–26.

Eyde, L. D., Moreland, K. L., Robertson, G. J., Primoff, E. S., & Most, R. B. (1988). *Test user qualifications: A data-based approach to promoting good test use.* Washington, DC: American Psychological Association.

Goldman, B. M. (2001). Toward an understanding of employment discrimination claiming: An integration of organizational justice and social information processing. *Personnel Psychology, 54,* 361–386.

Green, B. F. (1981). A primer of testing. *American Psychologist, 36,* 1001–1011.

Guion, R. M. (1998). *Assessment, measurement, and prediction for personnel decisions.* Mahwah, NJ: Lawrence Erlbaum Associates.

Hunter, J. E., & Hunter, R. F. (1984). Validity and utility of alternate predictors of job performance. *Psychological Bulletin, 96,* 72–98.

Lowman, R. L. (1998). *The ethical practice of psychology in organizations.* Washington, DC: American Psychological Association.

Lyman, H. B. (1971). *Test scores and what they mean.* Englewood Cliffs, NJ: Prentice-Hall.

McDaniel, M. A., Whetzel, D. L., Schmidt, F. L., Hunter, J. E., Mauer, S., & Russell, J. (1988). The validity of employment interviews: A review and meta-analysis. *Journal of Applied Psychology, 79*(4), 599–616.

Prien, E. P., & Macey, W. H. (1984, August). *Multi-domain job analysis of the industrial-organizational psychologist job.* Paper presented at the American Psychological Association Convention, Toronto, Canada.

Ryan, A. M., & Sackett, P. R. (1992). Relationships between graduate training, professional affiliation, and individual psychological assessment practices for personnel decisions. *Personnel Psychology, 45,* 363–387.

Schmitt, N., Gooding, R. Z., Noe, R. A., & Kirsch, M. (1984). Meta-analysis of validity studies published between 1964 and 1982 and the investigation of study characteristics. *Personnel Psychology, 37*, 407–422.

Schmitt, N., & Landy, F. J. (1993). The concept of validity. In N. Schmitt & W. Borman (Eds.), *Personnel selection in organizations* (pp. 275–309). San Francisco: Jossey-Bass.

Society for Human Resource Management. (2001). Four surveys and revised ethics code are released by SHRM. *HRFocus, 78*(8), 9.

Society for Human Resource Management. (n.d.). *SHRM code of ethical and professional standards in human resource management.* Retrieved September 24, 2002, from http://www.shrm.org/ethics/

Society for Industrial and Organizational Psychology. (1987). *Principles for the validation and use of personnel selection procedures* (3rd ed.). College Park, MD: Author.

Tett, R. P. Jackson, D. M., & Rothstein, H. (1991). Personality measures as predictors of job performance: A meta-analytic review. *Personnel Psychology, 44*, 703–742.

Turner, S. M., DeMers, S. T., Fox, H. R., & Reed, G. M. (2001). APA's *Guidelines for test user qualifications*: An executive summary. *American Psychologist, 56*(12), 1099–1113.

Uniform Guidelines on Employee Selection Procedures, 43 Fed. Reg. 38295–38309 (1978).

Vinchur, A. J. (1993). The prediction of predictability revisited: Differential predictability applied to managerial selection. *Educational and Psychological Measurement, 53*(4), 1085–1094.

Wiesner, W. H., & Cronshaw, S. F. (1988). A meta-analytic investigation of the impact of interview format and degree of structure on the validity of the employment interview. *Journal of Occupational Psychology, 61*, 275–290.

8

Final Thoughts
and Prognostications

The practice of individual assessment has a very nearly invisible past and is only sporadically discussed in the present, yet it is a very extensive area of professional practice. From a research and professional perspective, assessment is most closely aligned with the field of industrial and organizational (I/O) psychology. In fact, individual assessment is viewed as one of the 21 core competency areas of the I/O field (Prien & Macey, 1984; Turner, DeMers, Fox, & Reed, 2001), along with practice areas like personnel selection, performance appraisal, training and development, and organization analysis and development. However, whereas burgeoning literatures already exist in these other areas, there is virtually no research being conducted (or at least reported) in the area of individual assessment.

As has been mentioned in various places in previous chapters, the practice of individual assessment, though generally recognized, is still hidden in the closet. From our perspective, individual assessment must come out of the closet if the multitude of questions about the process and practice are ever to be answered by research and evaluation. It is this fundamental research that will be required in order to realize the full potential of individual assessment in the context of the identification and utilization of human resource talent. As it stands at the present time, individual assessment is generally hidden from view, or critique for that matter, and everyone believes that they are entitled to do it their own way. Furthermore, there are no published standards, though a parallel form of standardization was developed

187

with reference to the assessment center model, which has many similar facets or aspects (Bray & Thornton, 1989; Thornton & Byham, 1982).

Similarly, from an applied perspective, individuals practicing individual
assessment, either in their own organizations or as external consultants, are
frequently viewed as mystical priests or powerful, but somewhat shadowy,
clerics. It is very rare to see a clear, detailed description or display of their
work. Furthermore, there are few training programs or discussion groups designed to promote or share best practices. Of course, there have been several
half-day workshops sponsored by SIOP and a 2-day offsite workshop was
conducted by Prien, Schippmann, Hughes, and Sale (1991). In that single
2-day workshop, the individual assessment practice was, for the first time,
displayed in a comprehensive way that included not only the detailed process and procedures, but also assessment models and samples and the opportunity to develop and practice the acquired competencies.

In view of the dearth of published research, one might ask, "What is going
on here?" Have biased critical reviews like Martin Gross's *The Brain
Watchers* (1962) driven the practice under ground? Have uncertainties
about how to respond to a potential legal challenge created a universal desire to keep a low profile or are practitioners simply protecting a competitive
market space? More simply, are the practitioners just too busy conducting
assessments to spend the time and energy to conduct and report research?

Even more compelling are questions about the future of individual assessment practice. In terms of product life cycle concepts, has the awareness among
consumers reached the point of moving from the introduction stage to the
growth stage (Krell, 1981)? Will the surge of interest in management development and executive coaching create initiatives and thus create additional opportunities for individual assessment? Will advances in computer adaptive
testing and on-line administration change, or simply be incorporated into, the
existing structure (such as it is) and practice of individual assessment?

In 1998, Robert Guion commented bravely on the practice of individual
assessment, recognizing that, as a business, the practice very likely belies the
level of activity described in somewhat more formalized business settings.
Guion went on to say: "Little research on individual assessment has been reported, and most published reports are old. Nevertheless, individual assessment is alive and well as an area of professional practice, if not as an area of
research" (p. 631). In the footnote Guion continued:

> I recognize that individual assessment for personnel decisions is done all the
> time by people who are not psychologists. Trainers, managers, former
> schoolteachers, and others who are "nice people who get along well with
> others" assess candidates for various opportunities. For all I know, they may
> do it as well as or even better than psychologists, but the lack of systematic
> procedure is even more pronounced if we extend the field so widely. Ryan
> and Sackett (1987) restricted their definition to psychologists as the asses-

sors, and I do likewise rather than try to unravel the additional range of idiosyncratic procedures introduced by expanding it. (p. 631)

In our view, as long as the practice of individual assessment remains cloaked in secrecy, all efforts to improve, control, or even simply organize the practice are doomed and the result will be a stealth form of practice that continues to fly just below the radar screen of scholarly research and systematic review.

Although an official head count of active practitioners is not possible, it is reasonable to include all those instances of individual assessment where a measurement procedure (i.e., tests) is used for decision making in the $n = 1$ setting, as described by Sackett and Arvey (1993). This definition would then exclude only those settings where purely mechanical decisions are made based on validated test selection programs representing a large-scale sampling. All other instances, where a clinical decision is made, come under the umbrella of the individual assessment model. The defining feature or characteristic is that one person is assessed at a time, and the results of that idiosyncratic procedure are processed using an integrative strategy to yield a decision at the individual case level. In view of what appear to be voluminous test sales, there is indeed an enormous potential for individual assessment activity. About the only baffling notion here is why recognition of this practice activity appears to remain hidden from public view.

If one reads what Guion (1998) wrote with some care, there are literally thousands of people who are conducting what is basically individual assessment in business and industry today. This does not mean that one is entitled to identify individuals who are conducting individual assessments following some particular and peculiar set of beliefs that may constitute a lot of fiction: Neither I/O psychologists nor any other psychologists can police the world. As was stated elsewhere in this book, the best approach to dealing with these phenomena is via education, training, and practice. It is known that there are thousands of instruments designed to measure individual difference characteristics; these may be formal, informal, or simply scavenged from different magazines or Web sites. This is a sorry state of affairs, and we do not mean to imply that some form of licensing control should be used, but, to the extent possible, potential assessors, regardless of the level or facet of the job content model being examined, need to use the best tools and sources of information.

Thus, there should be no question that the individual assessment business is extensive. Furthermore, for all intents and purposes, the practice, which is most closely aligned with the field of I/O psychology, has been treated very much as an orphan child is treated by a mean stepmother. The practice of individual assessment has enormous potential, but it remains largely outside the scope of I/O or, more generally, outside of the practice of professional psychology. An important first step to resolving this situation would seem to be a comprehensive and generally accepted practice model.

As noted previously, the barriers to increased research in the area include self-preservation, proprietary interests, and time. In addition, there is the widely held belief that the practice does not lend itself to evaluative research. In the typical setting, the application of individual assessment practice will run the complete gamut from entry-level position candidates through senior-level executives. Confounding this paradigm is the variability in job type and occupational characterization that is related to the specific areas of competency, such as sales and marketing versus manufacturing versus administration, and so forth. A recent review by Highhouse (2002) elaborates upon this conundrum. Although he focused primarily on executive assessment, we would have to use all our fingers and toes to count the number of active consulting organizations who are known to be active in the individual assessment business. Furthermore, the Highhouse review was thorough, as far as it went, but he essentially stopped short of the key or critical research that underlies the IA practice.

What we have attempted to do in this book is to recognize the practice as a legitimate, widespread activity and to give it some of the technical and professional foundation that it has lacked in the past. To begin, a critical factor in conducting the individual assessment is to place it in an organizational context. The organization's values and goals will drive the purpose of the assessment and will have a strong influence on how decisions are made in designing and conducting the assessment. As discussed in previous chapters of this book, the purpose of the individual assessment ranges along a continuum, with pure selection on one end and pure development on the other end of the spectrum.

A significant hurdle to the evolution of the practice is the perception that individual assessment practice is somehow restricted to licensed individuals who are the only ones to be permitted access to available methods or procedures. Although there are restrictions that apply to various states' licensing agencies, those constraints do not apply within the private sector. Indeed, many individuals in general management positions are actively engaged in some level of assessment practice that is clearly incorporated in Guion's (1988) general definition. However, what is mentioned in some settings is the licensing of test instrument sales and materials as a means of control to represent partisan, self-serving interests.

One of the core issues that we have puzzled over and worried about until we have worn it down to a frazzle concerns the role of education and training prerequisites in using the tools that produce input information in individual assessment practice. We know from previous survey research that there is a very extensive practice of individual assessment, including those practitioners who may not have the benefit of extensive education or training in the area. Individuals in the human resource area have varying degrees of competence based on varying amounts of education, training, and experience, ranging from a zero base rate up to high levels of expertise. The only systematic treatment of this phenomenon, in terms of efforts to potentially enhance the utility of the practice, is represented by the work of Ann Marie Ryan and Paul Sackett (1987). This work was descriptive in nature, not evaluative, and was essentially limited to practice conducted by licensed professional I/O psychologists. However, as discussed, practice by I/O psychologists represents only the tip of the iceberg in terms of actual work activities. What is desperately needed is either draconian control, to prevent incompetent practice, or establishment of a program of training and development, to develop competencies among potential practitioners.

Furthermore, individual assessment should make use of the best sources of information about foundational subjects, and then use that information in the most appropriate way in the process of utilization of human talent. The kinds of information that go into the practice include what is conventionally thought of as the product of a job modeling effort, in terms of work activities, and individual difference characteristics, represented in terms of competencies. This information is then linked in some systematic way to characterizations of individual difference performance, otherwise known and labeled as criteria. We use the term *criteria* in the plural, because in the most appropriate model implied throughout the preceding chapters it is multidimensional and is best represented in all its complexity. The overriding element, though, is the appreciation of contextual variables somehow embedded or reflected in the organization character, mission, or culture climate. Although our treatise is that we are looking at these phenomena in behavioral terms, each facet of the process and processes is characterized somewhat differently. In this model, it is only when all facets of an individual assessment are completely identified, defined, and understood that the practice can be justified and rationalized. In short, the espoused position here is the same as that described years ago by Dunnette (1963), which is fundamental to the practice, except that Dunnette did not emphasize the $n = 1$ feature.

In practice and research on individual assessment, what should be remembered and accepted is that there is already a very comprehensive foundation of information available about the tools and procedures. What is probably the most fundamental database is already available and should be used; this is the base rate of validity of different individual difference measures with reference to various aspects of criterion measurement. There are a variety of meta-analyses of different facets of measurement. The general mental ability data by Schmidt, Hunter, Croll, and McKenzie (1983) and Schmidt, Gooding, Noe, and Kirsch (1984), which are the most comprehensive and compelling in this respect, are also supported by the work by Schippmann, Prien, and Katz (1990) on the in-basket and by Vinchur, Schippmann, Switzer, and Roth (1998) with reference to sales performance. There are, of course, other approaches and studies, such as projective techniques and measures and the work by Reilly and Chao (1982) on work sample tests. All these studies are linked to various aspects of the three-facet model that constitutes the foundation for individual assessment practice. These three facets are content and structure of work activities, content and structure of the competencies, and, finally, the very extensive array of performance behaviors linked to different levels of criterion performance.

Regardless of the licensing issue, a variety of human resource associates or staff personnel are, or can be, quite adequately trained to perform these activities. The fact is that anyone can have access to the typical paper-and-pencil tests commonly used at some level of expertise, except those instances where a service feature is added at a fee, where the service is regulated in private business. In other words, a private employer can legally conduct individual assessment activities without fear of violating a business ethic or legal guideline. The business ethic or professional guideline issue is only relevant when a service is offered to the public for a fee and the service provider is legally licensed.

Next, the practice of individual assessment does lend itself to systematic research and evaluation. The history of research and development on job analysis and modeling, along with research on individual difference measurement, is absolutely compelling. The fact that research data focused on the case level are not readily available appears to be a consequence of proprietary interests and lack of initiative among the practitioners with a felt need to publish. Note that, in a typical active individual assessment practice, it is quite possible to conduct from 5 to 20 individual assessments each month, possibly covering many different and unique job assignments. Thus, a more systematic research design is required, possibly an extension of the job component validity model. However, this would also require focusing attention on the criterion problem, which possibly could also be handled using the same analytical model. This in no way justifies our observation that the practice is flawed. There are numerous practitioners who are in possession of extensive databases and assessment algorithms, including criterion references based on the synthetic validity model, that remain hidden in research files and documents.

From a limited perspective, reviewing the results of meta-analytic studies could lead to the conclusion that the best, and perhaps the one and only, predictor of human performance effectiveness is a measure of g, or general intelligence. It is uniformly agreed upon that, if given a choice of only one measure, it would be a measure of g. This is probably the most practical and utilitarian characterization of individual difference characteristics. However, once the consequences of education, training, and experience are factored in, the phenomena (the multifaceted criterion construct) immediately beckon for more and better measurement. The question here, or the one that should be asked by assessors, is: "What do I need to know about an individual with reference to the different specific facets of the different models that we have described earlier in this book?" In the abstract, that is the issue raised by Messick (1995) in his discussion of psychological assessment.

Obviously, it is impractical to think in terms of a specific set of performance behaviors representing a criterion dimension for each of the models that we presented earlier in the book. We used three different models, ranging from 6 factors up to the 27 dimensions for the administrative competency model. This is, indeed, a very complex array of specifications and, realistically, it is imperative that we somehow systematize this total display and begin to examine the overlap among the different levels of definition and the different models. Just as we cannot be all things to all people, it would be impractical to deal with all of the individual competency dimensions represented by these models, multiplied by a number of different possible individual difference measures (tests) that could be used in the individual assessment process.

To systematize the individual assessment practice for research and development, we conducted a variety of factor analytic studies, using test dimensions as the database, to analyze dimensionality of measurement and to derive an overlapping set of competency models that reduce to about 10 factors. This work included five separate individual assessment databases collected from colleagues (each with more than 500 cases). Although the mix of assessment tests included in each database varied considerably, the factor analysis results of each clearly indicated a high degree of consistency. If the analysis is conducted at the item level, the result would be a much more complex set of dimensions, but that would have the appearance of an obsessive-compulsive approach to minutiae in terms of measurement and prediction.

In general, there are very extensive avenues available for trained, conscientious persons to conduct activities leading to a personnel decision. The notion that a license or some form of certification is required for approval of the activity, whether this decision be selectional, deselectional, or developmental in nature (the medical/legal model), leads to restrictions in the marketplace and serves to ensure protection of vested interests. Although there is certainly the possibility of corruption and harm in any human endeavor, the most realistic remedy and constructive influence is education and training. The philosophy espoused here is that there are relatively few settings or conditions that mandate official and coerced control. The licensing of human resource management practice activities, which includes individual assessment practice, is certainly no exception. The differentiation in the marketplace will provide the quality control via client feedback just as soon as the supply of trained and experienced talent exceeds the demand—thus, the most pragmatic answer is to educate and train more individual assessors.

One of the main issues following from the work we have done on developing an individual assessment model is the question of what one must know in order to conduct an individual assessment competently and effectively. This is an issue of assessor competencies and, as noted previously, we have developed a picture of this comprehensive data set in terms of three components: work activities, competencies, and the third facet, a much more extensive and comprehensive array of performance behaviors that characterizes the criteria one wishes to predict. One of the main sources of information here is the accumulated database characterizing performance behaviors at different levels of effectiveness across the entire dimensionality for a particular model. For example, for the management model consisting of 13 work activity dimensions, the different levels can be represented by the behaviorally anchored set of performance descriptors as a reference database. What needs to be known and understood is this complex model of work activities on one dimension, competencies on the other, and then probably 10 steps characterizing the performance behavior model in terms of a criterion array. This constitutes what an individual assessment practitioner needs to know in order to function effectively.

There is no question that people in the business of identifying and using human talent need to possess identifiable competencies, but the scope and array of the assessment talent database is extremely broad and needs to be identified, defined, and appropriately directed. A reasonable estimate of the potential head count of all partially to completely qualified HR professionals could easily exceed 20,000 individual practitioners. Even if this is an overestimate, application of this talent to the practice of assessment and the resulting improvement in selection could easily produce a significant increase in organization effectiveness, measured in profits and increased shareholder value (Pfeiffer, 1994, 1998).

There is a considerable amount of information available or, rather, questions that need to be addressed and resolved concerning the issues of cross-cultural approaches to individual assessment. What is not known are the answers to questions concerning the impact of language barriers, and also cultural barriers, on assessment practice. International organizations are conducting practice without constraints or restrictions but with apparent influence on domestic practice.

In addition, there are myriad questions about possible race and gender effects, standards for decision making for the different competency models, the use of cut scores, and, finally, the linkage of the individual assessment process to training and development. There is an age and experience issue as well and one that needs to be explored and handled in some way in order to make sense of the total system. The most egregious issue is the flagrant waste of talent attributable to underemployment in various sectors of the national economy. Continuation of discrimination practices that exist in the marketplace can only be labeled as unconscionable ignorance. Eventually, what is not known will be damaging.

What is known is that there is a conceptual base and logic to support individual assessment practice. The fundamental concept is clearly represented in the writings of Meehl (1954), Sawyer (1966), Trankell (1959), Messick (1965, 1975, 1985, 1995) and Matarazzo (1990). The assessment model can be described and characterized in terms of a system of work activities, competencies, and performance behaviors linked to different levels of criterion performance, with the fourth component being the individual test measurement array. It is imperative to develop the five-facet model system, which includes contextual features, to fully characterize what the individual assessment practitioner must do to conduct an individual assessment that is both rational and realistic. It is possible to muddle through this morass and develop a model that in some way allows an understanding of the process and procedure and thus of an individual. This process in terms of different sources of information is the result of scoring the work activity, competency requirements, the criterion dimensionality and level, and then, finally, the test scores.

One simple approach to learning what needs to be considered is the process of retranslation of test scores to both work activity dimensions and competency dimensions. That linkage information already exists in a number of different studies of performance behaviors linked to competency dimensions and performance behaviors by work activity dimensions. In order to complete this linkage matrix, it is necessary to link the test data model to both the work activity and the competency dimensionality. The conceptual structure is already well represented in the various criterion and content validation strategies, which, together with the extant databases, amply demonstrate that people behave and perform as expected at knowable levels of accomplishment.

What more is required? Prediction is an imperfect practice and, if by some purposeful endeavor general productivity can be enhanced in terms of one or another criterion measure, then researchers will have made a significant contribution to our society. It is not essential to have a measure of the ultimate criterion in every study, but only a conceptualization of some facet of value as Messick (1975, 1995) described in terms of his aims for psychological assessment.

However, moving forward, there are a variety of specific problems and ideas that require attention in the area of individual assessment. These ideas are not necessarily in any order of priority, but require a degree of attention in the context of the system that we have proposed.

1. In recent years, there has been increased interest in computerized testing (not computer adaptive testing) using internet-based delivery systems (Fowler, 1985). This is similar to the work that was originally produced by Vale, Keller, and Bentz (1986). During recent years, however, technology has advanced to the point that the use of statistical algorithms and perhaps artificial intelligence technology can be used to produce reports that bear considerable resemblance to reports composed by a single individual. Reports developed using this technology may represent the first step regarding the demise of the individual assessment practitioner, but would not replace the one-on-one or face-to-face contact between the individual client and the assessment practitioner service provider. The issue of context and performance, as well as interaction between the practitioner and the client, will give rise to questions concerning the final decision and action-based recommendation.

2. A related issue to computerized testing is the issue of sales and marketing of online services under the rubric of e-commerce. What has evolved from the development of information technology on the Internet is a commercialized practice of testing and assessment. At the

present time, the Internet communication system is relatively unregulated and, thus, becomes a delivery system for various "snake oil" marketing activities.

3. The structured interview as a source of information and data collection has a considerable history. In the individual assessment practitioner paradigm, the interview protocol is a measuring device or instrument to enhance what has been learned about the individual through the use of standardized testing or other measurement procedures. The history includes the scored patterned interview and other procedures going back over at least a 50-year period, but, in order to develop the individual assessment practitioner activity or paradigm, it would seem appropriate to begin structuring the interview so that there is a discernible linkage between the information gathered and the competency dimensions or constructs (Maurer & Russell, 1985). This would go a long way toward a more systematic evaluation of the assessment paradigm and development of criterion-related evidence of validity.

4. One of the developments in personality assessment using the Big Five constructs raises a number of questions. The Big Five instrument uses a self-description format (not a forced choice format) and thus there is an element of social desirability in the item response. Some of the linkage research represented in the work of Guion (1998) and enhanced by Wooten, Prien, and Prien (2000), Hughes and Prien (1989), and Vinchur, Prien, and Schippmann (1993) is relevant here in that, in the grand scheme of things, we would advocate linking together all four facets in the assessment test measurement model. Raymark, Schmit, and Guion (1997) and Sinclair and Michel (2001) established some of the relationship between the work activity analysis-based description of personality constructs and the more objective presentation of competencies. This requires further investigation in order to expand on the total system that leads to a more comprehensive understanding of the individual.

5. A thorn in the collective side of researchers is the lack of research on individual assessment. There is a paucity of research on the practice of individual assessment and there seems to be no interest in opening the door to introduce seasoned practitioners to potential researchers. What has been learned comes from a variety of piecemeal studies, including those by Albrecht, Glaser, and Marks (1964), Bartlett and Green (1966), DeNelsky and McKee (1969), Gilbert (1981), Gordon (1967), Guion (1961), Hilton, Bolin, Parker, Taylor, and Walker (1955), Mahoney, Jerdee, and Nash (1961), Miner (1970), Trankell (1959), and all the articles making up the Western Reserve University Studies (see Campbell, 1962, and Campbll, Otis, Liske, & Prien, 1962), as described in the Research Context section of chapter 1.

6. We have repeatedly discussed the assessor's ability to make judgments about other people, which we view as a construct in the assessment practice. We have referred to structured interviews, job analysis instru-

ments focused on work activities or on competencies, and the entire array of organization-related instrumentation to help guide the practice of judging others in the individual assessment paradigm. One should refer to the research by Taft (1955), Cronbach (1955), and Schmidt, Hunter, Croll, and McKenzie (1983) and examine the potential for development of the system. Furthermore, there is additional wisdom to appreciate in the writings by Holt (1958, 1970), Matarazzo (1990), Meehl (1954), Messick (1965, 1975, 1995), and Sawyer (1966).

7. One of the hidden issues in individual assessment is that of gender. Almost all individual assessment work done in the past was conducted by males, if only because the majority of professional work was done by males. I/O psychology, until recently, has been a male-dominated profession. Only in the last 10 years has there been a very visible presence of females as practitioners. If our paradigm in individual assessment is followed, one should find that assessor gender does not produce an effect, although it is known that in performance appraisal gender is a factor. This is evident, for example, in performance appraisal of police officer applicants.

8. An issue that requires some attention is that of resistance to training and education in relation to facilitating performance among certain segments of the population. There has been considerable interest in the past in reference to the hardcore unemployed, but there are several case studies that warrant and require some attention. This is an area of human performance where there is some involvement of criteria and also of factors that affect performance and the relationship between predictors and criteria.

9. In the broader sense, one of the essential issues in individual assessment is the concept of the criterion, particularly in terms of the different models. An assessor must have extensive knowledge and understanding of the various facets of performance variability, dimension by dimension, and in relation to the level and complexity of difficulty of the job. For various areas of the job or occupational spectrum, the relationship between criterion elements and contextual factors is very complex and dynamic. This is one of the elements in the five-component model that we have presented here, which needs some clarification and is part of the context of performance.

10. One of the areas of human performance is that which concerns culture variables. There is very little research on acculturation and the implications for human performance. It has been learned in recent years, through work with foreign nationals in the United States, that people do behave quite differently. The same is true for U. S. citizens who sojourn abroad and remain for various relatively short periods of time but become adapted to their host's culture. This whole phenomenon has received some attention, but not with respect to individual assessment models and paradigms.

11. An idea we have proposed in terms of education and training approaches for individual assessors is the exercise to study and learn about job content in terms of work activity, competency, performance behavior by level and effectiveness, the individual test measurement array, and, finally, contextual factors. This is the five-component model that we have discussed and it represents a possible training exercise in which assessors would acquire appreciation of the relationships among the five components of the model. This appreciation should enhance their effectiveness, as both assessors and predictors of the criterion. In this particular area, one of the potentially powerful tools available is the linkage procedure (Hughes & Prien, 1989; Vinchur, Prien, & Schippmann, 1993; Wooten, Prien, & Prien, 2000). This particular experimental design has not been used to the extent that it is available, although it is known that educated, trained, and experienced persons can conduct individual assessments and do so with accuracy. This is demonstrated by comparing mechanically produced predictions with idiosyncratic predictions derived through the individual assessment process. One test exercise that could be used to evaluate this research potential of the linkage operation would be to structure an assessment using the four facets of the measurement and then look for the interjudge reliability as an experimental procedure. In this approach, it is possible to collect data for four or five cases using a sample of cases, each a replication with repetition. The analytical strategy will be complex, but can use the inverse design and enter the data matrix using different entry points. The advantage of this design is the increased numerosity to reach statistical stability through imposed replication to enhance interpretability. A related and salient issue concerns the education, training, and experience requirements for the individual assessment practice. As we described previously, there are several levels of assessment ranging from the relatively direct, based on a relatively simple model, to the highly complex model. The entry-level expertise competencies can be acquired and employed by a broad range of individuals, but the more complex applications require greater expertise.

12. A final and very important issue is the diversity of measurement procedures and the concurrent uniqueness of practitioner and scientists. Practitioners appear to judge that they have little to gain via collaboration, and that each one has a unique method, procedure, or process to reach assessment conclusion. This is similar to the dynamics in studies of organization climate and culture and other similar measurement practice: The problem is lack of emphasis on replication. Uniqueness is good, replication is bad.

In conclusion, there are so many opportunities, so many questions to be answered, that the individual assessment journey will be a long one, and this is only a beginning.

REFERENCES

Albrecht, P. A., Glaser, E. D., & Marks, J. (1964). Validation of a multiple assessment procedure for managerial personnel. *Journal of Applied Psychology, 48,* 351–360.

Bartlett, C. J., & Green, C. G. (1966). Clinical prediction: Does one sometimes know too much? *Journal of Counseling Psychology, 13,* 267–270.

Bray, D., & Thornton, G. (1989). Guidelines and ethical considerations for assessment center operations. *Journal of Business and Psychology, 4*(2) 259–273.

Campbell, J. T. (1962). Assessments of higher-level personnel: I. Background and scope of the research. *Personnel Psychology, 15,* 57–74.

Campbell, J. T., Otis, J. L., Liske, R. E., & Prien, E. P. (1962). Assessments of higher-level personnel: II. Validity of the over-all assesment. *Personnel Psychology, 15,* 63–74.

Cronbach, L. J. (1955). Processes affecting scores on "understanding of others" and "assumed similarity." *Psychological Bulletin, 52,* 177–193.

DeNelsky, G. Y., & McKee, M. G. (1969). Prediction of job performance from assessment reports: Use of a modified Q-sort technique to expand predictor and criterion variance. *Journal of Applied Psychology, 53,* 439–445.

Dunnette, M. D. (1963). A modified model for test validation and selection research. *Journal of Applied Psychology, 47,* 317–323.

Fowler, R. D. (1985). Landmarks in computer assisted psychological assessment. *Journal of Consulting and Clinical Psychology, 53*(b), 748–759.

Gilbert, P. J. (1981). An investigation of clinical and mechanical combination of assessment center data. *Journal of Assessment Center Technology, 4,* 1–10.

Gordon, L. V. (1967). Clinical, psychometric, and work-sample approaches in the prediction of success in Peace Corps training. *Journal of Applied Psychology, 51,* 111–119.

Gross, M. L. (1962). *The brain watchers.* New York: Random.

Guion, R. M. (1961). Criterion measurement and personnel judgments. *Personnel Psychology, 14,* 141–149.

Guion, R. M. (1998). *Assessment, measurement, and prediction for personnel decisions.* Mahwah, NJ: Lawrence Erlbaum Associates.

Highhouse, S. (2002). Assessing the candidate as a whole: A historical and critical analysis of individual psychological assessment for personnel decision making. *Personnel Psychology, 55,* 363–396.

Hilton, A. C., Bolin, S. F., Parker, J. W., Taylor, E. K., & Walker, W. B. (1955). The validity of personnel assessments by professional psychologists. *Journal of Applied Psychology, 39,* 287–293.

Holt, R. R. (1958). Clinical and statistical prediction: A reformulation and some new data. *Journal of Abnormal and Social Psychology, 56,* 1–12.

Holt, R. R. (1970). Yet another look at clinical and statistical prediction: Or is clinical psychology worthwhile? *American Psychologist, 25,* 337–349.

Hughes, G. L., & Prien, E. P. (1989). Evaluation of task and job skill judgments used to develop test specifications. *Personnel Psychology, 42*(2), 283–292.

Krell, T. C. (1981). The marketing of organizational development: Past, present, and future. *Journal of Applied Behavioral Science, 17*(3), 309–323.

Mahoney, T. A., Jerdee, T. H., & Nash, A. N. (1961). Predicting managerial effectiveness. *Personnel Psychology, 13*, 147–163.

Matarazzo, J. D. (1990). Psychological assessment versus psychological testing. *American Psychologist, 45*, 999–1017.

Maurer, S. D., & Russell, J. S. (1985, August). *Validity of the employment interview revisited: A meta-analysis of existing research.* Paper presented at the annual meeting of the Academy of Management, Boston.

Meehl, P. E. (1954). *Clinical versus statistical prediction: A theoretical analysis and a review of the evidence.* Minneapolis: University of Minnesota Press.

Messick, S. (1965). Personality measurement and the ethics of assessment. *American Psychologist, 20*, 136–142.

Messick, S. (1975). The standard problem: Meaning and values in measurement evaluation. *American Psychologist, 30*, 955–966.

Messick, S. (1985). Response to changing assessment needs: Redesign of the national assessment of educational progress. *American Journal of Education, 94*(1), 90–105.

Messick, S. (1995). Validity of psychological assessment. *American Psychologist, 50*, 741–749.

Miner, J. B. (1970). Psychological evaluations as predictors of consulting success. *Personnel Psychology, 23*, 393–405.

Pfeiffer, J. (1994). *Competitive advantage through people: Unleashing the power of the work force.* Boston: Harvard Business School Press.

Pfeiffer, J. (1998). *The human equation: Building profits by putting people first.* Boston: Harvard Business School Press.

Prien, E. P., & Macey, W. H. (1984, August). *Multi-domain job analysis of the industrial-organizational psychologist job.* Paper presented at the American Psychological Association Convention, Toronto, Canada.

Prien, E. P., Schippmann, J. S., Hughes, G. L., & Sale, F., Jr. (1991, June). *An introduction to individual assessment.* Paper presented at the Society for Industrial and Organizational Psychology workshop, Baltimore, MD.

Raymark, P. H., Schmit, M. J., & Guion, R. M. (1997). Identifying potentially useful personality constructs for employee selection. *Personnel Psychology, 50*, 723–736.

Reilly, R. R., & Chao, G. T. (1982). Validity and fairness of some alternative employee selection procedures. *Personnel Psychology, 35*, 1–62.

Ryan, A. M., & Sackett, P. R. (1987). A survey of individual assessment practices by I/O psychologists. *Personnel Psychology, 40*(3), 455–488.

Sackett, P. R., & Arvey, R. D. (1993). Selection in small N settings. In N. Schmitt, W. C. Borman, & Associates (Eds.), *Personnel selection in organizations* (pp. 418–447). San Francisco: Jossey-Bass.

Sawyer, J. (1966). Measurement and prediction, clinical and statistical. *Psychological Bulletin, 66*, 178–200.

Schippmann, J. S., Prien, E. P., & Katz, J. A. (1990). Reliability and validity of in-basket performance measures. *Personnel Psychology, 43*, 837–859.

Schmidt, F. L., Hunter, J. E., Croll, P. R., & McKenzie, R. C. (1983). Estimation of employment test validities by expert judgment. *Journal of Applied Psychology, 68*, 590–601.

Schmidt, N., Gooding, R. Z., Noe, R. A., & Kirsch, M. (1984). Meta-analyses of validity studies published between 1964 and 1982 and the investigation of study characteristics. *Personnel Psychology, 37*, 407–422.

Sinclair, R. R., & Michel, R. P. (2001, April). *A construct-oriented approach to modeling entry-level job performance.* Paper presented at the Society for Industrial and Organizational Psychology conference, San Diego, CA.

Taft, R. (1955). The ability to judge people. *Psychological Bulletin, 52*, 1–23.

Thornton, G. C., III, & Byham, W. C. (1982). *Assessment centers and managerial performance.* New York: Academic.

Trankell, A. (1959). The psychologist as an instrument of prediction. *Journal of Applied Psychology, 43*, 170–175.

Turner, S. M., DeMers, S. T., Fox, H. R., & Reed, G. M. (2001). APA's guidelines for test user qualifications: An executive summary. *American Psychologist, 56*(12), 1099–1113.

Vale, C. D., Keller, L. S., & Bentz, V. J. (1986). Development and validation of a computerized interpretation system for personnel tests. *Personnel Psychology, 39*(3) 525–542.

Vinchur, A. J., Prien, E. P., & Schippmann, J. S. (1993). An alternative procedure for analyzing job analysis results for content-oriented test development. *Journal of Business and Psychology, 8*(2), 215–226.

Vinchur, A. J., Schippmann, J. S., Switzer, F. S., & Roth, P. L. (1998). A meta-analytic view of predictors of job performance for sales people. *Journal of Applied Psychology, 83*(4), 586–597.

Wooten, W. A., Prien, E. P., & Prien, K. O. (2000, June). *The development of an integrated job task and competency model for clerical occupations.* Paper presented at the International Personnel Association Assessment Council (IPMAAC) conference, Arlington, VA.

Appendix A

Primer of Measurement Terms and Concepts

Individual assessment involves the use and application of measurement procedures to arrive at valid and defensible conclusions about people. For many I/O psychologists, these methods and procedures are as familiar as the back of their hands. However, for some practitioners, including people whose training is in human resource management or other specialties in psychology, the content may not be quite as familiar.

For this reason we have included a brief primer of measurement terms. Although the listing of tests in Table 3.1 is extensive, some of the definitions and terminology necessary for full understanding of testing and measurement may not be as familiar to the reader. Similarly, a full understanding of the ideas and conclusions described in the Research Context sections of the chapters may be improved after a careful reading of this appendix material.

The material that follows is in three parts. First, we present a glossary of measurement terms, arranged in a categorical sequence, to focus attention on the key measurement concepts and ideas. Second, we present a primer of statistical procedures and definitions, which is primarily technical in nature and of interest to those planning to engage in validation research. The third section is a review of the multitrait-multimethod approach to assessment.

GLOSSARY OF TERMS

Types of Tests

There is a wide variety of test types and each has its place in the individual assessment practice. Each type of test has a particular purpose and design that differentiates it from other types of tests in terms of application and use. There exist hundreds of specific measures, some of which are virtually identical to others, differing only in name or other details. Thus, two tests with identical norms may result, in application, in quite different results. Similarly, two tests with quite different names may give virtually identical results in application. Thus, test names are not themselves the tests—they are just identifying labels.

- *Ability test:*   Ability is the power to perform a mental or physical work behavior that results in an observable product. For example, an assessee may have the ability to provide constructive feedback to subordinates. In this instance, the result or product is a more effective subordinate. An ability test is designed to measure an individual's ability or abilities in a particular area, such as interpersonal relations, mathematics, or spatial reasoning.

- *Achievement test:*   An achievement test measures the level of accomplishment, knowledge, or skill that the individual has acquired through education, training, or experience and is able to display and/or demonstrate in a specific work activity. A test of an assessee's knowledge of good supervisory skills or a vocabulary test are both achievement tests.

- *Aptitude test:*   An aptitude test measures the combination of characteristics that indicates the capacity of an individual to develop proficiency in some skill after training. Aptitude does not imply competency; a person may have a high level of mechanical aptitude, yet not know which end of a screwdriver is the business end.

- *Battery test:*   A test battery is a group of several tests. The results of each test are of value individually and, when used in combination, produce a composite score. Individual tests can be aggregated using unit weights, standard scores, or differential weights (often based on the results of a more complex statistical analysis).

- *Cognitive tests:* Cognitive tests measure characteristics (cognitive factors) of the person that differentiate among individuals in terms of mental ability or intelligence. Cognitive factors may be *general* (*g*, or general ability) or *specific*, such as social intelligence, mechanical ability, or verbal ability.

- *Equivalent forms:* Equivalent forms are any of two or more forms (or versions) of a test that are usually (but not always) *standardized* on the same population and published at the same time. These forms are designed to be similar in item content and difficulty, so that scores on the forms will be similar. The standards for determining or demonstrating equivalence include the same statistical parameters: equal mean, standard deviation, and factor composition. Normally, equivalent forms are prepared for achievement or ability tests, where there are right and wrong answers. Equivalent forms are useful when an assessee is being followed over time or in a large-scale testing or assessment program in a single organization, where "correct" answers may be passed around.

- *Inventory:* An inventory is a term commonly used to describe a paper-and-pencil test of personality, interest, attitude, or the like.

- *Ipsative test:* An ipsative measure contains multiple scales, the scores on which are not independent of one another. On an ipsative test, a high score on one scale may result in a low score on a second scale. The defining characteristic of an ipsative measure is that the test will consist of a fixed number of scored items that are linked to the various scales. The scale, however, may also include unique items, so that, for a 100-item test measuring 10 scales, only a proportion of the items are scored on multiple scales. The total count of responses may total 150 and, thus, scale scores are correlated (because of duplicate items) among the scales. Ipsative measurement is often found in personality measurement; the Gordon Personal Profile/Inventory (Gordon, 1993; see Table 3.1) is a typical ipsative test.

- *Objective test:*   An objective test is a test for which the scoring procedure is specified completely in advance, thereby permitting complete agreement among different scorers.

- *Omnibus test:*   In an omnibus test, many different types of items are used in obtaining a single overall total score. The test usually has one set of directions and one overall time limit.

- *Performance test:*   Broadly speaking, every test is a performance test, whether the performance is oral responses to questions, written responses to an essay test or an objective test, or the application of manual skills in a test situation. However, pencil-and-paper or oral tests are not usually regarded as performance tests. Performance tests generally require the use and manipulation of physical objects and the application of physical and manual skills in situations not restricted to oral and written responses.

- *Personality test:*   Personality is the sum total of everything that constitutes a person's mental, emotional, and temperamental makeup. Personality refers to the manner and effectiveness with which whole individuals meet their personal and social problems and, indirectly, the manner in which they impress their fellows. Personality is not directly observable or measurable, but instead is measured as a construct.

- *Standardized test:*   A standardized test is composed of empirically selected materials that have definite directions for administration, scoring, and use, are backed up with data on reliability and validity, and have adequately determined norms.

- *Work sample test:*   A work sample test evaluates the examinee's response to a simulated real-life problem or situation, such as a management in-basket or a typing test.

Describing Test Scores

"Describing Test Scores" maybe a misleading title, but the intent in this section is to differentiate tests from one another in terms of what the score means. Test score meaning is a critical step in using tests. To develop meaning, to determine what the test reveals about the person, requires developing and applying rules to interpret the outcome. Any test will produce a range of scores from one end of the distribution to the other and, when assessors see where in that range a person scores, they learn something about the person.

- *Anchor:*   An anchor is a test or other measured variable that is used to ensure the comparability of two or more forms of a defined instrument or measurement procedure.

- *Correction for guessing:*   This is a technique devised to adjust the number of right answers on a test by subtracting some portion of the wrong answers, which are presumed to be random answers and guesses. Standardized achievement tests, such as the SAT or GMAT, use this correction (Murphy, Impara, & Plake, 1999).

- *Cut or cutting score:*   A cutting score is a minimum passing score designed to differentiate among individuals who pass or fail in terms of some reference standard. The most familiar use of cutting scores is in education, where a score of 60% or 65% is normally the passing score. The cutting score may be determined through statistical analysis in relation to a defined criterion reference, through normative comparison of score distributions for defined samples of applicants, or with reference to business-related outcomes for a defined sample of the population.

- *Norm:*   The norm is the average, normal, or standard for a group of specified status (e.g., of a given age or grade placement). In the assessment process, some tests may be relatively immune to these factors; that is, test scores are consistent across groups and the appropriate comparison group is "general population." Other tests may be very sensitive to these mitigating factors. When using tests in the assessment process, considerable care should be taken to ensure appropriate interpretation of test scores with reference to the competency being assessed. Most test manuals will provide different normative score distributions for different occupational groups, when this is appropriate. Generally speaking, the rule of thumb in selecting the appropriate normative comparison is to use one standard deviation difference of mean scores as a guide to selecting the appropriate normative comparison. A more precise statistical test is available (see Appendix B) to determine when two test score distributions are different and warrant different interpretation or treatment. This becomes an issue of determining when score differences constitute differences in test score interpretation and is a significant issue in fair employment practices when scores are used for decision-making purposes.

- *Normed score:* A score is normed by converting the raw score to a percentile, using a table representing values descriptive of the performance on a test of some specified group.

- *Scaled score:* A scaled score is a unit in a system of equated scores established for the raw scores of a test so that the scaled score values may themselves be interpreted. The scaled score is normally representative of the mean performance of certain reference groups. Intervals between any pair of scaled scores may be interpreted as differences in terms of the characteristics of the reference group.

- *Standard score:* A standard score is a raw score (e.g., percentage of items correct), converted to a score based on a distribution with a known mean and standard deviation.

- *Criterion keyed test:* Criterion keying is the act or process of developing a test and its scoring key empirically, through noting characteristic differences in answers made by different groups of individuals. A test of management aptitude could be developed through criterion keying by comparing the answers of successful and unsuccessful managers.

- *Maximum-performance test:*   A maximum-performance test is any test on which the examinee is directed, at least implicitly, to achieve the best or highest score possible (e.g., intelligence, aptitude, and achievement tests). Contrast to the typical-performance test.

- *Typical-performance test:*   A typical-performance test is designed to measure what an examinee is really like, rather than any intellective or ability characteristic; this category includes tests of personality, attitude, and interest, and is used in opposition to a maximum-performance test.

- *Work-limit test:*   On a work-limit test, sufficient time is allowed for all or nearly all individuals to complete their work.

Using Tests

Anyone can score tests and use those test scores to differentiate among different persons. However, it takes a different feature to determine the meaning and usefulness of the test score. Drawing tests and test scores out of a hat is a meaningless gesture. It is only when a test and the underlying test score distribution can be related to a criterion that the measure has value in application. The criterion makes the test; in the absence of a criterion reference, a test score is only a meaningless number.

- *Adverse impact:*   Adverse impact is a differential rate of selection in hiring, promotion, or other decision-making procedures, which works to the disadvantage of a defined group of individuals, normally in a protected class. The presence of adverse impact (also referred to as disparate impact) is determined through statistical examination of differential hiring rates (the 4/5 rule).

- *Assessment:*   Assessment is the act or process of determining the present level of proficiency or accomplishment of an individual in comparison with independently described groups or standards.

- *Criterion/Criteria:*   A criterion is an outcome measure of performance with reference to an individual difference construct or a measure of performance or accomplishment at a point in time. A criterion measure may be immediate, representing the current status; proximate, representing a plateau of maturity; or ultimate, representing the hypothetical final career achievement of an individual. Normally, the criterion for selection and development activities is some measure (or measures) of job performance. *Criteria* is the plural form of the term, indicating multiple measurement procedures. These procedures may be combined, using either statistical or subjective methods, to arrive at a final outcome that can be used to place individuals along a valued dimension. For example, job performance for a sales representative might include the dollar volume of sales, a supervisor rating of performance, and a measure of customer satisfaction.

- *Selection ratio:* The selection ratio is the proportion of the number of persons selected to the number of persons tested; other things being equal, lower ratios (i.e., more people tested in order to select a given number) result in a higher proportion of those who succeed among those selected.

Basic Measurement and Statistical Terms and Concepts

Assessors can select a test and administer the measure to yield an outcome, which tells them something about the person in terms of a useful outcome: the criterion. However, it is also essential to look beyond the administration, application (scoring), and meaning as represented in the questions. For every test, there are contingencies that must be incorporated or attached to the application.

- *Correlation coefficient:* The correlation coefficient (r) is the most commonly used measure of relationship between two or more variables. The range of possible values is from -1.00 (for a perfect negative relationship), to values of 0.00 (no relationship), to $+1.00$ (a perfect positive relationship between variables). For example, height and weight are correlated, in that taller people are generally heavier than shorter people. However, this correlation is not perfect, as a look around your office or classroom will show. When three or more variables are measured simultaneously, a multiple correlation coefficient can be calculated to arrive at an index of agreement to predict a final outcome or criterion score.

- *Cross-validation:*

Cross-validity is the process of checking whether a decision derived from one data set is truly effective when the decision is applied to another independent data set. Cross-validation involves two variables, first, the criterion as a measure of success and, second, the predictor that is a measure of individual differences (see *validity*).

- *Error:*

Error is a generic term for those elements in a test and testing situation that operate to keep a test from giving perfectly valid results. *Constant errors* have a direct adverse effect on validity, but may not affect reliability (e.g., having arithmetic items in an English test). *Variable* (or *random*) *errors* reduce reliability directly and validity indirectly (e.g., nonstandard conditions of test administration, ambiguous wording of test items, etc.).

- *Heterogeneity:*

A heterogeneous group possesses a great deal of variability, such as, in testing, a test with a great variety of content or a group that varies considerably in the attribute tested.

- *Homogeneity:*

A homogenous group has little variability, such as, in testing, a test composed of items that vary little in type or a group that varies little in the attribute tested.

- *Mean:*

The mean, more commonly known as the average, is the most widely used measure of central tendency. The mean is equal to the sum of scores divided by the number of examinees. In psychometric measurement and in assessment work, users should carefully select the comparison group when interpreting test scores. The mean or average score for a test may vary considerably from one group to another. For example, mean scores on a test of management knowledge would be quite different in a group of experienced managers versus a group of factory operatives. Most important in this respect are variables such as the amount of education, the amount of training, specific occupation-related experience, and other such factors that may influence scores such as race, gender, age, and national origin. (The Civil Rights Act of 1991 forbids the practice of subgroup norming, i.e., establishing separate norm groups by protected class characteristics [age, gender, race, national origin]. However, many test manuals, especially personality inventories, will present norms by gender or age.)

• *Median:*

Next to the mean, the median is the most common measure of central tendency; it is the point on the scale of score values that separates the group into two equal subgroups, the 50th percentile (P_{50}), second quartile (Q_2), or fifth decile (D_5).

• *Mode:*

The mode is also a measure of central tendency, that is, the score value that has the highest frequency, or the score obtained by more examinees than any other.

• *Normal distribution:*

The normal distribution, also known as the bell curve, is a useful mathematical model representing the distribution expected when an infinite number of observations (e.g., scores) deviate from the mean only by chance. Although a perfectly normal distribution can never be attained in reality, many actual distributions do approach this model. The curve drawn to portray the normal distribution is a symmetrical bell-shaped curve whose properties (the shape and the range, measured in terms of standard deviations) are completely known. The normal distribution is the product of a frequency distribution.

• *Reliability:*

Reliability is the degree to which a person would obtain the same score if the test were re-administered to the person (assuming no additional learning, practice effects, etc.). Reliability is a measure of the trustworthiness of scores. Several types of reliability coefficients should be distinguished:
1. Coefficient of internal consistency is a measure based on internal analysis of data ob-

tained on a single trial of a test. The Kuder-Richardson or coefficient alpha is the most widely used measure.

2. *Coefficient of equivalence* is the correlation between scores from two forms given at the same time.

3. Coefficient of stability refers to a correlation between test and retest with some period of time intervening. The test–retest situation may be with two forms of the same test.

4. *Split-half coefficient* is a method of estimating the reliability of a power test by splitting it into comparable halves (usually the odd-numbered items and the even-numbered items, whose respective means and variances are equal), correlating the scores of the two halves, and applying the Spearman-Brown prophecy formula to estimate the correlation.

- *Standard deviation:* The standard deviation (SD) is a statistic used to describe the variability of a population or sample. The SD expresses the extent of the deviations from the mean for the distribution. It is obtained by taking the square root of the mean of the squares of the deviations from the mean of a distribution. If the group tested were a normal one, their scores, if plotted graphically, would yield a normal distribution curve. Approximately two thirds (68.3%) of the scores would lie within the limits of one standard deviation above and one standard deviation below the mean. One third of the scores would be above the mean by one standard deviation and one third below the mean by one standard deviation. About 95% of the scores lie within the limits of two standard deviations above and below the mean. About 99.7% of the cases lie within the limits of three standard deviations above and below the mean.

- *Standardization sample:* The standardization sample is that part of the reference population that is selected for use in norming a test. This sample should be representative of the reference population in essential characteristics, such as geographical representation, age, occupational group, or other demographic variables. Test score interpretation, particularly in the case of individual assessment, should place particular emphasis on the characteristics of the standardization sample in reference to test score interpretation.

- *Validity:*

A test is valid to the extent that what it measures or predicts is known. The two basic approaches to the determination of validity are empirical analysis and logical analysis.

1. *Criterion-related validity* is demonstrated by empirical data showing that the selection procedure is predictive of, or significantly correlated with, important elements of work behavior or criterion performance. Criterion validity may be determined on a concurrent or a predictive basis. *Concurrent validity* refers to how well test scores match measures of contemporary criterion performance. Concurrent validity is affected by the distribution of the range of scores attributable to prior use of the test in other selection procedures. *Predictive validity* relates to how well predictions made from the test are confirmed by data collected at a later time.

2. *Content validity* is a logical approach to validity. It refers to how well the content of the test samples the subject matter or situation about which conclusions are to be drawn. Content validity is especially important in an achievement test.

3. *Construct validity* concerns the underlying psychological qualities (or constructs) that a test measures. Using both logical and empirical methods, the theoretical variable (construct) underlying the test is validated. Construct validity is most commonly seen in the measurement of personality variables or other individual difference characteristics.

- *Variance:*

The variance is a statistic, equal to the square of the standard deviation (SD^2), widely used in research.

PRIMER OF STATISTICAL PROCEDURES
AND DEFINITIONS

Kinds of Variables

Basically, there are two kinds of variables that are measured when assessing people: categorical and linear variables. The distinction between these two types of variables is of more than academic interest, because what can be done with the information is dependent on the type of variable.

Categorical variables place people into categories or groups based on one or more characteristics of the person, that is, the population is divided into categories or groups. Group labels are given for convenience and have no meaning apart from that. For example, assessment candidates could be placed into two categories: inside applicants and outside applicants. These categories could, however, just as easily be labeled Group 1 and Group 2 or Mushrooms and Beans.

What the label is does not matter and, thus, one cannot perform mathematical operations on the label, even if it appears in numeric form. For example, there might be 75 male applicants, coded as "1," and 25 female applicants, coded as "2." Does this mean that the average gender is 1.25? What does a person whose gender is 1.25 look like?

For categorical variables, what can be known is limited to how many. Therefore, it is possible to look at distributions or proportions, but nothing more. In the examples that follow, both counts (Fig. A1) and percentages (Fig. A2) are shown. Some categorical variables have the appearance of order or numerical meaning. In the first example, the category is level of education. However, it is still not possible to determine an average level of education from that information. In order to do that, it would be necessary to know how many years of education were represented in each category. With the simple category labels, it is not possible to tell, for example, if "High School" means 12 years, 11 years, 13 years, or a combination of all of these.

Linear variables, on the other hand, represent a continuum. A particular property—age, weight, or annual sales—is measured numerically. Continuous variables are counted; linear variables are *measured*. Age, for example, is a linear variable. An individual can be 6 years old, 21 years old, or 34.5 years old. As a result, it is possible to perform a wider variety of mathematical operations on linear variables. As Fig. A3 shows, it is possible to compute an *average* (mean) value that represents the population. The characteristics of the population can also be represented by a *median* or by the *standard deviation*. It is also possible to look at the relationship among variables. For example, can an individual employee's annual sales be predicted from years of sales experience? Linear variables can also be represented graphically, using a scatterplot, showing the relationship of two linear variables, as shown in Fig. A4.

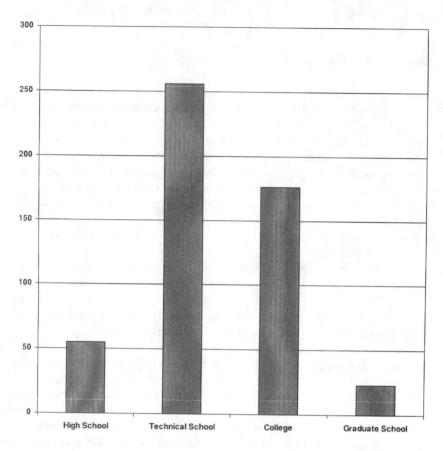

FIG. A.1.   Type of education of current applicants (count).

Describing a Data Set

The first step in looking at data about people is to numerically summarize the data. There are numerous techniques that can be used with linear variables, as described in the following list:

- *Measures of position:*   Measures of position are numbers that tell where a specified person or a particular score value stands within a set of scores. In a graph, any measure of position is located as a point on the baseline.

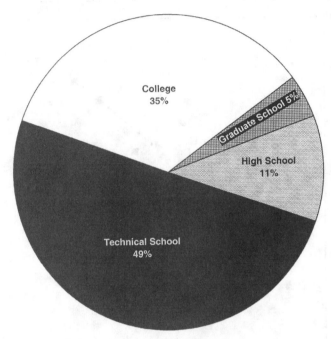

FIG. A.2.   Type of education of current applicants (percentage).

AGE	NUMBER OF APPLICANTS
18	43
19	52
20	63
21	58
22	64
23	43
24	39
25	41
26	29
27	25
28	18
29	23
30	12
Average age	22.66 years

FIG. A.3.   Applicant age.

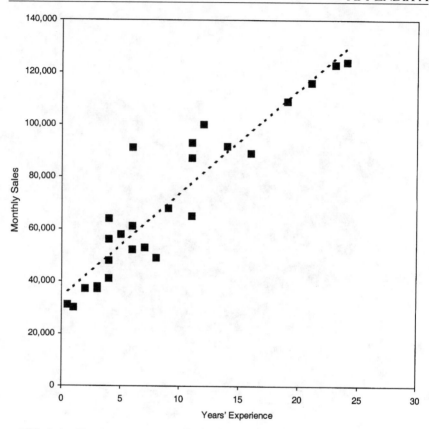

FIG. A.4.   Years' experience and sales performance.

- *Rank:*

Rank is the simplest description of position—first for the best or highest, second for the next best, third, and so on to last. It is familiar and simple, but its interpretation is so dependent on the size of the group that it is less useful than one might think at first. Generally, it is used informally in describing test results.

- *Percentile rank:*

Percentile rank is a better position indicator because it makes allowance for difference in the size of a group. Percentile rank is a statement of a person's relative position within a defined group—thus, a percentile rank of 38 indicates a score that is as high as or higher than those made by 38% of the people in that particular group. Percentile ranks are widely used as a type of test score.

Measures of Central Tendency (Averages)

A measure of central tendency is designed to provide a single value that is most characteristic or typical of a set of scores. Three such measures are fairly common in testing: the mean, median, and mode. Each of these may be located as a point along the baseline of a graph.

- *Mean:*

  The most common measure of position and of central tendency is the *arithmetic mean* (usually called simply the mean). This is nothing more than the average value. The mean is the most descriptive measure of a population. To compute the mean, one must total the values and divide by the number of cases:

  $$\overline{X} = \frac{\sum X}{N}$$

  where:

  $\overline{X}$ = Mean of x

  $\sum$ = Add the values of

  X = Scores on x

  N = Number of cases

- *Median:*

  With many types of data, there may be one very high value (or, at best, a very few high values) and many more lower values. The result is that the mean tends to exaggerate (that is, it pulls toward the extreme values) and the median becomes the preferred measure. The *median* is that value above which fall 50% of the cases and below which fall the other 50%; thus, it is less likely to be drawn in the direction of the extreme cases.

- *Measures of variability:*

  It is possible for two distributions of scores to have similar (or even identical) central tendency values and yet be very different. The scores in one distribution, for example, may be spread out over a far greater range of values than those in the other distribution. These next statistics show how much variability (or dispersion) there is in a distribution; that is, they show how scattered or spread out the scores are. In graphic format, each of these measures can be represented by a distance along the baseline.

- *Range:*

The range is a familiar concept, representing as it does the difference between highest and lowest scores. The range is easily found and easily understood, but is valuable only as a rough indication of variability. It is the least stable measure of variability, depending entirely on the two most extreme (and, therefore, least typical) scores. It is less useful in connection with other statistics than other measures of variability.

- *Standard deviation:*

Although it lacks the obvious rationale of the preceding measures of variability, the standard deviation is the best measure of variability. It is the most dependable measure of variability, for it varies less than other measures from one sample to the next. It fits mathematically with other statistics. It is widely accepted as the best measure of variability and is of special value to test users because it is (a) the basis for standard scores, (b) a way of expressing the reliability of a test score, (c) a way of indicating the accuracy of values predicted from a correlation coefficient, and (d) a common statistical test of significance. This statistic, in short, is one that every test user should know thoroughly: *The standard deviation is equal to the square root of the mean of the squared deviations from the distribution's mean.* (Read that last sentence again—it is not really that hard!) Although more efficient formulas exist, the standard deviation may be computed from the following formula:

$$S_x = \sqrt{\frac{\sum (X - \overline{X})^2}{N}}$$

where:

s_x = Standard deviation of x

$\sqrt{}$ = Take the square root of

$\sum$ = Add the values of

X = Scores on x

$\overline{X}$ = Mean of x

N = Number of cases

As a measure of variability it can be expressed as a distance along the baseline of a graph. The standard deviation is often used as a unit in expressing the difference between two specified score values; differences expressed in this fashion are more comparable from one distribution to another than they would be if expressed as raw scores. The standard deviation is also frequently used in making interpretations from the normal curve. In a normal distribution, 34.13% of the area under the curve lies between the mean and a point that is one standard deviation away from it, whereas 68.26 % of the area lies between a point that is one standard deviation below the mean and a point that is one standard deviation above the mean.

- *Correlation coefficient:* An additional commonly used statistic is the correlation coefficient. The correlation coefficient, represented by the symbol r, represents the degree and direction of linkage between two variables. The correlation coefficient is computed using the following formula:

$$r_{xy} = \frac{\sum (X - \overline{X})(Y - \overline{Y})}{N s_y s_y}$$

where:

r_{xy} = Correlation coefficient between x and y

$\sum$ = Add the values of

X = Scores on x

$\overline{X}$ = Mean of x

Y = Scores on y

$\overline{Y}$ = Mean of y

N = Number of cases

s_x = Standard deviation of x

s_y = Standard deviation of y

In conducting statistical analysis, care must be taken when defining the variables and their individual characteristics, particularly with reference to the range of scores and normative and ipsative characteristics.

More Statistics

The basic descriptive statistics described previously will serve most of the needs of the individual assessment practitioner. However, there are several additional statistical concepts that warrant mention.

In order to determine whether two populations are statistically equivalent, one can look at the *mean score difference*, or *t-test*. With this test, it can be determined whether a difference in average scores between groups reflects an actual difference in the underlying distribution of scores or if it is a result of chance alone. In order to conduct this test, one begins by computing a *t* ratio. The second step is to compare the *t* ratio to a significance table, to determine whether the difference in mean scores is a real or a chance occurrence. Today, of course, all of these steps are completed by a computer program, such as SAS (SAS Institute, Inc., 2000) or SPSS (Norusis, 2000), but a look at the actual equation is worthwhile, if only to have a better understanding of the theory underlying the printouts:

$$t = \frac{\overline{X} - \overline{Y}}{\sqrt{\dfrac{s^2}{N_x} + \dfrac{s^2}{N_y}}}$$

where:

$t = t - \text{ratio}$

$\overline{X}$ = Mean of x

$\overline{Y}$ = Mean of y

N = Number of persons tested in each group

s^2 = Shared variance, computed as follows:

$$s^2 = \frac{\sum(x-\bar{x})^2 + \sum(y-\bar{y})^2}{Nx + Ny - 2}$$

x = Values of x

y = Values of y

The *standard error of the mean* is a statistic used to determine whether the mean score value from a sample of individuals is representative of the underlying population from which the sample is drawn. In application (a rule of thumb), this means that it is possible to determine whether it is appropriate to use a particular normative database for interpreting a group's test scores. First, one computes the mean and the standard error of the mean for the sample or subgroup. If the mean for the sample differs from the normative mean by more than the value of the standard error of the mean, it would be appropriate to compute a separate mean, standard deviation, and score distribution for the sample or subgroup. The standard error of the mean is computed as follows:

$$SE_{\bar{x}} = \sqrt{\frac{s}{N-1}}$$

where:

$SE_{\bar{x}}$ = Standard error of the mean of x

s = Standard deviations of x

N = Number of cases

Factor analysis is also a statistical tool. The purpose of factor analysis is not to describe a group or to describe the relationship between two groups, but rather to reduce a large number of measurements to a smaller group of underlying constructs. For example, an individual might complete an extensive battery of tests. The individual's performance can be described or characterized by the entire array of scores, or these scores can be collapsed into several factors, such as *cognitive ability, interpersonal skills,* and *mechanical skills.* A full discussion of the underlying mechanisms of factor analysis is far beyond the scope of this text, but standard statistical packages fortunately make detailed knowledge unnecessary.

MULTITRAIT-MULTIMETHOD APPROACH

One of the most interesting and useful concepts and procedures in individual assessment measurement is the multitrait-multimethod (MT-MM) design. Although the subject is generally primarily of interest to researchers and measurement specialists interested in test construction, its usefulness in the individual assessment practice represents a powerful tool for understanding the individual assessee.

In a very pragmatic sense, in the effort to learn about a person, it is desirable and perhaps essential to use a number of different test scores to describe the person, to answer the question: "How do I know this individual?" One unwelcome, though undeniable, fact is that, for any single test, there exists the possibility of error in measurement. Less directly, there may also be some compensatory or countercompensatory influence on the examinee's performance in the assessment. Either of these factors—error or compensatory—influence the measurement of competencies in the assessment process. In practice, the experienced assessor will purposefully employ similar or overlapping measures, comparing the results of the measures to arrive at an answer to the question: "What kind of person is this?" Furthermore, in application, this multiple measures design represents a very powerful tool in the practice of individual assessment.

The fundamental background of the MT-MM model can be traced back to the APA's *Technical Recommendations for Psychological Tests and Diagnostic Techniques* (1954). The 1954 APA committee proposed construct validation, using MT-MM as a procedure to be used when validating the theory underlying the tests. At that time, construct validity was distinguished as a separate type of validity in an attempt to deal with the problem in test validation for which conventional forms of validity had not yet found an answer. The problem concerned the fact that psychological tests were often derived from a particular theoretical basis or model and attempted to measure individual variability on a theoretical construct continuum. Cronbach and Meehl (1955) provided a comprehensive statement in which the authors defined the concept of MT-MM and placed it within a logical, philosophical framework. The definition employed by Cronbach and Meehl described construct validity as the type of validation involved "whenever a test is to be interpreted as a measure of some attribute or quality which is not operationally defined" (p. 282). They then defined a construct as "some postulated attribute of people assumed to be reflected in test performance" (p. 295). Construct validity was placed by the authors within the philosophical framework of the "nomological net." The nomological net referred to a system of interlocking laws that made up a theory. Then, in order for a construct to be valid, according the authors, it must occur within a nomological net and must be related in some way to observable behaviors. The network would state the investigator's behavioral observations, the inferences linking these observations, and the hypothesis generated by the resulting network of observations and inferences. The formulation of an experimental design (test construction) to test the hypothesis would then follow, leading to data collection that would hopefully verify the hypothesis in terms of prediction.

As could be expected, any theoretical innovation would likely be challenged and that challenge occurred shortly after. In fact, Loevinger (1957) further defined the term *construct* in order to avoid what she saw as a possible philosophical confusion surrounding the use of the term. Loevinger proposed that the terms *trait* and *construct* be used in the same manner as the terms *parameter* and *statistic*. Trait would refer to the actual phenomenon to be understood and construct would refer to our current best estimate of it. This development obviously led to continuing discussion and some controversy regarding the meaning of the terms and the implications of the definitions. This is a matter of historical record, but at this point in the development—the late 1950s—the pragmatic aspects of individual assessment practice became paramount.

A number of enhancements to this theoretical design examined the idea of measurement errors and the source of those measurement errors. Orne (1962) suggested that one of the sources of error in measurement would be confounded by the "good subject" error, in both research and practice. Likewise, Webb, Campbell, Schwartz, and Sechrest (1966) suggested obtaining multiple behavioral references to enhance the development of a nomological net. Multiple measures would provide multiple events to test predictions resulting from hypotheses generated by a network. The problem described by Webb et al. incorporates a source of error, for example, when an interview would be considered an example of a single measurement class by taking multiple measures from within a single measurement class. Webb et al. advocated converging data from several classes as well as converging data from a single class and called this approach "triangulation of measurement procedure" (p. 84).

Completing the evolution of the MT-MM model, Campbell and Fiske (1959) proposed convergent and discriminate procedures in terms of a formal MT-MM matrix as a means of alleviating error in measurement. Thus, the MT-MM matrix based on a correlation matrix of several traits and several measures is the final theoretical development. However, discussion of the controversy would continue (e.g., Barker, 1968; Dawson, 1962; Fiske, 1971; Frederikson, 1972; Owens & Henry, 1966; Sells, 1963), all of these researchers contributing their ideas to the refinement of MT-MM theory and practice.

Considering this very extensive theoretical background, it is obviously incumbent on the practitioner in the individual assessment business to keep in mind and understand the beauty of the nomological net. As a conceptual framework, the nomological net is a pragmatic method for test construction, validation, and theory building. It is also, in application, an approach to understanding an individual at the case level. Thus, researchers and practitioners are obliged to collect data (to develop understanding of a person) that has both convergent and discriminant validity and that has generalizability across settings. This means collecting data using multiple methods of measurement to arrive at a convergent, discriminative protocol.

In practice, the use of a full MT-MM matrix will add unacceptably to the length and scope of the individual assessment. The obvious compromise is to administer two maximum performance measures of a similar dimension or to use multiple personality measures, again of similar traits, such as conscientiousness or integrity. Although this would not completely fulfill the expectations or requirements of the MT-MM design, some confirmation would be gained. Other, more independent, measures would be even more useful. Thus, competency-related interview judgments and conventional affective personality test dimension scores would be viewed as being more independent and as better multiple measures of a trait. Similarly, a maximum performance test of a dimension, combined with a competency-based, scaled, in-basket measure score would contribute to the confirming or disconfirming inference about the competency of the applicant. Simple repetition of the tests within a class, collected in situ, would be less desirable and less informative. Additionally, using contrived situations or using deception (such as the flat tire experiment of altruistic behavior) would certainly detract from the utility of this very powerful design for assessment (Bryan & Test, 1968).

In general, measurement obtained from the individual assessment test situation should reflect some degree of the measurement of an enduring trait or construct continuum in the behavior of an individual at the case level. This is then the preferred design in the idiosyncratic approach to individual assessment leading to prediction and decision making. In this way, the multitrait-multimethod-multisetting paradigm provides the optimum solution to this measurement dilemma.

The ultimate advice then leads assessment practitioners to carefully consider their selection of tests and to carefully evaluate the resulting array of scores. This test score array should incorporate some degree of redundancy or overlap of measurement. The redundant or overlapping areas must be examined to identify the areas where confirmations—or disconfirmations—can be found. A critical component of this process is the knowledge of tests and their properties, the properties of test scores and norms, and the nomological net, which facilitates the assessor's analysis, evaluation, and conclusions.

REFERENCES

American Psychological Association. (1954). Technical recommendations for psychological tests and diagnostic techniques. *Psychological Bulletin, 51*(Supp. 2), 1–38.

Barker, R. G. (1968). *Ecological psychology*. Stanford, CA: Stanford University Press.

Bryan, J. A., & Test, M. A. (1968). A lady in distress: The flat tire experiment. *Journal of Personality and Social Psychology, 41*, 10.

Campbell, D. T., & Fiske, D. W. (1959). Convergent and discriminant validation by the multitrait/multimethod matrix. *Psychological Bulletin, 14*, 619–629.

Civil Rights Act of 1991 (Pub. L. 102-166) (CRA).

Cronbach, L. J., & Meehl, P. E. (1955). Construct validity in psychological tests. *Psychological Bulletin, 52,* 281–302.

Dawson, R. E. (1962). Simulation in the social sciences. In H. Guetzkow (Ed.), *Simulation in social sciences: Readings* (pp. 1–15). Englewood Cliffs, NJ: Prentice-Hall.

Fiske, D. W. (1971). *Measuring the concepts of personality.* Chicago: Aldine.

Frederikson, N. (1972). Toward a taxonomy of situations. *American Psychologist, 27*(2), 114–123.

Gordon, L. V. (1993). *Gordon Personal Profile and Gordon Personal Inventory.* San Antonio, TX: The Psychological Corporation.

Loevinger, J. (1957). Objective tests as instruments of psychological theory. *Psychological Reports, 9,* 636–694.

Murphy, L. L., Impara, J. C., & Plake, B. S. (1999). *Tests in print (V).* Lincoln, NE: The Buros Institute of Mental Measurements.

Norusis, M. J. (2000). *SPSS 10.0 guide to data analysis.* Upper Saddle River, NJ: Prentice-Hall.

Orne, M. (1962). On the social and psychological experiment: With particular reference to demand characteristics and their implications. *American Psychologist, 17,* 776–783.

Owens, W. A., & Henry, E. R. (1966). *Biographical data in industrial psychology: A review and evaluation.* Greensboro, NC: Creative Research Institute of the Richardson Foundation.

SAS Institute, Inc. (2000). *SAS/STAT user's guide, version 8.* Cary, NC: Author.

Sells, S. B. (1963). *Stimulus determinants of behavior.* New York: Ronald Press.

Webb, E. J., Campbell, D. T., Schwartz, R. D., & Sechrest, L. (1966). *Unobtrusive measures: Nonreactive research in the social sciences.* Chicago: Rand McNally.

Appendix B

Management and Executive Model: Work Activities and Competencies

MANAGEMENT AND EXECUTIVE
Work Activities

FACTORS	DIMENSIONS

PEOPLE MANAGEMENT

I.   Staffing
II. Supervise People
III. People Development
IV. Personnel Administration
V.   Labor Relations
VI. External Relations

GENERAL OPERATIONS MANAGEMENT

VII. Supervise Work Operations
VIII. Materials Management
IX.   Information Management
X.   Facilities & Security Management
XI.   International Operations & Alliances

FUNCTIONAL MANAGEMENT

XII.   Research & Development Management
XIII. Accounting & Financial Management
XIV.   Marketing & Sales Management
XV.   Strategy Development & Deployment
XVI.   Internal Consulting

I. Staffing

1. Examine strategic business objectives to identify staffing issues related to achieving these objectives.
2. Review the organization structure (e.g., reporting relationships, responsibility flowcharts) of a work group or division to ensure it supports the business vision and strategy.
3. Identify employees in own department, or in other parts of the organization, who are backups to replace key individuals who may be promoted, leave the organization, and so forth.
4. Identify the relevant work activities and associated skills, knowledge, and experiences needed to successfully perform a role or job.
5. Evaluate the cost and effectiveness of recruiting efforts to guide changes in recruiting focus, sources, strategies, and so forth.
6. Conduct screening or employment interviews to collect information relevant for a target role or job.
7. Monitor state, federal, and local legislation, bulletins, and guideline updates for changes that affect the staffing process.

II. Supervise People

8. Assign work assignments and priorities to employees to ensure the best distribution of individual talents.
9. Establish performance standards for employees to clarify goals and performance expectations.
10. Design individual and/or work group goals that are mutually supportive to encourage cooperation and discourage competition.
11. Meet with employees to discuss their perceptions of the work they do to clarify role requirements and work responsibilities.
12. Measure employees' progress toward goals or assignment completion to evaluate individual performance and provide performance-related feedback.
13. Identify opportunities for rewarding positive work behavior and outcomes to reinforce activities that are aligned with the goals of the work group and the organization.

III. People Development

14. Conduct informal or formal orientation of new hires to provide new employees with an overview of the organization's policies, work rules, role or job responsibilities, and so forth.
15. Review the current job assignments of employees and, with reference to their individual performance, identify assignments or work experiences that will be challenging and require growth and development.

16. Identify performance deficiencies or training needs of individual employees to guide coaching efforts, training interventions, and the creation of individual development plans.
17. Select training courses or developmental interventions for individuals or groups of employees that address competency gaps resulting from the introduction of new technology, new work processes, redesigned jobs, and so forth.
18. Deliver training courses, seminars, or workshops designed to develop a job-related expertise, skill, or awareness.
19. Evaluate the effectiveness of training courses, workshops, or other developmental interventions that have been designed to address the training needs of individuals or groups of employees.

IV. Personnel Administration

20. Explain personnel policies, programs, procedures, rules, and so forth for employees to ensure understanding.
21. Conduct exit interviews to identify reasons for the separation.
22. Conduct personnel research (e.g., turnover or job classification analyses) designed to provide broader management with information for use in evaluating organization practices, interventions, policies, and so forth.
23. Develop and administer policies related to working hours and absences, work and vacation schedules, and so forth.
24. Conduct job evaluation research and compensation surveys to evaluate wage and salary equity and make recommendations to broader management.
25. Administer and monitor expenditures for various benefit programs such as workman's compensation, unemployment compensation, layoff income benefits, and so forth.
26. Maintain employee files to systematically document information related to employee performance, compensation, development, and so forth.

V. Labor Relations

27. Investigate employee grievances (e.g., collect facts, identify issues, research organization policies) to build a basis for discussions.
28. Develop negotiation strategies for dealing with union demands based on research of union expectations, grievance analyses, contract analyses, and so forth.
29. Develop relations with employee representatives from unions, professional groups, and so forth to lay the groundwork for future negotiations.

30. Review labor contract proposals to identify implications and bargaining points having to do with issues like job security, compensation, working conditions, grievance procedures, and union security.
31. Represent the organization's interests and strategy in negotiations with employee bargaining groups.
32. Monitor state or federal legislation, professional regulations, and so forth to stay abreast of changes that may affect employee relations activities, contracts, and negotiations.

VI. External Relations

33. Provide the board of directors, or other external advisory or oversight groups, with verbal or written updates to communicate trends or deviations from plans and highlight financial changes or operating results.
34. Develop a portfolio of regular contacts within the financial community (e.g., security analysts, financial press) to develop a financial public relations program.
35. Communicate planned organization actions (e.g., expansions, acquisitions, changes in operational focus, personnel changes) to local press, radio, and television outlets.
36. Represent the organization at community affairs and public functions to promote awareness and create goodwill.
37. Develop and/or administer corporate giving policies (i.e., relating to charities, fundraisers, donations to foundations) designed to promote goodwill and create a sense of positive corporate citizenship.
38. Respond to inquiries or requests for information from external sources such as the press or representatives from other organizations interested in benchmarking.
39. Consult with community and governmental representatives, or other economic partners, on ways to improve the business climate.

VII. Supervise Work Operations

40. Coordinate work with other groups to ensure smooth progress and a seamless integration of effort.
41. Develop flowcharts that describe the relationship of one process to another via visual descriptions of the work cycle to guide the creation of new work systems or procedures.
42. Identify inefficiencies or roadblocks in work procedures to guide change in work flow, physical layout of the work area, work processes, and so forth.
43. Chart business measures of timeliness, quality, and quantity (e.g., sales billed, orders received, products returned) for work groups or depart-

ments to help understand variations and their causes, and to communicate information to others.

44. Set timetables and intermediate checkpoints for others to follow in order to keep track of progress toward objectives.

45. Prepare reports of business activities or projects in one's own area of responsibility to update management.

46. Conduct cost–benefit analyses to determine the productivity and efficiency payoff of purchasing new technology, updating existing equipment, purchasing additional equipment, and so forth.

VIII. Materials Management

47. Evaluate potential vendor or supplier options to identify agreements that match needs of the organization in terms of price, delivery, service, technical assistance, and so forth.

48. Monitor the delivery of materials and supplies to count-check amounts against requisitions, ensure quality of deliverables, oversee proper storage and placement, and so forth.

49. Develop inventory monitoring systems to track stock, material, or resource availability, allow for checks of perpetual inventories, and so forth.

50. Monitor the flow of materials or the delivery of services throughout the logistics system to audit the efficiency and cost effectiveness of materials movement or service delivery.

51. Develop inventory control policies to hold inventory investments within bounds consistent with efficient operation.

52. Create master schedules for production, processing, or service delivery to guide workload distribution, efficient purchasing of materials or supplies, identify subcontracting needs, and so forth.

53. Conduct capacity utilization analyses to identify bottlenecks in production, processing, or service delivery centers.

IX. Information Management

54. Conduct information needs analyses to determine the information and reporting requirements of an individual manager, department, business area, and so forth.

55. Utilize computer-aided software engineering (CASE) products to facilitate data modeling and the design of database management systems.

56. Interpret business data for the purpose of identifying patterns, trends, and variances in company operations.

57. Create data flow diagrams to illustrate business procedures or processes and flows among these procedures/processes.

58. Develop database strategic plans that map specific subject databases against their prospective uses for supporting management's monitoring, analyzing, and planning activities.
59. Monitor information processing systems and specific processing outputs to ensure data quality.

X. Facilities and Security Management

60. Monitor facility/store/plant operations to assess compliance with industry regulations, state or federal laws, or company policies.
61. Review quality control and reliability data to ensure procedural compliance and identify areas in need of improvement.
62. Develop and/or monitor the implementation of policies designed to promote safety or security, reduce accidents, and control work hazards.
63. Inspect buildings, facility layout and functioning, and so on to determine their soundness, operational status, conformity to security guidelines, and so forth.
64. Research potential facility/store/plant location sites to maximize sales and productivity, minimize labor and transportation costs, and so forth.
65. Design facility/store/plant physical layouts to accommodate optimum product/process flow, maximize space utilization, incorporate requisite handling and transportation equipment, and so forth.

XI. International Operations and Alliances

66. Identify communications technology that may be used to facilitate the transmission of data and ideas across international boundaries.
67. Negotiate license agreement terms to achieve international objectives for penetrating foreign markets.
68. Conduct import product analyses to develop cost of business computations that take into account finding fees, FOB and freight costs, U.S. duty, wharfage, cartage, warehouse expenses, and so forth.
69. Investigate culture, education, and business training variables to determine the feasibility of delegating management functions to foreign nationals.
70. Research issues related to financing facilities for short-term credit or equity-capital needs, trademarks, licenses, trade names, patents, copyrights, and other intangible assets when conducting business abroad.
71. Evaluate the political, social, economic, and competitive conditions and long-range requirements of a potential host country to assess the attractiveness of investing in, or relocating, all or part of a business.

XII. Research and Development Management

72. Evaluate the strategic fit of research and development projects with the organization's objectives to guide the allocation of human, financial, and technological resources.
73. Generate and inventory basic and applied research ideas to develop a portfolio of future business possibilities.
74. Identify new products, product uses, processes, process or system improvements, ways to utilize by-products, waste, and so on that may contribute to an organization's existing stable of offerings.
75. Evaluate the technical feasibility of research and development ideas to guide recommendations concerning the allocation of human, financial, and technological resources.
76. Oversee research and development work conducted by outside facilities, such as independent laboratories, research institutes, academic institutions, consultants, trade associations, and so forth.

XIII. Accounting and Financial Management

77. Use spreadsheet or specialized financial software programs to analyze cash flow, sales forecasts, budget forecasts, staffing projections, and so forth.
78. Develop a budget or annual profit plan, including planned operations, time schedules, utilization of funds, anticipated financial position, and so forth, to be used in broader management planning and control.
79. Monitor expenditures to identify trends and evaluate variances in relation to an established budget.
80. Review subdepartmental budgets to reconcile differences and make sure that an overall budget includes comprehensive data for determining general costs for items such as supplies, staff personnel, facilities management, and so forth.
81. Review contracts, purchase agreements, and other financial arrangements to ensure compatibility with business goals and expectations about profitability.
82. Forecast the impact of business decisions and expected outcomes on overall financial results.
83. Monitor financial and economic information to identify trends and indicators that may impact business operations, planning, investments, and so forth.
84. Evaluate the profitability of new investments to guide decision making using standard measures of investment worth such as payback period, book return on book investment, internal rate of return, and contribution to net present worth.

XIV. Marketing and Sales Management

85. Research customer product or service needs to develop proposals, make recommendations for change in existing product or service lines, and so forth.
86. Monitor competitor pricing of equivalent products or services to help others make pricing decisions.
87. Evaluate packaging (i.e., both functional and merchandising) and branding recommendations for specific products or services.
88. Research markup and cost factors of a product or service to guide price setting.
89. Develop advertising or promotional strategies designed to attract customers, compete successfully with other comparable businesses, promote company image, build employee morale, and so forth.
90. Evaluate the sales performance of groups or regions to identify areas in need of additional coverage, training, realignment, special sales actions, and so forth.
91. Prepare status reports on sales, results of promotional programs, impact of pricing changes, and so on to update management.

XV. Strategy Development and Deployment

92. Review statistical data and other economic, political, and market information to identify opportunities and risks associated with potential business decisions.
93. Establish profit objectives (e.g., profit growth, level, and stability) for a business or business unit to guide long-range planning.
94. Evaluate the growth of a business enterprise to identify a course of competitive action for moving into the future by considering variables like market size and scope, market maturity, competitor rivalry, changes in product demand, access to capital, and so forth.
95. Evaluate the human, technological, infrastructural, financial, and cultural strengths and weaknesses of an organization or business to see what there is to work with when responding to opportunities and threats in the external environment.
96. Review or propose business strategies designed to achieve targeted returns for shareholders, owners, employees, customers, and so forth.
97. Identify specific revenue-generating or cost savings initiatives in one's own functional area to bring business operations in alignment with the broader organizational strategy.

XVI. Internal Consulting

98. Read manuals, books, technical journals, research publications, and so forth to stay abreast of new developments in one's own area of expertise.

99. Research the relevant literature (e.g., manuals, books, technical journals, research publications) to find information for answering specific questions or to build a base of information for supporting a specific action or decision.

100. Provide professional advice or specialized assistance and technical instruction to other employees with questions in one's own area of expertise.

101. Attend conferences, seminars, professional association meetings, and so forth to stay informed about industry and competitor practices.

102. Investigate problems (involving equipment, hardware, business processes or operations, etc.) requiring the application of technical or sophisticated procedures, tools, analysis techniques, and so forth.

103. Monitor the organization's practices or operations with reference to laws, regulations, guidelines, industry practices, and so forth to assess compliance, risk, and exposure.

MANAGEMENT AND EXECUTIVE
Competencies

FACTORS	DIMENSIONS
THINKING	I. Analytical Ability II. Creativity III. Short-Term Planning IV. Strategic Thinking V. Business Specific Knowledge
COMMUNI-CATIONS	VI. Verbal Communications VII. Written Communications VIII. Listening Skills IX. Public Speaking
INTER-PERSONAL	X. Business Relationships/Teamwork XI. Influencing Skills XII. Adaptability XIII. Dependability & Trust
LEADERSHIP	XIV. Supervisory Skills XV. Motivation Skills XVI. Decisiveness XVII. Work Commitment
GENERAL OPERATIONS	XVIII. Materials Management XIX. Facilities & Security XX. Information Management & Computers XXI. International Operations & Alliances
FUNCTIONAL KNOWLEDGE	XXII. Economics XXIII. Accounting & Finance XXIV. Marketing & Sales XXV. Human Resources

I. Analytical Ability

1. Skill in breaking down issues or problems into component parts to identify underlying issues.
2. Skill in recognizing gaps in existing information, which is important for fully understanding an issue or problem.
3. Skill in quickly gaining job-related knowledge and using newly acquired knowledge to help understand issues or solve problems.
4. Willingness to reflect on and analyze one's own mistakes to try to learn from experience.
5. Skill in grasping the complexities and understanding intricate relationships among issues or problems.

II. Creativity

6. Skill in analyzing issues or problems from different points of view to identify alternative courses of action.
7. Skill in generating ideas and solutions in response to business issues and problems.
8. Skill in making intuitive, inferential leaps in thinking that are logically grounded.
9. Willingness to develop solutions or consider proposals that challenge status quo assumptions or pro forma operations.
10. Willingness to face challenges or problems with an open mind and sense of curiosity.

III. Short-Term Planning

11. Skill in analyzing the work flow to ensure existing processes facilitate, rather than hinder, the accomplishment of work.
12. Skill in translating business or work group strategies into specific objectives and tactics.
13. Skill in balancing day-to-day activities with long-term objectives.
14. Skill in estimating the time and resources required to carry out a work objective.
15. Skill in coordinating the activities of multiple work groups to eliminate duplication of effort and inefficiencies in getting work accomplished.
16. Skill in identifying the most appropriate sequence in which activities should be conducted to efficiently complete a project.

IV. Strategic Thinking

17. Skill in identifying the most probable long-term consequences of an action or decision given a large number of possible future outcomes.

18. Skill in recognizing the broad or long-term implications of business decisions and plans.
19. Skill in recognizing strategic business opportunities resulting from changes in the economic, technological, political/legal, or social environments.
20. Skill in seeing the relationship between one's own work group or business unit and other departments or functions in the organization.
21. Skill in recognizing alliances, either internal or external to the organization, that are complimentary and that benefit the competitive position of multiple parties.
22. Knowledge of the microenvironment variables that can impact the strategic management process (e.g., buyer switching costs, concentration of customers, competitor business strategies).
23. Knowledge of variables in the organization environment that can impact competitive positioning and long-term business planning (e.g., morale and commitment of key talent, technological assets available to the organization, organizational structure, and decision-making styles).

V. Business Specific Knowledge

24. Knowledge of competitors' products, strategies, and business philosophies.
25. Knowledge of the organization's mission, goals, product and service lines, associated competitive strengths and weaknesses, and so forth.
26. Knowledge of how other parts of the organization function (e.g., in other functional or geographic divisions, practice areas, and business units).
27. Knowledge of the perspectives and agendas of key decision makers in the organization that may impact project planning, policy development, resource distribution, and so forth.
28. Knowledge of who in the organization needs to be involved if decisions are to be well received.

VI. Verbal Communications

29. Skill in organizing thoughts or facts in verbal communications in such a way that they facilitate understanding.
30. Skill in adapting speaking style (e.g., enthusiasm and expressiveness) to fit the situation and the audience.
31. Skill in selecting words that convey the intent of a verbal message precisely and without ambiguity.
32. Skill in using non-verbal behavior (e.g., gestures and eye contact) to underscore important points in verbal communications.

33. Skill in using questions and verbal probes to elicit information or clarify issues with others.

VII. Written Communications

34. Skill in preparing written communications that express information clearly and concisely.
35. Knowledge of basic rules of grammar, punctuation, and sentence structure.
36. Skill in scanning reports, memos, or other documents to identify key points.
37. Skill in creating written material that has a logical flow of thoughts and ideas.
38. Skill in reviewing reports, memos, or other written material for flaws in logic or unsupported recommendations.
39. Skill in preparing reports, manuals, or other documents that contain complex information and that are intended to be read by others without a technical background.

VIII. Listening Skills

40. Skill in interpreting the nonverbal messages (e.g., crossed arms, facial expressions) that accompany a speaker's verbal communications.
41. Skill in using open-ended verbal probes to get others to open up and elaborate on a topic.
42. Skill in using paraphrasing and summarizing techniques to clarify the content of a speaker's verbal communications.
43. Willingness to listen to, and demonstrate empathy for, the concerns of others.
44. Willingness to listen to others express disagreements in an effort to understand issues or explore another point of view.

IX. Public Speaking

45. Skill in anticipating the interests and expectations of an audience when preparing a presentation.
46. Skill in demonstrating confidence and poise during large group discussions or formal presentations.
47. Skill in controlling the timing and sequence of events during a formal presentation.
48. Knowledge of various visual aids (e.g., slides, flipcharts, videos, computer presentation software) that may be used to augment a presentation and an understanding of the advantages and disadvantages of each.

49. Knowledge of social codes and standards governing behavior in business or social settings where one is identified with the organization.
50. Skill in thinking quickly on one's feet and handling questions from the floor during large group discussions or formal presentations.

X. Business Relationships/Teamwork

51. Willingness to be proactive and work at connecting and building cooperative relationships with others.
52. Willingness to ignore personal likes and dislikes in work relationships and focus on the work at hand.
53. Willingness to consider the feelings or concerns of other team members when making decisions.
54. Skill at anticipating the reactions of other people in response to comments and feedback, decisions, and so forth.
55. Willingness to demonstrate an interest in the work-related and personal concerns of other team members.
56. Willingness to confront racist, sexist, ethnocentric, or other insensitive behavior in the workplace.
57. Willingness to promote work policies and structures that promote teamwork or enhance the functioning of work teams.

XI. Influencing Skills

58. Skill in assertively presenting one's own point of view without offending or alienating others.
59. Skill in building a strong logical argument and compelling rationale to support one's ideas and recommendations.
60. Knowledge of effective negotiating tactics and techniques (e.g., reframing vs. rejecting outright another party's position, specifying how one's objectives will benefit the other party).
61. Skill in investigating and understanding another person's needs or negotiating position to guide the development or framing of one's own argument.
62. Skill in creating a strong personal presence that commands attention and respect in groups.

XII. Adaptability

63. Skill in adjusting one's work pace to keep up with rapidly changing events.
64. Skill in shifting one's attention between multiple activities and competing demands.
65. Willingness to accept criticism without overreacting or becoming defensive.

66. Willingness to remain open to, and assimilate, new information or data which impacts a previous decision, course of action, and so forth.
67. Skill in keeping a cool head and positive focus in stressful situations.

XIII. Dependability and Trust

68. Willingness to follow through on commitments and promises.
69. Skill in communicating information in an open and sincere manner that promotes credibility (e.g., honest answers to tough questions).
70. Willingness to act carefully and responsibly with sensitive or classified information (e.g., compensation figures or proprietary technical information).
71. Willingness to accept responsibility for one's own mistakes.
72. Knowledge of theories and techniques for enhancing an organization's ethical and moral consciousness.
73. Knowledge of social responsibility concepts in business and industry (e.g., concepts of relativism and stakeholder analysis).

XIV. Supervisory Skills

74. Skill in conveying a sense of urgency to others to help team members focus on a limited set of priorities.
75. Willingness to focus on employee development and training activities despite the daily rush to get work done.
76. Knowledge of existing development resources that can be used to support the skill development of team members (e.g., books, seminars, training programs).
77. Skill in identifying assignments for others that are designed to stretch and develop their capabilities.
78. Willingness to monitor work assignments to stay on top of work progress.
79. Skill in communicating the goals of a work group or business unit to team members so that individual work behavior is aligned with broader strategies.
80. Skill in setting priorities and work directions for others so they have a clear idea of performance expectation.
81. Skill in assigning the appropriate level of authority to coincide with delegated work activities.

XV. Motivation Skills

82. Knowledge of basic principles of motivation and theories of work behavior.
83. Skill in creating an energetic and enthusiastic work environment where people have positive attitudes about their work.

84. Willingness to take the time to track and reinforce positive work behaviors in others.
85. Skill in conveying to others the feeling that their work is valued and that they are an important member of the team.
86. Willingness to involve others in planning and decision making.

XVI. Decisiveness

87. Willingness to take a stand on important matters when faced with difficult dilemmas or decisions.
88. Willingness to make decisions in the face of uncertainty or when tough choices are required.
89. Skill in setting priorities and developing a work direction in ambiguous situations.
90. Skill in delivering clear and action-oriented instructions in crisis situations requiring quick action.
91. Willingness to step forward and champion new initiatives and improvements in the organization that require broad commitment or change.

XVII. Work Commitment

92. Willingness to persist in the face of difficulties (e.g., when work becomes complex, intellectually challenging, politically complicated).
93. Skill in maintaining a high energy level to keep up with the pace of daily work activities.
94. Willingness to set high standards of personal performance.
95. Willingness to take the initiative in seeking out new work challenges and increase the variety and scope of one's job.
96. Willingness to bring issues to closure by pushing forward until a resolution is achieved.
97. Skill at staying focused on work priorities and working through or around frequent interruptions.
98. Willingness to pursue continuous learning to stay current with advances in one's own area of expertise.

XVIII. Materials Management

99. Knowledge of purchasing fundamentals and techniques (e.g., forecasting techniques, purchasing control processes, procedures for establishing and maintaining vendor relations).
100. Knowledge of storage and inventory concepts (e.g., methods for determining storage layout, coding and marking, balancing and controlling inventory costs).

101. Knowledge of order processing (e.g., methods for entering orders, invoicing orders, measuring customer service).
102. Knowledge of logistics engineering (e.g., procedures for measuring reliability and maintainability, analyzing system functions, analyzing logistics support).
103. Knowledge of work process planning (e.g., job design concepts, work measurement procedures, variables impacting capacity planning and facilities layout).
104. Knowledge of process design and implementation (e.g., production and service designs, quality improvement concepts, project management and control).
105. Skill in setting clear priorities and work directions for others.
106. Skill in communicating the goals of a work group or business unit to individuals on one's team.

XIX. Facilities and Security

107. Knowledge of facilities tactical planning (e.g., general site/location analysis, basic ergonomics, regulatory laws governing facilities).
108. Knowledge of preventative maintenance guidelines and procedures for equipment and facilities.
109. Knowledge of start-up procedures and facility implementation (e.g., procedures for monitoring equipment and furniture installation, obtaining municipality permits, contracting outside services).
110. Knowledge of procedures for establishing physical security (e.g., intrusion prevention techniques and devices, fire protection techniques and devices, disaster recovery plans).
111. Knowledge of procedures for establishing personnel security (e.g., background investigation procedures, monitoring techniques and tools, checks and balances and separation of duties).

XX. Information Management and Computers

112. Knowledge of information systems and information management (e.g., techniques for defining user requirements and data structures, statistical procedures for analyzing system functioning).
113. Knowledge of database manipulation and management (e.g., techniques for designing databases, storage and access methods in computer systems, CASE tools and data modeling).
114. Knowledge of project management tools and techniques.
115. Knowledge of decision support and expert systems in information management (e.g., neural networks, platform design features, compatibility issues).
116. Knowledge of computer hardware and peripheral devices (e.g., storage media such as tape drives, imaging devices, file server setup and configuration).

117. Knowledge of computer operations and support tools (e.g., software utilities, job schedulers, data transfer tools).
118. Knowledge of computer network management tools (e.g., wireless technology, LANs and WANs, system network architecture).
119. Knowledge of computer information system development tools (e.g., program development standards, compilers and linkers, automated debugging and testing tools).

XXI. International Operations and Alliances

120. Knowledge of international economics (e.g., variables impacting international trade and capital flows, production mobility factors, trade policy assessment).
121. Knowledge of international marketing (e.g., business customs and practices in global marketing, export trade mechanics and logistics, international distribution systems).
122. Knowledge of global human resources management (e.g., ethical issues in international management, impact of different value systems on decision making, cultural diversity influences, organizational behavior).
123. Knowledge of international corporate finance (e.g., currency trading and parity relationships, economic and political risk evaluation, international monetary arrangements).

XXII. Economics

124. Knowledge of basic economic concepts and theories (e.g., marginal cost and benefit evaluations, production and consumption relationships and measurement).
125. Knowledge of microeconomics (e.g., variables involved in understanding consumer behavior, procedures for determining optimal input combinations and cost functions for an organization).
126. Knowledge of macroeconomics (e.g., commodity and credit markets, factors impacting capital accumulation and economic growth, variables impacting the demand for money).
127. Knowledge of labor economics (e.g., wage determination tables, stagflation concepts, trade union organization and functioning).
128. Knowledge of econometrics (e.g., descriptive statistics, linear regression models, disequilibrium models).
129. Knowledge of economic development (e.g., social aspects of development, trade policies of developing countries, agriculture policy and relationships to economic development).
130. Skill in using economic indicators to forecast trends and business cycles.

XXIII. Accounting and Finance

131. Knowledge of financial statements and analysis (e.g., balance sheets, cash flow statements, equity analysis).
132. Knowledge of management accounting procedures (e.g., cost–volume–profit analysis, return on investment calculations, capital budgeting).
133. Knowledge of auditing procedures (e.g., payroll and personnel cycles, sales and collection cycles, divisible profit calculations).
134. Knowledge of basic principles of finance (e.g., calculating net present value, risk assessment, asset pricing models).
135. Knowledge of corporate finance principles (e.g., debt financing, credit and cash management, methods for evaluating market efficiency).
136. Knowledge of corporate investment management (e.g., tax shelters, contrarian investment strategies and stock reversals, diversification concepts).
137. Knowledge of financial markets (e.g., primary and secondary markets, monetary and fiscal policy, security analysis).
138. Knowledge of financial risk measurement and management (e.g., volatility forecasting, risk capital calculations, credit risk management).
139. Skill in analyzing financial statements to evaluate an organization's fiscal health and locate causes of variance in business operations.

XXIV. Marketing and Sales

140. Knowledge of marketing research and analysis (e.g., sales forecasting, product and pricing research, marketing research designs).
141. Knowledge of product design and management (e.g., new product development strategies, product life-cycle concepts, market segmentation and positioning).
142. Knowledge of retail marketing and merchandising (e.g., techniques for modifying store image, planogram uses and misuses, pricing and promotion strategies).
143. Knowledge of consumer behavior (e.g., marketing communications that impact consumer behavior, economic and psychological theories about consumer behavior, sociocultural factors affecting consumer behavior).
144. Knowledge of sales management (e.g., methods for analyzing existing accounts, techniques for estimating sales based on trends).
145. Knowledge of territory management (e.g., procedures used to establish territory boundaries, methods for monitoring territory performance).
146. Skill in evaluating what constitutes desirable features or options in a product/service with reference to potential customer base or target market.

147. Skill in identifying customer needs and careabouts and matching or modifying products/services accordingly.

XXV. Human Resources

148. Knowledge of strategic human resource planning (e.g., techniques for inventorying internal labor supplies, modeling personnel flows, forecasting resource requirements).
149. Knowledge of labor laws and government regulations impacting human resource management (e.g., EEOC and OFCCP regulations, Civil Rights laws, labor laws such as the Wagner Act and Taft-Hartley Act).
150. Knowledge of job modeling techniques and outputs (e.g., interview and questionnaire approaches, creating models of work for jobs or groups of jobs).
151. Knowledge of employee selection and placement methods (e.g., interviewing best practices, ability and personality testing, validating decision-making processes).
152. Knowledge of employee compensation and reward systems (e.g., strategies for designing pay systems, conducting pay surveys, creating incentive programs).
153. Knowledge of performance appraisal approaches and methods for tracking individual performance (e.g., requirements of a relevant appraisal system, pros and cons of different methods, potential uses and misuses of appraisal data).
154. Knowledge of training programs and techniques (e.g., on-the-job methods, the use of simulations, training evaluation methodology).
155. Knowledge of procedures and techniques for organization analysis and development.
156. Knowledge of employee and health and safety issues and regulations (e.g., health programs for employees, OSHA standards, reporting and enforcement, worker compensation and disability programs).

Appendix C

Supervisory Model: Work Activities and Competencies

SUPERVISORY
Work Activities

FACTORS	DIMENSIONS

PEOPLE MANAGEMENT

   I.   Staffing
  II.   Supervise People
 III. People Development
 IV. Personnel Administration
  V.   Labor Relations

GENERAL OPERATIONS MANAGEMENT

  VI.   Supervise Work Operations
 VII. Equipment & Materials Management
VIII. Information Management
 IX. Facilities & Safety Management

FUNCTIONAL- MANAGEMENT

  X.   Research & Development Management
 XI. Accounting & Financial Management
XII. Marketing & Sales Management

I. Staffing

1. Identify the relevant work activities and associated skills, knowledge, and experiences needed to successfully perform a role or job.
2. Interview job candidates to determine qualifications and their suitability for employment in specific positions.
3. Monitor state, federal, and local legislation, bulletins, and guideline updates for changes that affect the staffing process.
4. Review manpower or personnel data to discern trends in absenteeism, tardiness, or turnover to facilitate development of personnel policies.

II. Supervise People

5. Conduct or originate staff meetings to exchange information, define objectives, establish priorities and develop solutions for emerging problems.
6. Obtain and/or clarify information from employees relevant to work procedures and standards.
7. Present work-related information (such as work or safety procedures, scheduled downtime) to subordinates or coworkers through memoranda or notices.
8. Establish performance standards for employees to clarify goals and performance expectations.
9. Inform subordinates about work methods, objectives, progress, and expected changes.
10. Encourage a subordinate's contributions and high-quality performance through words of encouragement, praise, direct assistance, and so forth.
11. Review a subordinate's work and provide action-oriented feedback to correct performance deficiencies.
12. Identify and address a subordinate's personal problems that affect job performance.
13. Distribute work assignments based on workload, work priorities, and worker capabilities.
14. Develop and maintain up-to-date manuals of department or job practices and procedures to standardize the activities of subordinates.
15. Meet with employees to discuss their perceptions of the work they do and to clarify role requirements and work responsibilities.
16. Measure employees' progress toward goals or assignment completion to evaluate individual performance and provide performance-related feedback.
17. Identify opportunities for rewarding positive work behavior and outcomes to reinforce activities that are aligned with the goals of the work group and the organization.
18. Conduct employee disciplinary interviews.

III. People Development

19. Conduct on-the-job training by demonstrating job activities and directly supervising practice.
20. Conduct informal or formal orientation of new hires to provide new employees with an overview of the organization's policies, work rules, role or job responsibilities, and so forth.
21. Review the current job assignments of employees and, with reference to their individual performance, identify assignments or work experiences that will be challenging and require growth and development.
22. Identify performance deficiencies or training needs of individual employees to guide coaching efforts and training interventions.
23. Select training courses or developmental interventions for individuals or groups of employees that address competency gaps resulting from the introduction of new technology, new work processes, redesigned jobs, and so forth.

IV. Personnel Administration

24. Explain personnel policies, programs, procedures, rules, and so forth for employees to ensure understanding.
25. Conduct exit interviews to determine causes for separation and to identify trends that have policy implications.
26. Develop and administer policies related to working hours and absences, work and vacation schedules, and so forth.
27. Administer and monitor expenditures for various benefit programs such as workers' compensation, unemployment compensation, layoff income benefits, and so forth.
28. Maintain employee files to systematically document information related to employee performance, compensation, development, and so forth.
29. Make recommendations for pay adjustments for subordinates.

V. Labor Relations

30. Intervene to resolve disagreements or interpersonal difficulties among employees.
31. Identify situations that, if unchanged, could lead to conflict among employees.
32. Investigate recurrent disputes among employees to determine causes and contributing factors.
33. Review and evaluate employee relations activities to determine their effectiveness.
34. Review local conditions or situations to predict labor relations problems.

35. Investigate employee grievances (e.g., collect facts, identify issues, research organization policies) to build a basis for discussions.
36. Develop relations with employee representatives from unions, professional groups, and so forth to lay the groundwork for future negotiations.

VI. Supervise Work Operations

37. Establish production schedules and allocate direct labor to achieve and maintain production line balance and product flow.
38. Determine changes in equipment layout and staffing to be made in response to changes in product mix.
39. Adjust work schedules or project priorities to meet emergencies or changing conditions.
40. Coordinate multiple and/or competing activities and assignments for efficient use of time and resources.
41. Evaluate the production schedule in order to anticipate required changes in personnel assignments.
42. Identify inefficiencies or roadblocks in work procedures to guide change in work flow, physical layout of the work area, work processes, and so forth.
43. Set timetables and intermediate checkpoints for others to follow in order to keep track of progress toward objectives.
44. Prepare reports of business activities or projects in one's own area of responsibility to update management.

VII. Equipment and Materials Management

45. Develop sequenced action plans to rectify identified problems with equipment or production lines.
46. Examine equipment to determine primary and/or contributory factors of equipment failure.
47. Monitor in-progress products to identify potential problems or needed adjustments to production equipment or procedures.
48. Monitor the delivery of materials and supplies to count-check amounts against requisitions, ensure quality of deliverables, oversee proper storage and placement, and so forth.
49. Develop inventory monitoring systems to track stock, material, or resource availability, allow for checks of perpetual inventories, and so forth.
50. Monitor the flow of materials or the delivery of services throughout the logistics system to audit the efficiency and cost effectiveness of materials movement or service delivery.
51. Conduct capacity utilization analyses to identify bottlenecks in production, processing, or service delivery systems.

VIII. Information Management

52. Conduct information needs analyses to determine the information and reporting requirements of an individual manager, department, business area, and so forth.
53. Interpret business data for the purpose of identifying patterns, trends, and variances in company operations.
54. Create data flow diagrams to illustrate business procedures or processes and flows among these procedures or processes.
55. Monitor information-processing systems and specific processing outputs to ensure data quality.

IX. Facilities and Safety Management

56. Monitor facility/store/plant operations to assess compliance with industry regulations, state or federal laws, or company policies.
57. Review quality control and reliability data to ensure procedural compliance and identify areas in need of improvement.
58. Develop and/or monitor the implementation of policies designed to promote safety or security, reduce accidents, and control work hazards.
59. Inspect buildings, facility layout and functioning, and so forth to determine their soundness, operational status, conformity to security guidelines, and so forth.

X. Research and Development Management

60. Identify new products, product uses, processes, process or system improvements, ways to utilize by-products and waste, and so forth that may contribute to an organization's existing stable of offerings.
61. Evaluate the technical feasibility of research and development ideas to guide recommendations concerning the allocation of human, financial, and technological resources.
62. Oversee research and development work conducted by outside facilities, such as independent laboratories, research institutes, academic institutions, consultants, trade associations, and so forth.

XI. Accounting and Financial Management

63. Use spreadsheet or specialized financial software programs to analyze cash flow, sales forecasts, budget forecasts, staffing projections, and so forth.
64. Monitor expenditures to identify trends and evaluate variances in relation to an established budget.
65. Review contracts, purchase agreements, and other financial arrangements to ensure compatibility with business goals and expectations about profitability.

XII. Marketing and Sales Management

66. Research customer project or service needs to develop proposals, make recommendations for change in existing product or service lines, and so forth.
67. Monitor competitor pricing of equivalent products or services to help others make pricing decisions.
68. Evaluate packaging (i.e., both functional and merchandising) and branding recommendations for specific products or services.
69. Prepare status reports on sales, results of promotional programs, impact of pricing changes, and so forth to update management.

SUPERVISORY
Competencies

FACTORS	DIMENSIONS
THINKING	I. Analytical Ability II. Project Planning III. Business Specific Knowledge
COMMUNI-CATIONS	IV. Verbal Communications V. Written Communications
INTER-PERSONAL	VI. Business Relationships/Teamwork VII. Work & Organization Adaptation VIII. Dependability & Trust
LEADERSHIP	IX. Management of Performance Quality X. Supervisory Skills
GENERAL OPERATIONS	XI. Materials Management XII. Facilities & Security XIII. Information Management & Computers
FUNCTIONAL KNOWLEDGE	XIV. Personnel & Staffing

I. Analytical Ability

1. Skill in identifying the relevant facts underlying conflicting claims or issues.
2. Skill in recognizing what additional information about a problem situation should be collected.
3. Skill in taking various points of view in analyzing, interpreting, and evaluating data.
4. Skill in breaking down a complex situation into its primary components.
5. Skill in evaluating conflicting alternatives based on partial or incomplete information.
6. Skill in identifying primary and/or contributory causes of equipment or manufacturing problems.

II. Project Planning

7. Knowledge of factors that have an effect on work assignment completion time.
8. Skill in coordinating the activities of other individuals or departments on joint projects.
9. Skill in scheduling multiple projects that compete for limited resources (e.g., time, equipment, personnel, etc.).
10. Skill in establishing project priorities based on relative merits, demands, or requirements.
11. Skill in sharing attention among multiple simultaneous projects or assignments.
12. Skill in adjusting project schedules or work assignments in response to changes in conditions or priorities.

III. Business Specific Knowledge

13. Knowledge of competitors' products, pricing, features, merchandising efforts, and so forth.
14. Knowledge of how other parts of the organization function (e.g., in other work teams, functional or geographic divisions, and business units).
15. Knowledge of when to go into the organization to obtain necessary information or data.
16. Knowledge of the organization's goals, product and service lines, associated competitive strengths and weaknesses, and so forth.

IV. Verbal Communications

17. Skill in soliciting information through interviews or conversation.

18. Skill in conveying information in a concise fashion without losing necessary detail.
19. Skill in helping others to clarify a request, question, or response that is not clear.
20. Skill in identifying the important points of information in a conversation.

V. Written Communications

21. Skill in translating informal conversation into action-oriented memoranda.
22. Skill in summarizing activities occurring in one's area of responsibility in written reports.
23. Knowledge of basic rules of grammar, punctuation, and sentence structure.
24. Skill in preparing reports, manuals, or other documents that are intended to be read and used by others.

VI. Business Relationships/Teamwork

25. Skill in maintaining perspective and composure in personally stressful times.
26. Skill in predicting the reaction of others to information, events, or conditions.
27. Skill in the application of timing, tact, and discretion in communicating business-related information.
28. Skill in recognizing interpersonal problems that interfere with work group performance.
29. Skill in recognizing and capitalizing on social and interpersonal cues in dealing with others.
30. Willingness to ignore personal likes and dislikes in work relationships and focus on the work at hand.

VII. Work and Organization Adaptation

31. Skill in pacing work activities and maintaining a sense of urgency and level of attention to detail essential to complete work assignments and goals.
32. Skill in identifying the setting and the conditions that determine when an individual is representing the organization.
33. Knowledge of the protocol regarding meetings, conferences, events, appointments, and authority relationships.
34. Knowledge of company standards regarding dress, language, personal hygiene, attendance, and expressed attitudes toward coworkers or customers.

35. Skill in identifying and adapting to the conditions and circumstances of the work, organization, rules, and regulations necessary to maintain a smooth-running and efficient organization.

VIII. Dependability and Trust

36. Willingness to follow through on commitments and promises.
37. Skill in communicating information in an open and sincere manner that promotes credibility (e.g., honest answers to tough questions).
38. Willingness to accept responsibility for one's own mistakes.
39. Knowledge of proprietary restrictions regarding discussion of organization operations, plans, problems, or relationships with other organizations.

IX. Management of Performance Quality

40. Skill in explaining and demonstrating work procedures to others.
41. Skill in distinguishing between effective and ineffective procedures or job performance.
42. Skill in communicating evaluative judgments and descriptive comments on the job performance of subordinates.
43. Knowledge of alternative techniques and procedures for training and their relative advantages or disadvantages.
44. Skill in recognizing signs or symptoms of personal problems that might affect job performance.
45. Skill in coaching subordinates to correct ineffective work practices or to remedy performance deficiencies.

X. Supervisory Skills

46. Skill in recognizing situational restrictions or conditions that affect choice of supervisory style.
47. Skill in addressing conditions that interfere with the performance of employees.
48. Willingness to act immediately in emergency situations.
49. Skill in assigning tasks and delegating authority in relation to a subordinate's capabilities and developmental needs.
50. Skill in recognizing and capitalizing on conditions or situations that would be perceived as rewarding by a subordinate.
51. Skill in adjusting one's actions in relation to changes in situational cues.

XI. Materials Management

52. Knowledge of purchasing fundamentals and techniques (e.g., forecasting techniques, purchasing control processes, procedures of establishing and maintaining vendor relations).
53. Knowledge of storage and inventory concepts (e.g., methods for determining storage layout, coding and marking, balancing and controlling inventory costs).
54. Knowledge of order processing (e.g., methods for entering orders, invoicing orders, measuring customer service).
55. Knowledge of logistics engineering (e.g., procedures for measuring reliability and maintainability, analyzing system functions, analyzing logistics support).
56. Knowledge of work process planning (e.g., job design concepts, work measurement procedures, variables impacting capacity planning and facilities layout).
57. Knowledge of process design and implementation (e.g., production and service designs, quality improvement concepts, project management and control).

XII. Facilities and Security

58. Knowledge of facilities tactical planning (e.g., general site/location analysis, basic ergonomics, regulatory laws governing facilities).
59. Knowledge of preventative maintenance guidelines and procedures for equipment and facilities.
60. Knowledge of start-up procedures and facility implementation (e.g., procedures for monitoring equipment and furniture installation, obtaining municipality permits, contracting outside services).
61. Knowledge of procedures for establishing physical security (e.g., intrusion prevention techniques and devices, fire protection techniques and devices, disaster recovery plans).
62. Knowledge of procedures for establishing personnel security (e.g., background investigation procedures, monitoring techniques and tools, checks and balances and separation of duties).

XIII. Information Management and Computers

63. Knowledge of information systems and information management (e.g., techniques for defining user requirements and data structures, statistical procedures for analyzing system functioning).
64. Knowledge of database manipulation and management (e.g., techniques for designing databases, storage and access methods in computer systems, CASE tools and data modeling).

65. Knowledge of computer hardware and peripheral devices (e.g., storage media such as tape drives, imaging devices, file server setup and configuration).
66. Knowledge of computer operations and support tools (e.g., software utilities, job schedulers, data transfer tools).
67. Knowledge of computer network management tools (e.g., wireless technology, LANs and WANs, system network architecture).

XIV. Personnel and Staffing

68. Skill in assessing the morale of subordinates.
69. Skill in enforcing rules and regulations without alienating others.
70. Skill in applying personnel rules in a fair and consistent manner.
71. Skill in evaluating relevant applicant background and job skills through review of resumes and application forms or through personal interviews.
72. Skill in assessing the capabilities and limitations of individuals in order to allocate personnel or make job assignments.
73. Skill in estimating time and labor requirements for work activities in order to determine staffing levels.

Appendix D

Administrative Model:
Work Activities
and Competencies

ADMINISTRATIVE
Work Activities

FACTORS	DIMENSIONS

PEOPLE

I. Supervise Clerical Employees
II. Organize, Schedule, Assign, & Monitor Work
III. Perform Receptionist Activities
IV. Public & Customer Relations
V. Sell Products & Services
VI. Employee Communications

DATA

VII. Analyze, Interpret, & Report Business Data
VIII. Computer, Verify, & Record Business Data
IX. Code & Transcribe Data
X. Receive & Disburse Cash
XI. Perform Bookkeeping & Billing Activities
XII. Handle Loan & Credit Information
XIII. Data Entry Operations

THINGS

XIV. Purchase & Maintain Supplies
XV. Type Written Materials
XVI. File & Retrieve Materials
XVII. Administrative Secretarial Duties
XVIII. Process Written Materials
XIX. Take Dictation
XX. Receive, Ship, & Distribute Mail
XXI. Computer Operations
XXII. Maintain Personnel Records
XXIII. Paralegal Activities
XXIV. Operate & Maintain Equipment

I. Supervise Clerical Employees

1. Review the work of others, return it for revision, and provide feedback and instructions as necessary.
2. Plan and coordinate the assignment or execution of duties performed by other individuals.
3. Conduct interviews with individuals and make decisions regarding selection or dismissal of employees.
4. Assign and monitor routine work activities.
5. Train new workers or other staff in the knowledge and procedures for doing their jobs.

II. Organize, Schedule, Assign, and Monitor Work

6. Monitor and evaluate the performance of other personnel.
7. Assign individuals to specific duties and locations and direct individuals in the performance of their assigned duties.
8. Estimate materials, labor, and time requirements for specific projects.
9. Organize work received from different individuals according to overall priorities.
10. Set completion dates for forms, records, or reports.

III. Perform Receptionist Activities

11. Greet visitors and direct them to the appropriate individual.
12. Answer questions and give requested directions or other information directly or by telephone.
13. Verify or confirm the identity of phone callers prior to initiating actions.
14. Receive orders, requests, instructions, or information, personally or by telephone.
15. Sign or initial documents to acknowledge receipt of valuables.

IV. Public and Customer Relations

16. Provide information over the phone or in person (e.g., explaining regulations or policies).
17. Provide services (e.g., receiving purchase orders or handling complaints that require further processing) over the phone or in person.
18. Act as host in greeting groups of visitors, conducting tours, or orchestrating business or social events.
19. Assist customers in making purchases (other than checkout).
20. Contact organizations or individuals in person or by phone in order to resolve problems in schedules, deliveries, or commitments for goods or services.

V. Sell Products and Services

21. Prepare and maintain display of products and merchandise in public areas.
22. Operate cash register to receive money and make change.
23. Investigate and resolve customer problems with goods or services.
24. Prepare and deliver sales presentations describing accommodations, services or products.
25. Wait on customers and provide information, answer questions, or suggest alternatives.

VI. Employee Communications

26. Select, assemble, and arrange distribution of news articles or other materials (brochures, leaflets, etc.) of interest within the organization.
27. Assist in planning, coordinating, and administering sponsored activities for employees or visitors (e.g., meetings, banquets).
28. Provide information to employees on the availability and terms of company benefits and services.
29. Assist employees in obtaining benefits or services.
30. Maintain bulletin board or other displays of employee-relevant information.

VII. Analyze, Interpret, and Report Business Data

31. Prepare reports, based on information at hand, following standard procedures.
32. Prepare reports requiring the investigation of various sources of information and systematic organization and presentation.
33. Evaluate information requirements for financial report preparation.
34. Maintain custody of evidence presented at meetings (including written memoranda, documents, etc.) for incorporation into transcript and records.
35. Prepare analyses or summaries of programs, reports, specific operational items, or other data.

VIII. Compute, Verify, and Record Business Data

36. Maintain checklists, logs, worksheets, or other records used to monitor the status of a project or business activity.
37. Perform calculations following a multistep formula or procedure.
38. Develop forms for the recording of numerical and statistical information.
39. Check forms or records against documents, items, master forms, or other standards to ensure accuracy and completeness.

40. Compute statistics, such as means, medians, percentages, proportions, and so forth using a calculator or computer.

IX. Code and Transcribe Data

41. Prepare summary or data entry/coding sheets for computer processing from information contained in other sources.
42. Allocate charges or payments to individual departments and accounts using accounting codes.
43. Verify accuracy of data coding and make necessary corrections.
44. Code materials using number or letter codes.
45. Make out various routing forms such as checks, receipts, invoices, form letter addresses, time or cash reports, andd so forth according to standard operating procedure.

X. Receive and Disburse Cash

46. Perform cash transactions (cashing checks, petty cash reimbursements, etc.) with customers and employees.
47. Contact bookkeeping or accounting personnel to verify the accuracy of accounts or other financial records.
48. Verify funds against amount shown on a form or record by separating currency by denomination and counting.
49. Review financial transactions to determine compliance with applicable internal and external regulations.
50. Solicit payment of bills directly from individuals, make collection of money, and keep a record of each collection.

XI. Perform Bookkeeping and Billing Activities

51. Review accounting statements, expense reports, and standard forms for accuracy, completeness, and conformity to procedures.
52. Locate sources of errors revealed through trial balance or failure to balance to an established control figure by comparing two or more sources.
53. Allocate debits, credits, costs, charges, or other similar bookkeeping items of operational procedures to correct accounts or classification.
54. Post entries in financial journals, ledgers, or other financial records.
55. Make adjustments to journal, ledger, or other records to reconcile out-of-balance conditions or numerical figures.

XII. Handle Loan and Credit Information

56. Approve or reject applications, loans, requests, claims, or other items following operational policies or rules of action.

57. Conduct loan reviews to evaluate or determine compliance with loan agreements.
58. Recommend maturity of past-due accounts and charges to bad debt.
59. Determine status of accounts in relation to payments or billings.
60. Telephone customers to notify them of returned checks and obtain payment.

XIII. Data Entry Operations

61. Operate computer peripheral equipment (e.g., printer, forms burster, magnetic tape units).
62. Verify the accuracy of data entered into computer files using a printout or visual screen.
63. Select appropriate recording or transcribing programs based on the format of the coded data to be entered.
64. Operate computer or data entry terminals to enter, change, or establish customer account information files.
65. Analyze computer or computer equipment operation in relation to conditions displayed on screens, monitors, and so on.

XIV. Purchase and Maintain Supplies

66. Take physical inventory of supplies, materials or completed work products.
67. Sign or initial documents to acknowledge receipt of valuables and authorize payment of invoices.
68. Schedule the delivery of materials and supplies to others within the organization.
69. Evaluate needs and order necessary supplies, materials, or other items.
70. Prepare purchase orders and submit to purchasing department.

XV. Type Written Materials

71. Proofread reports or other correspondence for grammar or spelling.
72. Send standard letters, printed literature, or other materials in response to routine requests on predetermined conditions.
73. Compose letters, memos, or other documents for the supervisor's signature.
74. Type tables, graphs, charts, or diagrams based on data supplied from other sources.
75. Type drafts of legal documents or records.

XVI. File and Retrieve Materials

76. Review, update, or revise file contents to reflect current status of subject.
77. Place forms, records, correspondence, or other material in the correct location in a systematic file.
78. Classify or sort informational material, correspondence, records, business forms, merchandise, or other items following standard methods of systematized arrangement.
79. Search indices, manuals, files, records or other sources for desired or missing information on specific subjects.
80. Locate and retrieve filed or stored material.

XVII. Administrative Secretarial Duties

81. Notify or remind certain individuals or departments of meetings, scheduled dates, specific duties, or occurrences.
82. Maintain an appointment book or schedule for one's supervisor.
83. Coordinate the scheduling of meetings, facilities (conference rooms, etc.), or events (tours, banquets, etc.) with other individuals or groups.
84. Investigate the source of discrepancies in documentation or search for lost documents through coordination with others outside the department.
85. Prepare expense vouchers and travel authorization and complete travel or meeting arrangements for departmental personnel.

XVIII. Process Written Materials

86. Type material from copy or manuscript.
87. Check completed forms or correspondence for inaccuracies in spelling, punctuation, grammar, format, neatness, or general appearance.
88. Compose routine correspondence or memoranda following standard operating procedures.
89. Compose correspondence requiring specific knowledge of methods, procedures, policies, or other information.
90. Produce copies of correspondence, reports, or other numerical or verbal data using a computer, a copier, or printing equipment and prepare them for distribution.

XIX. Take Dictation

91. Take shorthand notes of material to be included in reports, letters, or documents.
92. Transcribe information from telephone or recording tape.
93. Take shorthand in meetings and conferences to produce notes and summary reports.

94. Use shorthand to record dictation and work instructions given by supervisor.
95. Transcribe shorthand or stenotype notes using a typewriter.

XX. Receive, Ship, and Distribute Mail

96. Certify, register, insure, or complete forms associated with special mail services such as overnight courier or registered mail.
97. Arrange for the delivery of confidential documents via courier or special messenger.
98. Deliver mail, materials, or supplies to appropriate individuals.
99. Distribute mail, bulletins, memos, and reports to employees and offices.
100. Sort incoming and outgoing mail.

XXI. Computer Operations

101. Determine computer processing priorities on the basis of processing time, equipment availability, or other parameters.
102. Prepare computer program control cards or codes for jobs.
103. Coordinate with users on preparation of computer operating instructions.
104. Load programs and data cards or tapes.
105. Select computer program subroutines to accomplish jobs received for processing.

XXII. Maintain Personnel Records

106. Check work and background references on prospective employees.
107. Compile and maintain records or confidential and regulated information, such as personnel records.
108. Accept and log in employment applications, resumes, or job bids.
109. Make employment recommendations about applicants based on reference checks.
110. Interpret regulations, manuals, or policies to determine their applicability or provisions under specific conditions (e.g., insurance claims, tax regulations, personnel policies, etc.).

XXIII. Paralegal Activities

111. Draft or review pleadings, briefs, contracts, or other legal documents to assist licensed attorney.
112. Research legal questions and summarize findings in a written report.
113. Notarize applications, licenses, or other documents.
114. Provide administrative assistance to official representatives at legal proceedings.
115. Read and interpret regulations, manuals or administrative orders.

XXIV. Operate and Maintain Equipment

116. Schedule equipment inspections to determine need for maintenance.
117. Schedule maintenance work for office equipment according to an established schedule or priority system.
118. Repair, adjust, clean, and otherwise service electrical and mechanical office machines.
119. Operate printing and microfilming equipment.
120. Operate packaging and mailing equipment.

ADMINISTRATIVE
Competencies

FACTORS	DIMENSIONS
THINKING	I. Scheduling & Coordinating II. Arithmetic Skills III. Research & Evaluation IV. Work & Organization Skills
COMMUNI-CATIONS	V. Communications Skills VI. Oral Communications Skills
INTER-PERSONAL	VII. Customer & Public Relations VIII. Work & Organization Adaptation
LEADERSHIP	IX. Supervisory Skills
GENERAL OPERATIONS	X. Process Written Materials XI. Computer Operations Skills XII. Data Entry Skills
FUNCTIONAL KNOWLEDGE	XIII. Bookkeeping & Accounting Skills XIV. Paralegal Skills XV. Merchandising XVI. Personnel Services XVII. Fund Transfer Procedures

I. Scheduling and Coordinating

1. Skill in making arrangements, scheduling, and completing other details for meetings.
2. Skill in planning and conducting multiple activities within a specified time frame to ensure goal or deadline achievement.
3. Skill in coordinating various short-term plans to achieve long-term strategies and organizational goals.
4. Skill in scheduling and managing job activities (e.g., to set activity priorities, sequence, and maintain time perspectives).
5. Knowledge of established procedures for developing work schedules and assigning overtime.
6. Skill in visualizing the end product of work activities.

II. Arithmetic Skills

7. Skill in detecting and correcting arithmetic errors.
8. Knowledge of forecasting or explanatory financial data analysis strategies (e.g., performance ratios, trend line analysis, value index equations, etc).
9. Skill in performing calculations involving algebraic formulas, statistical formulas, or complex procedures used in handling business data.
10. Skill in performing simple arithmetic calculations (adding, subtracting, multiplying, dividing).
11. Knowledge of procedures used to calculate discount and payment schedules.
12. Skill in identifying deviations or exceptions in accounts, records, and so forth requiring explanation or further action.

III. Research and Evaluation

13. Knowledge of procedures used to locate and obtain copies of lost or missing forms or information.
14. Skill in tracing sources of errors resulting from multiple possible origins.
15. Skill in identifying probable causes of discrepancies in company records.
16. Skill in identifying the sequence of activities to locate or retrieve lost or misplaced files, documents, and so forth.
17. Skill in recognizing what specific additional information about a problem or situation should be collected.
18. Knowledge of the nature and location of information contained in records and files.

IV. Work and Organization Skills

19. Skill in adjusting schedules to reflect changing situations, requirements, or priorities.
20. Skill in working without close supervision.
21. Skill in recognizing the impact of what other employees are doing upon one's own area of responsibility.
22. Skill in interpreting and implementing instructions issued by management.
23. Skill in following through on specific problems or programs and maintaining a continuous level of emphasis until completion.
24. Skill in distinguishing between problems that can be resolved through routine procedures from those that require specialized response or attention of other persons.

V. Communications Skills

25. Skill in conveying information in a concise fashion without loss of necessary detail.
26. Skill in organizing information in reports, correspondence, and so on, in a logical and meaningful manner.
27. Skill in providing spoken information or instructions to others.
28. Skill in soliciting information through personal interviews or personal conversations.
29. Skill in maintaining or projecting a positive image in face-to-face conversations as well as in telephone conversations.
30. Skill in recognizing and capitalizing on social cues that affect the outcome of business and personal dealings with other people.

VI. Oral Communications Skills

31. Skill in identifying the important points of information from spoken content.
32. Skill in understanding what others are saying.
33. Skill in orally summarizing activity occurring in an area of responsibility.
34. Knowledge of what information should be considered confidential.
35. Skill in translating spoken information to written action memos.

VII. Customer and Public Relations

36. Skill in tactfully answering customer or employee questions, suggestions, or complaints.

37. Knowledge of authority limitations in responding to and resolving customer complaints.
38. Knowledge of procedures and policies for determining the validity of a customer complaint.
39. Skill in recognizing opportunities to improve or develop customer relations.
40. Skill in dealing with confidential information to protect customer interests.

VIII. Work and Organization Adaptation

41. Skill in pacing work activities and maintaining a sense of urgency and level of attention to detail essential to complete work assignments and goals.
42. Knowledge of the protocol regarding meetings, conferences, events, appointments, and authority relationships.
43. Knowledge of the restrictions and proprietary standards regarding discussion of organization operations, plans, problems, or relationships with other organizations.
44. Knowledge of company standards regarding dress, language, personal hygiene, attendance, and expressed attitudes toward coworkers or people associated with the organization.
45. Skill in identifying the setting and conditions that determine when an individual is identified with or representing the organization.

IX. Supervisory Skills

46. Ability to evaluate and give others feedback on their job performance.
47. Ability to explain or demonstrate work techniques, safety procedures, and so forth to others.
48. Ability to deal with subordinate performance deficiencies in a constructive manner.
49. Knowledge of principles and methods for employee performance evaluation and counseling for performance improvement.
50. Skill in identifying strengths and weaknesses of subordinate performance and establishing plans for training and development.
51. Skill in delegating responsibilities based on subordinate strengths, developmental needs, and workload.

X. Process Written Materials

52. Skill in typing from manuscripts, draft copies, voice recordings, or dictation.
53. Knowledge of rules of grammar and punctuation.

54. Skill in detecting errors in grammar or punctuation or omissions through proofreading letters, reports, forms, tables, or codes.
55. Skill in spelling commonly used English words and business terms.
56. Skill in operating word processing equipment.
57. Knowledge of formats for various written communications (e.g., letters, memoranda, reports).

XI. Computer Operations Skills

58. Skill in operating computer test and data entry, retrieval terminals, and peripheral equipment.
59. Knowledge of procedures and codes to enter, change, or delete computerized information.
60. Skill in operating computer peripherals such as printers, tape and disk drives, and so forth.
61. Skill in using packaged computer software programs to analyze business data or arrange business information.
62. Knowledge of computer programs or formats required for use with various types of data.
63. Skill in translating a user's request into computer systems procedures.

XII. Data Entry Skills

64. Skill in performing key entry of alpha or numeric material.
65. Skill in entering numerical or coded data into a computer using keyboard operations.
66. Knowledge of data entry operations with reference to speed and accuracy.
67. Knowledge of procedures and codes used to enter, change, or delete computer data or information.
68. Knowledge of entry procedures to access computer system programs or files.

XIII. Bookkeeping and Accounting Skills

69. Knowledge of procedures used to credit or debit accounts based on activity in one's area of responsibility.
70. Knowledge of procedures used to post general ledger entries.
71. Skill in detecting errors or discrepancies in record entries, data postings, or other log entries.
72. Knowledge of the procedures used to calculate principle, interest, discounts, and payment schedules.

73. Knowledge of standard bookkeeping and accounting principles and procedures.

XIV. Paralegal Skills

74. Knowledge of requirements, procedures, and schedules for reporting business or operational information to regulatory agencies.
75. Knowledge of formats, procedures, and wording conventions of legal documents.
76. Skill in analyzing legal documents to extract required information.
77. Knowledge of sources of information regarding laws, codes, and regulations.
78. Knowledge of terminology used in defining legal research questions.
79. Skill in using citation indexes such as the BNA index to locate case summaries, decisions, and search leads for legal research.

XV. Merchandising

80. Skill in determining customer or client needs and preferences from nonspecific or incomplete information.
81. Knowledge of products or services available to match customer needs and preferences.
82. Knowledge of the sales and promotional features of products and services in a retail environment.
83. Skill in recognizing cues that would indicate an opportunity for a cross-sale.
84. Skill in explaining to or interpreting for customers the procedures used to calculate refunds or reimbursements.

XVI. Personnel Services

85. Knowledge of employee medical insurance policies, retirement plan coverage, and other employee benefits, services, and policies.
86. Knowledge of required forms for obtaining and processing applicant or employee information.
87. Knowledge of union contract provisions and organization policies regarding wage and salary administration.
88. Knowledge of policies and regulations concerning the collection, recording, and dissemination of personnel data.
89. Knowledge of the policies and procedures regarding selection, promotion, transfer, discipline, or discharge of employees.
90. Knowledge of EEOC and Affirmative Action guidelines with regard to recruitment, selection, promotion, and transfer actions.

XVII. Fund Transfer Procedures

91. Knowledge of security procedures related to the movement or transfer of funds.
92. Knowledge of procedures to resolve errors in the transfer of funds.
93. Knowledge of procedures used to transfer funds to and from customer accounts.
94. Knowledge of bank deposit and fund transfer procedures.
95. Skill in handling and sorting currency, checks, and so forth.

Author Index

A

Albrecht, P. A., 11, 15, 23, 196, 199
American Educational Research Association, 35, 50, 175, 185
American Psychological Association, 35, 50, 175, 176, 184, 185, 224, 226
Ansbacher, H. L., 7, 23
Antonioni, D., 71, 95
Aronowitz, S., 18, 23
Arthur, W., Jr., 54, 91, 111, 120
Arvey, R. D., 54, 55, 89, 189, 200
Ash, R. A., 20, 25, 28, 51, 70, 89
Ashworth, S., 67, 93
Atwater, L. E., 71, 95

B

Bachler, C. J., 104, 120
Baker, T. G., 69, 89
Barker, R. G., 225, 226
Barnwell, F., 73, 95
Barr, S. H., 128, 140
Barrett, R. S., 28, 50
Barrick, M. R., 66, 71, 93, 174, 185
Bartlett, C. J., 196, 199
Bass, B. M., 113, 120
Battista, M., 20, 25, 28, 51
Bendig, A. W., 113, 120
Benson, C., 68, 90
Bentz, V., 195, 201
Biersner, R. J., 73, 89
Black, J., 11, 15, 16, 23
Bleir, A., 41, 51
Bloom, B. S., 10, 12, 25
Bolin, S. F., 10, 12, 16, 24, 196, 199
Borman, W. C., 20, 25, 41, 50, 65, 72, 93, 94
Boudreau, J. W., 4, 23
Boyatzis, R. E., 38, 50

Bracken, D. W., 71, 89
Bray, D. W., 68, 89, 188, 199
Brickner, M., 127, 140
Bridges, W., 18, 23
Brush, D. H., 41, 50
Bryan, J. A., 226, 226
Burnett, J. R., 113, 120
Burtt, H. E., 8, 23
Byham, W. C., 68, 95, 152, 168, 188, 201

C

Cable, D. M., 54, 92, 113, 120
Camerer, C. F., 128, 139
Campbell, D. T., 22, 23, 225, 226, 227
Campbell, J. T., 11, 14, 23, 24, 196, 199
Campion, J. E., 54, 55, 89, 113, 120
Campion, M. A., 55, 89, 111, 113, 120
Carr, L., 20, 25, 28, 51
Carter, R. C., 73, 89
Cascio, W. F., 113, 120
Castle, P. F. C., 12, 23
Chao, G. T., 3, 25, 54, 66, 94, 191, 200
Chase, W. G., 128, 139
Christiansen, N. D., 66, 89
Church, A. H., 71, 89
Conrad, K. A., xvi, xxi
Conway, J. M., 55, 89
Croll, P. R., 72, 94, 191, 197, 200
Cronbach, L. J., 66, 89, 197, 199, 224, 227
Cronshaw, S. F., 54, 55, 95, 111, 121, 174, 186
Crooks, L. A., 67, 89
Cross, D., 113, 121

D

Dalessio, A. T., 71, 90
Dawes, R. M., 127, 139
Dawson, R. E., 225, 227
Day, D. A., 67, 90

Degroot, T., 113, *120*
DeMers, S. T., 176, *186*, 187, *201*
DeNelsky, G. Y., 11, 16, *23*, 196, *199*
DeNisi, A. S., 71, 73, 90, *92*
Dicken, C., 11, 15, 16, *23*
DiFazio, W., 18, *23*
Dipboye, R. L., 113, *121*
Dreher, G. F., 127, *140*
DuBois, P. H., 7, *23*
Duncan, D., 10, 12, *24*
Dunnette, M. D., 10, 13, *23*, 66, 73, *91*, 93, 191, *199*
Duran, A. S., 128, *140*

E

Earles, J. A., 55, *94*
Eaton, H. K., 66, *91*
Einhorn, H. J., 128, *139*
Elkins, T. J., 71, *90*
Ellingson, J. E., 66, *94*
Ericson, K. A., 128, *139*
Eyde, L. D., 20, *25*, 28, *51*, 176, *185*

F

Fan, C., 113, *120*
Farina, A. J., Jr., 43, *50*
Farr, J. L., 113, *121*
Feild, H. S., 69, *90*
Finn, R. H., 113, *120*
Fiske, D. W., 7, 9, 10, *24*, 225, 226, *227*
Flanagan, J. C., 11, 15, *23*, 129, *139*
Fleishman, E. A., 8, 20, *23*, *25*, 43, *50*, *51*, 65, 68, 90, *91*, 93
Fowler, R. D., 195, *199*
Fox, H. R., 176, *186*, 187, *201*
Fraser, S. L., 36, *51*
Frederickson, N., 225, *227*

G

Gael, S., 28, 41, *50*
Ganzach, Y., 127, 128, *140*
Garforth, F. I. de la P., 12, *23*
Gatewood, R. D., 69, *90*
Gaugler, B. B., 68, *90*
Gebhardt, D. L., 68, *90*, 93
Gellatly, I. R., 66, *90*
Ghiselli, E. E., 66, *90*
Ghorpade, J., 71, *90*
Gibson, J. W., 70, *90*
Gilbert, P. J., 196, *199*
Glaser, E. D., 11, 15, *23*, 196, *199*
Goffin, R. D., 66, 67, 89, *90*
Goldberg, L. R., 73, *91*
Goldman, B. M., 175, *185*
Gooding, R. Z., 3, *25*, 55, 66, *94*, 174, *186*, 191, *201*

Goodman, D. F., 55, *89*
Gordon, L. V., 11, 16, *23*, 196, *199*, 206, *227*
Gordon, T. R., 70, *92*
Gottier, R. F., 66, *91*
Grant, D. L., 68, *89*
Green, B. F., 183, *185*
Green, C. G., 196, *199*
Gross, M. L., 188, *199*
Gruys, M. L., 66, *94*
Guion, R. M., 3, *24*, 66, 68, 70, *91*, 172, *185*, 188, 189, 190, 196, *199*, *200*
Guterman, H. A., 41, *51*

H

Handyside, J., 10, 12, *24*
Hanfmann, E., 7, *24*
Hansen, C. P., xvi, *xxi*
Hanson, M. A., 67, *93*
Harris, E. F., 8, *23*
Harris, M. M., 54, 55, *91*
Hase, H. D., 73, *91*
Hasserbrook, F., 128, *140*
Hazucha, J. F., 71, *91*
Hellervik, L. W., 27, *50*
Helms, J. E., 152, 153, *168*
Hemphill, J. K., 8, *24*, 43, *50*
Henry, E. R., 225, *227*
Herold, D. M., 66, *91*
Hesketh, B., 20, *25*, 28, *51*
Hezlett, S. A., 71, *91*
Hicks, M. D., 27, *50*
Higgins, C. A., 54, *92*, 113, *120*
Highhouse, S., 190, *199*
Hilton, A. C., 10, 12, 16, *24*, 70, 71, *92*, 196, *199*
Hirsh, H. R., 72, *91*
Hitt, M. A., 128, *140*
Hoffman, C. C., 73, *91*
Hogan, J. C., 68, *91*
Hogue, J. P., 14, *24*
Holden, L. M., 73, *91*
Hollenbeck, G. P., xvi, *xxi*
Holt, R. R., 10, 13, *24*, 197, *199*
Holtzman, W. H., 9, 10, 13, 16, *24*
Horvath, J. A., 153, *168*
Hough, L. M., 66, 67, 70, 71, 72, 73, *91*, 93, *94*
House, R. J., 66, *91*
Houston, J.S., 73, *93*
Hudson, J. P., Jr., 113, *120*
Huffcutt, A. I., 54, *91*, 111, *120*
Hughes, G. L., xvi, *xxi*, 41, *51*, 69, *94*, 188, 196, 198, *199*, *200*
Hunter, J. E., 3, 4, *24*, *25*, 54, 55, 66, 69, 72, *91*, *94*, 111, *120*, *121*, 174, *185*, 191, 197, *200*
Hunter, R. F., 3, *24*, 54, 55, 69, *91*, 111, *120*, 174, *185*
Huse, E. F., 11, 14, 16, *24*

I

Impara, J. C., 20, *24*, 55, *92, 93*, 207, *227*

J

Jackson, D. M., 174, *186*
Jackson, D. N., 66, 73, 90, *92*, 95
Jako, R. A., 55, 89
Janz, T., 54, *92*, 111, *120*
Jeanneret, P. R., xvi, *xxi*, 20, *25*, 65, 73, *92, 93*
Jerdee, T. H., 196, *200*
Johnson, E. J., 128, *139*
Johnson, J. C., 70, 89
Johnson, P. E., 128, *140*
Johnston, N. G., 66, 67, 89, 90
Jones, L. V., 113, *120*
Judge, T. A., 54, *92*, 113, *120*

K

Kahneman, D., 127, *140*
Kamp, J. D., 66, *91*
Katz, J. A., 67, *94*, 191, *200*
Kehoe, J., 20, *25*, 28, *51*
Keller, L. S., 195, *201*
Kelly, E. L., 9, 10, *24*
Kelly, M. L., 67, *93*
Kirchner, W. K., 10, 13, *23*
Kirsch, M., 3, *25*, 55, 66, *94*, 174, *186*, 191, *201*
Klayman, N., 127, 128, *140*
Kleinmuntz, B., 128, *139*
Kleinmuntz, D. N., 128, *139*
Klimoski, R., 127, *140*
Kluger, A. N., 71, 90, *92*, 127, 128, *140*
Kopelman, R. E., 4, *24*
Krell, T. C., 188, *199*
Krug, R. E., 11, 15, *23*
Kuhnert, K. W., 113, *121*

L

Landy, F. J., 172, *186*
Latham, G. P., 111, *120*
Lavigna, R. J., 70, *92*
Lawrence, P. R., 38, *51*
Levine, E. L., 70, 89, *92*
Levine, J. M., 43, *51*
Lichtenfels, P. A., 54, 95, 111, *121*
Liske, R. E., 11, 14, *23*, 196, *199*
Lodge, M., 113, *121*
Loevinger, J., 73, *92*, 225, *227*
Lopez, F., 67, *92*
Lorsch, J. W., 38, *51*
Lowman, R. L., 183, *185*
Lozada-Larsen, S. R., 36, *51*
Lyman, H. B., 183, *185*
Lyons, T., 70, *92*

M

Maas, J. B., 113, *121*
Macan, T. H., 113, *121*
MacCrimmon, K. R., 126, *140*
Macey, W. H., 178, *185*, 187, *200*
MacKinnon, D. W., 7, *24*
Mael, F. A., 70, 71, *92*
Mahoney, J. D., 41, *51*
Mahoney, M. H., 67, 89
Mahoney, T. A., 196, *200*
Marks, J., 11, 15, *23*, 196, *199*
Marquardt, L. D., 73, *92*
Matarazzo, J. D., 194, 197, *200*
Maurer, S. D., 54, 55, *93*, 111, *121*, 174, *185*, 196, *200*
Maye, D. M., 70, *92*
McCall, M. M., 41, *51*
McClelland, D. C., 20, *25*
McCloy, R. A., 66, *91*
McCormick, E. J., 73, *92, 93*
McDaniel, M. A., 54, 55, 70, 89, *93*, 111, *121*, 174, *185*
McHenry, J. J., 67, *93*
McKee, M. G., 11, 16, *23*, 196, *199*
McKenzie, R. C., 4, *25*, 72, *94*, 191, 197, *200*
McLagan, P. A., 20, *24*
McManus, M. A., 67, *93*
McPhail, S. M., 73, *91, 93*
Mecham, R. C., 73, *92, 93*
Meehl, P. E., 127, *140*, 153, *168*, 194, 197, *200*, 224, *227*
Mendoza, J. L., 71, *94*
Meritt-Haston, R., 70, *93*
Messick, S., 152, 153, *168*, 192, 195, 197, *200*
Meyer, H. H., 10, 12, *24*
Meyer, J. P., 66, 90
Michel, R. P., 196, *201*
Miller, G. A., 127, *140*
Miller, J. D., 7, *24*
Miller, L., xvi, *xxi*
Miner, J. B., 11, 16, *24*, 196, *200*
Mintzberg, H., 38, *51*
Moller, J., 128, *140*
Moreland, K. L., 176, *185*
Morgan, R. B., 69, *93*
Most, R. B., 176, *185*
Mosteller, F., 113, *121*
Motowidlo, S. J., 113, *120*
Mount, M. K., 66, 71, *93*, 174, *185*
Muchinsky, P. M., 127, *140*
Muldrow, T., 4, *25*
Mumford, M. D., 20, *25*, 65, 68, 70, 90, *93*, 95
Munsterberg, H., 8, *24*
Murphy, L. L., 55, *93*, 207, *227*
Murphy, P. J., 41, *51*
Murray, H. A., 7, *24*
Myers, D. C., 68, *93*

N

Nash, A. N., 196, 200
National Council on Measurement in Education, 35, 50, 175, 185
Nisbett, R., 127, 140
Noe, R. A., 3, 25, 55, 66, 94, 174, 186, 191, 201
Norusis, M. J., 222, 227

O

O'Connor, E. J., 113, 120
Ogden, G. D., 68, 91
Ohmann, O. A., 8, 24
Organ, D. W., 153, 168
Orne, M., 225, 227
Otis, J. L., 8, 11, 14, 23, 24, 196, 199
Outerbridge, A. N., 4, 25
Owens, W. A., 70, 93, 95, 225, 227

P

Palmer, D. K., 55, 89
Parasuraman, R., 43, 51
Parker, J. W., 10, 12, 16, 24, 196, 199
Parry, M. E., 72, 93
Patrick, J., 73, 95
Paullin, C., 71, 91
Paunonen, S. V., 66, 90
Pearlman, K., 20, 25, 28, 51
Peterson, N. G., 20, 25, 65, 73, 93
Pfeiffer, J., 194, 200
Phelan, J. G., 11, 14, 25
Phillips, J. S., 71, 90
Pinto, P. R., 43, 51
Plake, B. S., 20, 24, 55, 92, 93, 207, 227
Polson, P. G., 128, 139
Posner, M. I., 127, 140
Price, S. J., 68, 93
Prien, E. P., xvi, xxi, 11, 14, 20, 23, 24, 25, 28, 41, 51, 67, 69, 70, 90, 94, 95, 178, 185, 187, 188, 191, 196, 198, 199, 200, 201
Prien, K. O., 196, 198, 201
Primoff, E. S., 176, 185
Pulakos, E. C., 72, 94
Pulakos, E. D., 113, 121
Pursell, E. D., 54, 95, 111, 120, 121

Q

Quaintance, M. K., 43, 50, 65, 90

R

Rader, M., 54, 94, 111, 121
Raymark, P. H., 196, 200

N

Reagan, R. T., 113, 121
Ree, M. J., 55, 94
Reed, G. M., 176, 186, 187, 201
Reilly, M. E., 65, 90
Reilly, R. R., 3, 25, 54, 66, 94, 191, 200
Rifkin, J., 18, 25
Robertson, D. W., 73, 94
Robertson, G. J., 176, 185
Rogelberg, S. G., 71, 89
Romashko, T., 43, 51
Ronan, W. W., 20, 25
Rosenthal, D. B., 68, 90
Ross, L., 127, 140
Rosse, R. L., 73, 93
Roth, P. L., 66, 67, 95, 191, 201
Rothe, H. F., 8, 25
Rothstein, H., 174, 186
Rothstein, M. G., 66, 67, 89, 90, 95
Russell, J. S, 174, 185, 196, 200
Ryan, A. M., xv, xxi, 43, 51, 54, 94, 177, 185, 188, 191, 200
Ryan, K., 153, 168

S

Saari, L. M., 111, 120
Sackett, P. R., xv, xxi, 43, 51, 54, 66, 94, 127, 140, 177, 185, 188, 189, 191, 200
Sale, F., Jr., xvi, xix, 188, 200
Sanchez, J. I., 20, 25, 28, 36, 51
SAS Institute, Inc., 222, 227
Sawyer, J., 127, 140, 153, 168, 194, 197, 200
Schemmer, F. M., 68, 90
Schippmann, J. S., xvi, xxi, 20, 25, 27, 28, 29, 31, 33, 34, 41, 51, 66, 67, 69, 94, 95, 153, 168, 188, 191, 196, 198, 200, 201
Schmidt, F. L., 3, 4, 25, 54, 55, 66, 72, 91, 93, 94, 111, 121, 174, 185, 191, 197, 200
Schmidt, N., 54, 55, 66, 94, 191, 201
Schmit, M. J., 196, 200
Schmitt, N., 3, 25, 113, 121, 172, 174, 186
Schneider, B., 38, 51
Schneider, R., 71, 91
Schoenfeldt, L. S., 71, 94
Schuh, A. J., 113, 121
Schwartz, R. D., 225, 227
Sechrest, L., 225, 227
Sells, S. B., 9, 13, 16, 24, 225, 227
Shane, S. A., 66, 91
Shartle, C. L., 8, 25
Shaw, J. B., 73, 92
Shore, L. M., 127, 140
Shore, T. H., 127, 140
Silverman, S. B., 67, 90
Silzer, R. F., xvi, xxi, 11, 17, 25
Simon, H. A., 127, 128, 139, 140
Sinclair, R. R., 196, 201
Slovic, P., 127, 140
Smith, J. E., 69, 93

Society for Human Resource Management, 176, 183, *186*
Society for Industrial and Organizational Psychology, 35, *51*, 176, *186*
Sommers, C., 27, *50*
Sparks, C. P., 35, *51*
Sparrow, J., 73, *95*
Spector, P. E., 113, *121*
Spencer, L. M., 20, *25*
Spencer, S., 20, *25*
Spreitzer, G. K., 41, *51*
Spurgeon, P., 73, *95*
Stanley, J. C., 22, *23*
Stead, N. H., 8, *25*
Stein, M. I., 10, 12, *25*
Stern, G. G., 10, 12, *25*
Sternberg, R. J., 153, *168*
Stokes, G. S., 70, *95*
Strong, E. K., 8, *25*
Summerlin, W., 70, *95*
Super, D. E., 70, *95*
Switzer, F. S., 66, 67, *95*, 191, *201*

T

Taft, R., 197, *201*
Tamir, L., xvi, *xxi*
Tanenhaus, J., 113, *121*
Taylor, E. K., 10, 12, 16, *24*, 196, *199*
Taylor, R. N., 126, *140*
Test, M. A., 226, *226*
Tett, R. P., 41, *51*, 66, *95*, 174, *186*
Theologus, G. C., 43, *51*
Thornton, G. C., III, 68, 90, *95*, 127, *140*, 152, *168*, 188, *199*, *201*
Thurstone, L. L., 113, *120*
Timmreck, C. W., 71, *89*
Toquam, J. L., 67, 73, *93*
Tornow, W. W., 43, *51*
Trankell, A., 11, 13, *25*, 194, 196, *201*
Trattner, M. H., 4, *25*
Trent, T. T., 73, *94*
Trumbo, D., 54, *95*
Turnage, J. J., 127, *140*
Turner, S. M., 176, *186*, 187, *201*
Tursky, B., 113, *121*

Tversky, A., 127, *140*

U

Ulm, R. A., 70, *92*
Ulrich, L., 54, *95*
Uniform Guidelines on Employee Selection Procedures, 35, *51*, 171, 172, *186*
U.S. Department of Labor, 34, *51*, 64, *95*
Urbrock, R. S., 8, *26*

V

Vale, C. D., 195, *201*
Vance, R. J., 113, *121*
Vernon, P., 9, 10, *26*
Vinchur, A. J., 66, 67, *95*, 173, *186*, 191, 196, 198, *201*
Viteles, M. A., 8, *26*
Vrazo, G. J., 27, *51*

W

Waclawski, J., 71, *89*
Wagner, R., 54, *95*
Wagner, R. K., 153, *168*
Waldman, D. A., 71, *95*
Walker, W. B., 10, 12, 16, *24*, 196, *199*
Ward, L. B., 67, *95*
Webb, E. J., 225, *227*
Wexley, K. N., 70, *93*
Wheaton, G. R., 43, *50*
Whetzel, D. L., 54, 55, *93*, 111, *121*, 174, *185*
Wiesner, W. H., 54, 55, *95*, 111, *121*, 174, *186*
Wiggins, J. S., 73, *95*, 122, *140*
Williams, W. M., 153, *168*
Wing, H., 73, *93*
Witt, L. A., 71, *93*
Wooten, W. A., 70, *95*, 196, 198, *201*
Wright, P. M., 54, *95*, 111, *121*

Y

Youtz, C., 113, *121*

Subject Index

A

Ability(ies), 20, 28
    competencies and, 29–30, 33–34
    defined, 204
Ability tests, 3–4, 204
Absolute scores, 124
Accommodation for disabilities, 96, 99
Accounting management
    management and executive model, 236
    supervisory model, 256
Accounting skills
    administrative model, 278–279
    management and executive model, 248
Achievement test, 204
Action verbs, use in reports, 146
Activity–attribute linkages, 73
Adaptability, management and executive model, 243–244
Adaptability Test (AT), 56
Administrative model, 41, 44
    competencies, 274–280
    work activities, 266–273
Advanced Mental Ability Test (AMAT), 56, 75, 78, 82–83
Adverse impact, 209
Age Discrimination in Employment Act (1967), 34, 172
Airline pilots, individual assessment research on, 11, 13–14
Alliance management, management and executive model, 235, 247
American Psychological Association, 8, 184–185
Americans with Disabilities Act (ADA) (1990), 34–35, 96, 99, 172
Analytical ability
    management and executive model, 240
    supervisory model, 259
Applied psychology, xvii
Aptitude tests, 3–4, 204

Arithmetic mean, 219
Arithmetic skills, administrative model, 275
Assessee
    background, 107–108, 142, 147
    feedback to, 103–104, 143–144, 153–154, 184
    follow-up with, 142–143, 151–152, 154
    relationship with assessor, 96, 100–102, 184
Assessment agreement form, 96, 99
Assessment center model, 68, 188
Assessment interview, 21, 52–53, 100–109
    dos and don'ts, 109
    ethical issues, 183
    evaluating data from, 110–112
    examples, 113–120
    legal issues, 109, 175
    questions, 19, 109, 111, 113
    research context, 111, 113
    structured, 111, 196
    worksheet, 107–108
Assessment of qualifications document, 69–70
Assessment protocol, 19–21, 41, 52–88
    examples, 74–88
    research context, 53–74
    tests and, 52–53
Assessment specifications, identifying, 33–42
Assessor, xvi
    ability to make judgments, 196–197
    competency of, 176–182, 193–194
    credibility of, 145–146
    differences attributable to, 13, 16
    gender of, 197
    multiple vs. sole, 144–145
    relationship with assessee, 96, 100–102, 184
Average(s), 215, 217, 219–222

B

Background, assessee, 107–108, 142, 147
Bar chart, 141

Base rate of validity, 191–192, *see also* Validity
  biographical inventories and, 70–71
  cognitive ability tests and, 55–60, 64–65
  interest inventories and, 67
  interviews and, 54–55
  personality tests and, 66–67
  reference checks and, 69–70
  360 degree ratings and, 71
  work samples and, 67–69
Basic Skill Measures, 60
Battery test, 204–205
Bennett Mechanical Comprehension Test
  (BMCT), 56
Biodata, 70–71
Biographical inventories, 53, 70–71
Bookkeeping/billing activity, administrative
  model, 269
Bookkeeping skills, administrative model,
  278–279
Brain Watchers, The, 188
British Foreign Service and Civil Service selec-
  tion program, 7, 9–10
Business consultants, individual assessment re-
  search on, 11, 16–17
Business data analysis, administrative model,
  268
Business data recording, administrative model,
  268–269
Business relationships/teamwork
  management and executive model, 243
  supervisory model, 260
Business Relations Skills Test (BRST), 56, 82–83
Business specific knowledge
  management and executive model, 241
  supervisory model, 259

C

California Psychological Inventory (CPI), 61,
  87–88
Campbell Interest and Skill Survey (CISS), 63
Can-do competencies, 28, 55
Career aspirations, 146, 148
Carnegie Tech group, 8
Case Western Reserve research, 14
Cash reception/disbursement, administrative
  model, 269
Categorical variables, 215
Central tendency errors, 112
Chunking, 127
Citizenship behavior, 153
Civil Rights Act of 1964, Title VII, 34, 172, 174
Civil Rights Act of 1991, 34, 172, 175, 212
Civil Service candidates, individual assessment
  research on, 9–10
Clerical employee supervision, administrative
  model, 267
Clinical assessment, 8, 127, 129
Clinically collected data, 124

Clinical psychologists, 8
Clinical psychologist trainees, individual assess-
  ment research on, 10
Clinical psychology, 177
Code of Conduct, 184–185
*Code of Ethical and Professional Standards in Hu-
  man Resource Management*, 176
Coefficient alpha, 213
Coefficient of equivalence, 213
Coefficient of internal consistency, 212–213
Coefficient of stability, 213
Cognitive ability tests, 53, 100, 205
  base rate validity and, 55–60, 64–65
Communication skills, administrative model,
  276
Competency(ies), 19
  assessor, 176–182, 193–194
  available vs. required, 34
  can-do, 28, 55
  defined, 20, 28
  historical assessment and, 7
  identifying, 5, 6, 33–36
  identifying job, 31–33
  identifying people, 28–30, 33
  individual assessment, 36, 179–182
  interpretation of assessment data and,
    126–127
  job-related, 108
  test scores and, 195
  will-do, 28, 66
Competency evaluation, 146, 148–150
Competency models, 41–42
  administrative, 41, 44, 274–280
  management and executive, 41, 229–249
  sales and customer relations, 42
  supervisory, 41, 258–263
  technical and analytical, 42
Competency profiles
  department manager, 79, 81
  division president, 84, 86
  sales associate, 75, 77
Competitive strategy, 31, 33–34
Computerized testing, 195
Computer operation work activities, administra-
  tive model, 272
Computer Programmer Aptitude Battery
  (CPAB), 57
Computer competencies
  administrative model, 278
  management and executive model, 246–247
  supervisory model, 262–263
Concurrent validity, 214
Confidentiality, 183
Configural rules, 128
Consent forms, 21
Constant errors, 211
Construct, defined, 224–225
Construct validity, 173, 214, 224
Consumers, of assessment services, xvii
Content validity, 173, 214

Contextual information, about assessee,
        107–109
Continuous variables, 215–216
Contrast errors, 112
Coordinating skills, administrative model, 275
Correction for guessing, 207
Correlation coefficient, 210–211, 221–222
Counseling, individual assessment competencies
        in, 182
Counseling Center at Stanford University, 15
Counseling psychology, 177
Creativity, management and executive model,
        240
Credibility, assessor, 145–146
Criterion/criteria, 191, 209–210
        concept of, 197
Criterion development, 5
Criterion group, 73–74
Criterion keyed test, 208
Criterion-related strategy, 4–6
Criterion validity, 172–173, 214
Critical Reasoning Test Battery (CRTB), 57
Critical Thinking Test (CTT), 57, 87–88
Cross-validation, 211
Cultural equivalents, 153
Culture variables, 197
Current job, of assessee, 107–108
Customer relations, administrative model, 267,
        276–277
Customer Relations Skills Test (CRS), 64
Customer Service Inventory (CSI), 64, 78–79
Cut/cutting score, 207

D

Data collection and analysis, individual assess-
        ment competencies, 180–181
Data entry operations, administrative model,
        270
Data entry skills, administrative model, 278
Data set, describing, 216, 218–219
Data transcription, administrative model, 269
Decision making, 126–129
Decisiveness, management and executive model,
        245
Department manager assessment
        assessment interview, 115–117
        establishing assessment protocol for, 79–84
        integration and interpretation stage,
                133–136
        job modeling, 46–48
        report, 154, 158–162
Dependability
        management and executive model, 244
        supervisory model, 261
Deselection, 37
Development
        individual assessment for, xv, 37–38
        management and executive model, 231–232

pure developmental assessments, 37
remedial developmental assessments, 37
report on prospects for, 142, 146, 150–152
supervisory model, 254
talent searches, 37–38
Dictation, administrative model, 271–272
Dictionary of Occupational Titles (DOT), 65
Differential Aptitude Test (DAT), 57
Discriminant validity, 12, 14–16
District marketing managers, individual assess-
        ment research on, 11, 15
Division president assessment
        assessment interview, 117–120
        establishing assessment protocol for, 84–88
        integration and interpretation stage,
                136–139
        job modeling, 48–50
        report, 162–168
Draw-a-Person Test, 12

E

e-commerce, individual assessment and,
        195–196
Economics, management and executive model,
        247
Education
        competencies and, 29–30, 33–34
        falsifying, 104–105
        for individual assessment practice, xvii, 188,
                190–192, 197
Edwards Personal Preference Schedule (EPPS),
        61, 87–88
EEOC (Equal Employment Opportunity Com-
        mission) laws, 172
Elementary school trainees, individual assess-
        ment research on, 10, 12
Elements of Supervision (EOS), 57, 82–83
Empathy, demonstrating to assessee, 101
Employee Aptitude Survey (EAS), 57
Employee communications, administrative
        model, 268
Employment testing, 3–6
        historical context, 7–8
Endorsement, in report, 142–143
Engineers, individual assessment research on,
        11, 15
Equal Pay Act of 1963, 34
Equipment maintenance, administrative model,
        273
Equipment management, supervisory model, 255
Equivalent forms, 205
Error, 211, 224
        measurement of, 225
Essential functions of job, 34
Ethical issues in individual assessment, 182–185
Ethical Principles of Psychologists, 184–185
Evidence, supporting assessment process,
        173–174

Executive assessment, 8
Executive model, 41
    competencies, 239–249
    work activities, 230–238
Executive Order No. 11246 (1978), 172
Expectations, of individual assessment, 38,
        102–103
Experience, competencies and, 29–30, 33–34
Experts, decision making and, 128
External relations, management and executive
        model, 233
External selection, 37

F

Facilities management
    management and executive model, 235, 246
    supervisory model, 256, 262
Factor analysis, 73–74, 223
False information, given in assessment, 104–105
Federal law, individual assessment and, 172
Feedback, to assessee, 19, 21–22, 103–104,
        143–144, 153–154, 184
Feeling and Doing test, 12
Financial knowledge, management and execu-
        tive model, 248
Financial management
    management and executive model, 236
    supervisory model, 256
First impression errors, 112
First-line supervisors, individual assessment re-
        search on, 11, 14–16
Five-facet model, 194, 198, see also Individual
        assessment model
Five-point rating scale, 110–111, 113
Flanagan Industrial Test (FIT), 58
Fleishman Job Analyses Survey (F-JAS), 65
Follow-up, 19, 22–23, 142–143, 151–152, 154
Foreign Service candidates, individual assess-
        ment research on, 9–10
Foundations for career success, 146–148
4/5 rule, 209
Fund transfer procedures, administrative model,
        280

G

Gender, assessment and, 194, 197
General Aptitude Test Battery (GATB), 55,
        64–65
General Electric supervisors, individual assess-
        ment research on, 10, 12–13
General mental ability measures, 56
German military, employment testing and, 7
Ghiselli Self Description Inventory (GSDI), 61,
        78–79
Global Personality Inventory (GPI), 61
GMAT (Graduate Management Admissions
        Test), 207
Goals, of assessee, 107–108

Gordon Personal Profile Inventory (GPPI), 62,
        75, 78, 82–84, 206
Government employees, individual assessment
        research on, 11, 16
Group discussions, leaderless, 68
Guessing, correcting for, 207
Guilford-Zimmerman Temperament Survey
        (GZTS), 62

H

Halo effects, 12
Halo errors, 112
Handbook of Human Abilities, 65
Heterogeneity, 211
Historical context, of employment testing, 7–8
Hogan Personality Inventory (HPI), 62
Homogeneity, 211
Human resource management, xvii
    individual assessment and expertise in,
        177–178
    management and executive model, 249

I

In-basket test, 67, 191
Individual assessment, 6–7, 209
    conceptual base, 194–195
    conducting, 19, 21, 96–100, see also Assess-
        ment interview
    cross-cultural approaches to, 194
    cultural variables and, 197
    defined, xv
    for development, see Development
    ethical issues, 182–185
    expectations of, 38
    extent of industry, 189, 193
    future of, 188–189
    history of, 7–8
    Internet and marketing of, 195–196
    legal issues in, 171–175
    professional issues in, 175–182
    research context, 9–18
    for selection, xv, 37
Individual assessment competencies, 179–182
Individual assessment model, 18–23, 198
    conducting assessment, 19, 21, 96–100, see
        also Assessment interview
    establishing assessment protocol, see Assess-
        ment protocol
    feedback, 19, 21–22, 103–104, 143–144,
        153–154, 184
    integration and interpretation, 19, 21–22,
        122–139
    job modeling, see Job modeling
    program evaluation, 22–23
    reporting, see Report/reporting
Industrial and organizational (I/O) psychology,
        8, 177–178, 187, 189, 191, 197

Industrial and organizational (I/O) psychologists, 8, 174, 177–178
Industrial Reading Test (IRT), 60
Industrial relations, xvii
Influencing skills, management and executive model, 243
Information
    overload, 127
    utility of, 152–153
Information management
    management and executive model, 234–235, 246–247
    supervisory model, 256, 262–263
Integration and interpretation, 19, 21–22, 122–139
    examples, 129–139
    research context, 126–129
    worksheets, 129–130, 134–135, 137–138
Intellectual functioning, 146–148, 159–160, 165
Intelligence, as predictor of human performance, 192
Interactive work samples, 67–69
Interest inventories, 13, 53, 63
    base rate validity and, 67
Interests, competencies and, 29–30, 33–34
Internal consulting, management and executive model, 237–238
Internal selection, 37
International operations, management and executive model, 235, 247
Internet
    computerized testing and, 195
    online assessment services and, 195–196
Interpersonal Style Inventory (ISI), 62
Interview, see also Assessment interview
    base rate validity of, 54–55
    structured, 54, 111, 196
    unstructured, 54, 111
Introduction
    assessment interview, 100–106
    individual assessment, 96–98, 100
    report, 146
    Inventory, 205, see also Test(s)
    biographical, 53, 70–71
    interest, 13, 53, 63, 67
Ipsative scoring, 124–126
Ipsative test, 205–206

J

Jackson Personality Test (JPS), 62
Job, 21
    defined, 18, 20
Job analysis, 35
    defined, 20
    interviews and, 54–55
    research on, 43

Job category, 6, 21, 36
Job descriptions, 40
Job expert, 41
Job family, 6
Job group, 6, 21, 36
Job modeling, 5, 17–20, 27–50
    assessment process evidence and, 173–174
    competency identification, 28–36
    defined, 20
    for department manager, 48
    for division president, 49–50
    examples, 44–50
    identifying assessment specifications, 36–42
    individual assessment competencies, 179
    individual assessment decision making and, 126–127
    interviews and, 54–55
    job competency identification, 31–33
    legal issues and, 35–36
    personal competency identification, 28–30
    psychological assessment and, 125
    questions, 40, 44, 46
    for sales associate, 45–46
Job modeling questionnaire, 41, 44, 75
Job Modeling Worksheet, 38–40
Job pyramid, 31–33
Job-related competencies, 108

K

Knowledge, skills, and abilities (KSAs), 20, 28
Kuder General Interest Survey (KGIS), 63
Kuder-Richardson coefficient, 213

L

Labor relations
    management and executive model, 232–233
    supervisory model, 254–255
Leadership Opinion Questionnaire (LOQ), 64, 83–84
Legal issues, 171–175
    individual assessment and, 34–36
    reference checks and, 69
Leniency errors, 112
Licensing, of individual assessment practitioners, 177–178, 190, 193
Linear rules, 128
Linear variables, 215
Line graph, 141
Linkage procedure, 198
Listening skills, management and executive model, 242
Loan and credit information, administrative model, 269–270
Lockheed engineers, individual assessment research on, 11, 15

M

Management and Organization Skills Test (MOST), 58
Management model, 41
  competencies, 239–249
  work activities, 230–238
Managerial jobs, cognitive ability tests and, 55
Managers, individual assessment research on, 11, 14–17
Manchester Personality Questionnaire (MPQ), 63
Marketing activities, management and executive model, 248–249
Marketing management
  management and executive model, 237
  supervisory model, 257
Materials management
  management and executive model, 234, 245–246
  supervisory model, 255, 262
Mathematical Reasoning Test (MRT), 60, 82–83
Maximum-performance test, 209
Mean, 211–212, 219
  standard error of the, 223
Mean score difference, 222–223
Measurement
  diversity in, 198
  errors in, 225
  individual assessment competencies, 180
  multiple, 53
  of nontraditional topics, 153
  objective, 124
  overlap in, 226
  subjective, 124
  terms/concepts, 210–214
Measures of central tendency, 219–222
Measures of position, 216
Measures of variability, 219–220
Mechanically collected data, 124
Median, 212, 215, 219
Menninger School of Psychology residents, individual assessment research on, 10, 13
Mental Measurements Yearbook, The, 20, 55
Merchandising, administrative model, 279
Method contamination, 144
Minimum qualifications, evaluation of, 69–70
Mission, organizational, 32–33, 39
Mode, 212
Motivation, 146, 148, 160–161, 165–167
  competencies and, 29–30, 33–34
  management and executive model, 244–245
Multiple cutoffs, 129
Multitrait-multimethod approach, 144, 223–226

N

Names, use in reports, 145
Narrative report, 142

National Institute of Industrial Psychology, 12
Negative leniency errors, 112
Nomological net, 224–226
Noninteractive work samples, 67–68
Norm, 207–208
Normal distribution, 212
Normative database, 124–126
Normed score, 208
Notes, from assessment interview, 106, 109
Novices, decision making and, 128
Numerical Computation Test (NCT), 60, 75, 78
Numerical Skills Profile (NSP), 60

O

Objective measurement, 124
Objective personality tests, 66
Objective test, 206
Occupational class, 21
Occupation information analysis, individual assessment competencies, 181
OFCCP (Office of Federal Contract Compliance Programs), 172
Office of Strategic Services (OSS), employment testing and, 7
Omnibus test, 206
O*NET, 65
Open-ended questions, 109
Organizational assessment
  department manager, 47
  division president, 49
  questions, 39, 44, 46
  sales associate, 45
Organizational behavior, individual assessment and expertise in, 177
Organizational charts, 40
Organizational context, individual assessment and, 38, 190–191
Organizational culture, assessee fit with, 145
Organizational psychology, 177–178
Organizational structure, 32
Organizational vision, 31–34
Organization Modeling Worksheet, 38–39
Orientation, for individual assessment, 21, 96–98, 100
Overgeneralizations, danger of, 112

P

Pair comparison model, 124
Paper-and-pencil test, 20–21, 52, 183
Paralegal activities/skills, administrative model, 272, 279
Past behavior, as predictor of performance, 109
Peace Corp. volunteers, individual assessment research on, 11, 16
Peer rankings, 15
People development, supervisory model, 254
People pyramid, 29–30

People supervision
    management and executive model, 231
    supervisory model, 253
Percentage, 217
Percentile rank, 218–219
Performance
    competencies and, 32
    defining, 28
    individual assessment and prediction of, 9
    intelligence as predictor of, 192
    measures of, 5
    objective personality measures and, 66
    past behavior as predictor of, 109
    work samples and prediction of, 68
Performance criteria, 17
Performance data, 5
Performance quality management, supervisory
        model, 261
Performance tests, 100, 206
Personal Audit Program, individual assessment
        research on, 10, 12
Personality, competency and, 28
Personality assessment, 70–71
Personality tests, 13, 53, 61–63, 100, 196, 206
    base rate validity and, 66–67
    objective, 66
    projective, 66
Personnel activities, supervisory model, 263
Personnel administration
    management and executive model, 232
    supervisory model, 254
Personnel records, administrative model, 272
Personnel research, 4–6
Personnel services, administrative model, 279
Planning
    management and executive model, 240
    supervisory model, 259
Planning and Organizing Skills Test (POST),
        82–83, 87–88
Planning, Organizing, and Scheduling Test
        (POST), 58
Population reference, 124–126
Position, 21
    as assessment target, 36
Position Analysis Questionnaire (PAQ), 73
Positive leniency errors, 112
Power tests, 53
Prediction, individual assessment and, 27–28
Predictive validity, 214
Pregnancy Discrimination Act (1978), 172
Premodeling questions, 36–41
Prework, 21, 96
Principles for the Validation and Use of Personnel
        Selection Procedures, 35, 176
Principles of Work Sample Testing, 68
Problem solving, intellectual functioning and,
        147–148
Productivity, employment testing and, 3–4
Professional issues, 175–182
Professional standards, 182

Program evaluation, 19, 22–23, 146
Projective personality tests, 66
Project planning, supervisory model, 259
Protocol worksheet
    department manager, 82–83
    division president, 84, 87–88
    sales associate, 78
Psychologists, clinical assessment and, 8
Public relations, administrative model, 267,
        276–277
Public service, employment testing and, 7
Public speaking, management and executive
        model, 242–243
Pure developmental assessments, 37

Q

Quantitative data, mechanical combination of,
        126–128
Questions, interview, 19, 109, 111, 113

R

Random errors, 211
Range, 220
Rank, 218
Ranking, percentile, 218–219
Rating scale
    for competencies, 149
    for interview data, 110–111, 113
Rational-theoretical approach, 73–74
Raven Progressive Matrices (RPM), 58
Reception activities, administrative model, 267
Recommendation, examples, 157, 161, 167–168
Reconciliation discussions, 144–145
Recruiters, standards for, 146
Reference checks, base rate validity and, 69–70
Reference population, 124–126, 213–214
Rehabilitation Act (1973), 172
Reliability, 212–213
Remedial developmental assessments, 37
Report/reporting, 6, 19, 22, 103–104, 141–143,
        144–167
    assessee background, 147
    competency evaluation, 148–150
    computer-generated, 195
    development suggestions, 150–152
    examples, 154–167
    formats, 141–142, 146
    intellectual functioning, 147–148
    legal issues, 175
    motivation and career aspirations, 148
    research context, 152–154
    social and personal functioning, 147
Research
    on assessment interview, 111, 113
    on assessment protocol, 53–74
    on assessment reporting, 152–154

on individual assessment, 9–18, 187–190, 196
on integration and interpretation, 126–129
on job modeling, 43
Research and development management
    management and executive model, 236
    supervisory model, 256
Research and evaluation, administrative model, 275
Role plays, 68–69, 87
Rorschach Ink Blot Test, 66

S

Safety management, supervisory model, 256
Sales Ability Test (SAT), 59, 78–79, 82–83
Sales activities
    administrative model, 268
    management and executive model, 248–249
Sales and customer relations competency model, 42
Sales associate assessment
    assessment interview, 113–114
    establishing assessment protocol for, 74–79
    integration and interpretation stage, 129–133
    job modeling, 44–46
    report, 154–157
Sales engineer, 42
Sales management
    management and executive model, 237
    supervisory model, 257
Sales Professional Assessment Inventory (SPAI), 59
SAS, 222
SAT (Scholastic Aptitude Test), 207
Scale construction literature, 73–74
Scaled score, 208
Scandinavian Airline pilots, individual assessment research on, 11, 13–14
Scatterplot, 218
Scheduling, administrative model, 275
SCOPES test battery, 15
Score(s)
    cut/cutting, 208
    normed, 208
    scaled, 208
    standard, 208
    weighting, 149–150
Score distributions, 125–126
Scoring system, evaluation of minimum qualifications and, 70
Selection
    deselection, 37
    external, 37
    individual assessment for, xv, 37
    internal, 37
Selection ratio, 210
Self-report questionnaires, 66

Selling Skills Series (SSS), 59
Semiskilled jobs, cognitive ability tests and, 55
Services, administrative model, 268
Short-term planning, management and executive model, 240
SHRM (Society for Human Resource Management), 185
Similar-to-me errors, 112
Simulations, 68
16PF, 63
Social and Business Judgment Skills (SBJS), 59, 82–83
Social and personal functioning, 146–147, 159, 164
Spearman-Brown prophecy formula, 213
Spearman-Brown rank correlation, 14
Specific ability measures, 56–59
Speed tests, 53
Split-half coefficient, 213
SPSS, 222
Staffing
    management and executive model, 231
    supervisory model, 253, 263
Standard deviation, 213, 215, 220–221
Standard error of the mean, 223
Standardization sample, 213–214
Standardized test, 206
Standard Oil Company, 8
Standards, for individual assessment, 187–188
Standards for Educational and Psychological Testing, 35, 175–176
Standard score, 208
Statistical procedures, 215–223
Statistical terms, 210–214
Stereotyping errors, 112
Strategic business initiatives, 31, 33–34
Strategic thinking skills, 30
    management and executive model, 240–241
Strategy development and deployment, management and executive model, 237
Structured interview, 54, 111, 196
Subjective measurement, 124
Success
    competencies and, 32
    defining, 28, 36
Succession planning, 151–152
Supervision of clerical employees, administrative model, 267
Supervision of people
    management and executive model, 231
    supervisory model, 253
Supervision of work operations
    management and executive model, 233–234
    supervisory model, 255
Supervisory model, 41
    competencies, 258–263
    work activities, 252–257
Supervisory positions, individual assessment research on, 10
Supervisory Practices Inventory (SPI), 59

Supervisory skills
    administrative model, 277
    management and executive model, 244
    supervisory model, 261
Supply maintenance, administrative model, 270

T

Talent searches, 37–38
Target job, defined, 6
Target job requirements, 6, 38, 41
Target population
    for cognitive ability tests, 56–60
    for interest inventories, 63
    for personality tests, 61–63
    for work style tests, 64
Taxonomies of Human Performance, 65
Teamwork and Organizational Skills Test
        (TOST), 59, 82–83
Technical and analytical competency model, 42
Technical jobs, cognitive ability tests and, 55
*Technical Recommendations for Psychological Tests
        and Diagnostic Techniques*, 224
Test(s), 52–53
    ability, 3–4, 204
    achievement, 204
    aptitude, 3–4, 204
    base rate of validity and, 174
    battery, 204–205
    cognitive ability, 53, 55–60, 64–65, 100, 205
    computerized, 195
    criterion keyed, 208
    establishing protocol and, 5
    evaluation of, 175–176
    individual assessment competencies and,
        180
    ipsative, 205–206
    maximum-performance, 209
    objective, 206
    omnibus, 206
    performance, 206
    personality, 13, 53, 61–63, 66–67, 100, 196,
        206
    power, 53
    relation to work activity and competency di-
        mensions, 195
    selecting, 6, 19, 72–74, 124–125
    speed, 53
    standardized, 206
    types of, 204–206
    typical-performance, 209
    using, 209–210
    weighting scores, 149–150
    work sample, 206
    work style, 64
Test administrator, 183–184
Test–criterion relationships, 5
Testing, 20–21
    administration of, 5, 183–184

    developing program of, 4–6
    employment, 3–8
    ethical issues in, 183
    individual assessment competencies in, 181
Test publishers, as gatekeepers, 178
Test score profile, 141
Test scores, describing, 207–209
Tests in Print, 55
Test User Qualification, 176
Thematic Apperception Test, 66
Three-facet model, 191–192
360-degree ratings, 53, 71
3M sales managers, individual assessment re-
        search on, 10, 13
Thurstone Temperament Schedule (TTS), 63
Thurstone Test of Mental Alertness (TMA), 56
Time frame, for assessment interview, 105
Title VII of the Civil Rights Act of 1964, 34,
        172, 174
Titles, use in reports, 145
Training
    competencies and, 29–30, 33–34
    in individual assessment practice, xvi, 188,
        190–192, 197
Trait(s), 225
    competencies and, 29–30, 33–34
Triangulation of measurement procedure, 225
Trust
    management and executive model, 244
    supervisory model, 261
T-test, 222–223
Turnover, employment testing and, 4
Typical-performance test, 209
Typing duties, administrative model, 270

U

*Uniform Guidelines on Employee Selection Proce-
        dures*, 35, 171–172, 179
United States, employment testing in, 7–8
Unskilled jobs, cognitive ability tests and, 55
Unstructured interview, 54, 111
USAF aviation cadets, individual assessment re-
        search on, 9–10, 12

V

Validity, 153, 172–174, 214
    base rate of, *see* Base rate validity
    concurrent, 214
    construct, 173, 214, 224
    content, 173, 214
    criterion, 172–173
    criterion-related, 214
    defined, 172
    job requirements and test, 54
    predictive, 214
    research, 179–180

Values
    competencies and, 29–30, 33–34
    organizational, 32–33, 39
Variable errors, 211
Variables
    categorical, 215
    continuous, 215–216
    kinds of, 215–216
    linear, 215
Variance, 214
Verbal communications
    management and executive model, 241–242
    supervisory model, 259–260

W

Watson Glaser Critical Thinking Appraisal
    (WGCT), 59, 87–88
Weighted application blank, 70–71
Weighting data inputs, 127–128
Weighting scores, 149–150
Western Reserve University Personnel Research
    Institute, 10, 12
Wide Range Achievement Test (WRAT-3), 60
Will-do competencies, 28, 66
Women, individual assessment research on, 16
Wonderlic Basic Skills Test (WBST), 60
Wonderlic Personnel Test (WPT), 56
Work activities, 31–34, 40
    administrative model, 266–273
    management and executive model, 230–238

supervisory model, 252–257
    test scores and, 195
Work activity profile
    department manager, 79–80
    division president, 84–85
    sales associate, 75–76
Work and organization adaptation
    administrative model, 277
    supervisory model, 260–261
Work and organization skills, administrative
    model, 276
Work assignment, administrative model, 267
Work commitment, management and executive
    model, 245
Work conditions, 32
Work context, 31, 33–34
Work culture, 38–39
Work operations supervision
    management and executive model, 233–234
    supervisory model, 255
Work sample tests, 52–53, 191–192, 206
    base rate validity and, 67–69
    interactive, 67–69
    noninteractive, 67–68
Work Skills Series Production (WSSP), 60
Work Styles Questionnaire (WSQ), 64
Work style tests, 64
Written communications
    management and executive model, 242
    supervisory model, 260
Written materials, administrative model,
    270–271, 277–278